Most self-help guides for couples focus on how to manage the difficulties that emerge within partnerships. Full of useful tips, real-life situations, and practical exercises, *Happy Together* spotlights how partners can best champion one another when experiencing external threats during instances of homophobia in a heterosexist world. Two decades of scholarship inform the warmhearted advice the seasoned authors offer here on how to be your partner's biggest ally and advocate. I highly recommend reading *Happy Together* with your loved one!

—**Dr. Bernadette Barton, PhD,** author of *Pray the Gay Away: The Extraordinary Lives of Bible Belt Gays*; Professor of Sociology and Women's Studies, Morehead State University, Morehead, KY

Same-sex couples and families are now among the norm across America—thanks, in no small part, to the groundbreaking research of Rostosky and Riggle. Who better, then, to create this important volume that covers all the bases related to families of choice? Any individual seeking to better understand the lived realities of same-sex families must have this comprehensive volume.

—**Douglas C. Haldeman, PhD,** Chair, Doctoral Program in Clinical Psychology, John F. Kennedy University, Pleasant Hill, CA

Rostosky and Riggle's research expertise enables them to stand way above the usual clichés about coming out and couple communication from which so many other self-help publications suffer. This book emphasizes the truly unique challenges of being a committed same-sex couple in contemporary society, including how to deal with the subtle and not-so-subtle signs of prejudice lesbian and gay couples face. I highly recommend it to all same-sex partners who are determined to see their relationship succeed.

—**Robert-Jay Green, PhD,** Founder, Senior Research Fellow, and Distinguished Professor Emeritus, Rockway Institute for Research in LGBT Psychology, California School of Professional Psychology, San Francisco

HAPPY
TOGETHER

HAPPY
TOGETHER

**Thriving as a Same-Sex Couple in
Your Family, Workplace,
and Community**

**SHARON S. ROSTOSKY, PhD, and
ELLEN D. B. RIGGLE, PhD**

AMERICAN PSYCHOLOGICAL ASSOCIATION • *Washington, DC*

Published by
APA LifeTools
750 First Street, NE
Washington, DC 20002
www.apa.org

To order
APA Order Department
P.O. Box 92984
Washington, DC 20090-2984
Tel: (800) 374-2721;
Direct: (202) 336-5510
Fax: (202) 336-5502;
TDD/TTY: (202) 336-6123
Online: www.apa.org/pubs/books
E-mail: order@apa.org

In the U.K., Europe, Africa, and the Middle East, copies may be ordered from
American Psychological Association
3 Henrietta Street
Covent Garden, London
WC2E 8LU England

Typeset in Sabon by Circle Graphics, Inc., Columbia, MD

Printer: United Book Press, Inc., Baltimore, MD
Cover Designer: Naylor Design, Washington, DC

The opinions and statements published are the responsibility of the authors, and such opinions and statements do not necessarily represent the policies of the American Psychological Association.

Library of Congress Cataloging-in-Publication Data
Rostosky, Sharon Scales.
  Happy together : thriving as a same-sex couple in your family, workplace, and community / Sharon S. Rostosky, Ellen D.B. Riggle. — First edition.
      pages cm. — (APA life tools)
  Includes bibliographical references and index.
  ISBN 978-1-4338-1953-7 — ISBN 1-4338-1953-8 1. Gay couples—Psychology.
2. Stress management. 3. Discrimination. I. Riggle, Ellen D. B. II. Title.
  HQ76.34.R67 2015
  306.84'8—dc23
                                        2014041616

British Library Cataloguing-in-Publication Data
A CIP record is available from the British Library.

Printed in the United States of America
First Edition

http://dx.doi.org/10.1037/14620-000

To our family of choice.

CONTENTS

Contents

PREFACE

"That couple drove over two-and-a-half hours just to talk to us!"

"Jane and Maya started telling us their story, and by the end we were reaching for a box of tissues, it was just so sweet!"

"Wow, that couple has been through a lot, but have you ever met such an optimistic pair? I want to be more like them!"

"Danny and Joey are so in love and committed to their relationship!"

These are just a few of the reactions we have shared with each other after interviewing a same-sex couple for one of the many research studies that we have conducted for well over a decade (and counting). This book is built around stories of the common challenges that couples face and the strength that they gain in the process of overcoming these challenges. These stories have enriched our professional lives as academics and scholars and have provided inspiration for our personal life as a same-sex couple. It has been a privilege to hear each couple's story.

Same-sex couples face some very real challenges in a society that still stigmatizes us for who we love. This cultural stigma touches all of us in one way or another. Yet, as couples interact with each other and with us, we are informed and touched by the satisfaction and fulfillment that they find in their everyday lives as a couple.

Although same-sex couples feel stigma and its impact, they are not victims. They are wise. They are funny. They are loving. They are hardworking couples leading lives of meaning and purpose in their families, workplaces, neighborhoods, and communities. They are our role models. As we illustrate in this book, same-sex couples find many positive, life-affirming ways to cope with, and even transform, the minority stress that they experience. They act with self-determination, creating happy, satisfying lives and relationships.

We live in a fast-changing social, cultural, and political land-scape. During the course of our studies, many states passed laws and constitutional amendments barring the recognition of same-sex relationships and marriages. Now a growing number of states have begun to recognize the civil marriages of same-sex couples, and the federal government has extended recognition to all couples who are married. More and more people, from high-profile celebrities and sports stars to regular, everyday folks, talk about their same-sex partner or spouse. Yet, until our society is no longer structured to sustain heterosexism, same-sex couples will not be entirely free of minority stress and the challenges that it brings.

Clearly, our wish is for all couples and their relationships to be treated with respect and dignity. We strive toward a minority-stress-free future, a future of full equality for all couples and their families. We offer this book as a resource for same-sex couples whose goals include creating and maintaining a happy, satisfying, and fulfilling relationship. The reason some couples drive hours to talk with us is that they are committed to each other and to helping build a better world for everyone. It is our intention to honor their commitment to their love and to social justice by sharing the stories that couples have shared with us about their relationship with each other, their families, and their communities.

We are deeply grateful to the many couples who have shared their stories with us. We also acknowledge others who have helped and supported us in the years leading up to the publication of this book. First, we thank the American Psychological Foundation's Wayne F. Placek Award for funding our research several times over the years. We thank the College of Education, the College of Arts and Sciences, and the vice president for research at the University of Kentucky for providing additional funding and support. Mark Frisiello and Phyllis Hoovler spent countless hours meticulously transcribing interviews. Susan Daole, our brilliant librarian, tracked down every obscure title we asked for. Dr. Greg Herek, Dr. Janis Bohan, and Dr. Bernadette Barton have gifted us with insightful feedback, inspiration, and encouragement. Likewise, we have benefited enormously from our research collaborations with Dr. Kimberly Balsam, Dr. Adam Fingerhut, Dr. Sharon Horne, and Dr. Esther Rothblum. We thank Dr. Dan Walinsky, Della Mosley, and Jennifer Cook for commenting on early drafts of sections of this book. Many of the graduate students on our research team (see www.prismresearch.org) also contributed to the original research studies as interviewers, coders, and coauthors. We are especially indebted to Dr. Kathleen Ritter and Dr. Glenda Russell for their substantial feedback and many helpful suggestions that improved every aspect of this final product. We are also grateful to the people at APA Books, and especially to Susan Herman, our development editor, and Nikki Seifert, our copy-editor, for all of their help in making our academic writing more accessible. Finally, we thank our own family, Brett, Laine, Matt, Phyllis (Mom), and Rea, and our many friends. You inspire us and keep us smiling with gratitude!

HAPPY
TOGETHER

INTRODUCTION

Same-sex couples can and do have stable, committed, satisfying relationships. In every healthy long-term intimate relationship, whether same-sex or different-sex,[1] partners need to develop good relationship skills and social support. In fact, same-sex and different-sex couples' relationships are more alike than different. There is one key difference, however: Unlike different-sex couples, same-sex couples face stigma, prejudice, and discrimination because of their same-sex attraction, their relationships, and the families they create. And they still do not enjoy the same access to social and institutional support for their relationship that different-sex couples often take for granted. These challenges, taken together, can cause a lot of stress—which we refer to as *minority stress* throughout this book. Same-sex couples need to learn positive coping skills and strategies so that they can meet the challenges of minority stress and thrive.

WHY WE WROTE THIS BOOK

Despite the unique challenges they face, same-sex couples have very few resources they can turn to. No one is more surprised by this fact than us! After all, the general alarm and anxiety about the fragility and instability of different-sex couples' relationships is palpable. A quick check of the self-help aisle at our local bookstore reveals titles that promise the "4 keys," "8 conversations," "7 habits," "5 lessons," or, our favorite, "12 hours to a happy, satisfying, loving, divorce-proof marriage." Search "couple relationships" on the Internet and you will find millions of links to websites, blogs, advice columns, books, workshops, weekend retreats, and a myriad of other resources.

The vast majority of these available resources, however, are written for different-sex couples. They often focus on how couples can address the conflicts that inevitably occur between the two of them because, supposedly, "men are from Mars, women are from Venus." Resources that include same-sex couples are rare. Even more uncommon is any discussion of the effects of minority stress on same-sex couple relationships.

We wrote this book to fill that gap. Same-sex couples should not have to translate books written for different-sex couple relationships to make them applicable. Instead, they deserve resources in which they can recognize themselves and their unique experiences. They deserve a book that addresses their specific needs.

We want same-sex couples to have access to custom-made tools that they can use to help their relationships thrive. Therefore, in this book we (a) illustrate how minority stress shows up in the everyday lives of real same-sex couples, (b) help couples recognize and label their own experiences of minority stress, and (c) offer a rich variety of suggestions and activities that will help couples positively cope and ultimately flourish.

This book is based on the research that we have conducted for more than a decade on same-sex couples; minority stress; and positive lesbian, gay, bisexual, transgender, and/or queer (LGBTQ) identity. As part of our research program (www.prismresearch.org),

4

we have interviewed more than 150 same-sex couples face-to-face about their relationships and their life experiences. We have also surveyed thousands of LGBTQ people, many in same-sex partnerships.

Many of the stories that couples have shared with us, the challenges they face, and the strategies that they have used to cope with minority stress are featured in the chapters that follow. Many couples we have interviewed shared their stories of successfully coping with minority stress. In this book, you will read many inspiring examples of resilience that illustrate how couples can address the minority stress in their lives in positive ways.

In every chapter, we build on the positive strategies that couples use and suggest others that can be helpful. You will see many examples of how you can build on your own strengths as a couple to create strategies that will work for you. You will find guidance for setting appropriate boundaries with others; using appropriately assertive communication skills; and creating positive social support in your family, workplace, and community. When we use positive strategies such as these, we begin to change our environment, making it a healthier place for us and for everyone else, too.

WHO SHOULD READ THIS BOOK

This book is written primarily for same-sex couples; same-sex–partnered individuals; and individuals who identify themselves as lesbian, gay, or bisexual. We think the book also presents information and resources for individuals who identify as transgender or queer. So, where appropriate we use *LGBTQ* to signify this broad application. Because we (the authors) are also members of this group, we do not hesitate to use the words *we* and *our* as we talk to our primary audience of other same-sex couples and LGBTQ-identified individuals. We want to explicitly join with our readers on a personal level, in solidarity and support for the joys and challenges that we all experience.

Although we recognize that not all close, committed relationships are pairs of individuals, we wrote this book with same-sex couples in committed relationships in mind. Individuals in other forms of relationships may also benefit from these examples and activities. Different-sex couples might even pick up a pointer or two to enhance their own relationships!

Same-sex couples are a very diverse group made up of individuals with endless combinations of complex intersecting identities and characteristics that cannot all be adequately illustrated in one book, such as this one. For this reason, we keep our focus on the minority stress experiences unique to being perceived as a same-sex couple. Unless it is directly relevant, we do not highlight or make assumptions about the other identities of individuals in the stories. For example, we do not label a specific couple member as identifying as bisexual or transgender or as a person with a disability unless that individual identity is directly pertinent to the minority stress that the same-sex couple is experiencing together. Our hope is that you will use the exercises in the book to reflect on how your own complex identities, personalities, histories, and social circumstances shape your unique experiences as a couple.

We also hope this book will be a resource for counselors, helping professionals (including medical and legal professionals), human resources personnel, clergy and spiritual leaders, and the family members and friends of individuals who identify as LGBTQ and of same-sex couples. Anyone who knows or works with a same-sex couple may benefit from reading about the everyday experiences of the many same-sex couples whose stories are featured in this book. By understanding the kinds of environments, supports, and strengths that help these couples to thrive and flourish, anyone can become a more effective ally and advocate.

HOW MINORITY STRESS AFFECTS SAME-SEX COUPLES

Most same-sex couples experience some form of minority stress—a concept that describes the unique, chronic stress experienced by people who are perceived to belong to a stigmatized social group. Minority stress is over and above the typical stressors that anyone might experience, such as the stress of driving home in rush-hour traffic or the stress of trying to balance a bank account so one can pay his or her bills. Minority stress includes (a) experiences of prejudice or discrimination, (b) anticipation and fear of rejection, (c) decisions about when to conceal or disclose our identity, (d) negative feelings we have internalized about our identity, and (e) efforts to cope with the stress that stigma creates.[2]

Although minority stress affects any person with one or more stigmatized social statuses (e.g., people who are African American or differently abled), in this book we use the concept to highlight the extra stresses that same-sex couples experience. Prejudice based on stigma can be expressed in both subtle and in blatant forms, which can make it difficult for couples to recognize and label these stressors. Sometimes couples don't realize the impact of these stressors until one or both partners begin to experience psychological or physical health symptoms.

The first step in dealing with minority stress is to recognize that it is a normal reaction to stigma. When we understand that stigma is at the root of the minority stress that we experience, we can begin to gain new insights and a new perspective into its effects on our daily lives as individuals and as a couple. These insights can help us transform stigma into an opportunity for positive growth.

As we say many times in this book, the problem is stigma. Same-sex couples are *not* the problem and are *not* to blame for minority stress. Stigma is toxic and must be eliminated for all families to have the opportunity to thrive.

Stigma is perpetuated by a culture that supports different-sex couples while devaluing or excluding same-sex couples from these same support systems. In the United States (and in other countries around the world), people grow up in a social system that supports *heterosexual privilege*, which is the unquestioned acceptance of heterosexuality as normal, natural, and expected. Teaching people that same-sex relationships (nonheterosexual) are inferior to different-sex relationships (heterosexual) and creating policies and stereotypes that support this belief is called *heterosexism*. Minority stress, as experienced by same-sex couples and people who identify as LGBTQ, results from living in a heterosexist society that privileges heterosexual identity and devalues nonheterosexual identities.

When we live in a toxic environment that is discriminatory or even dangerous, we have to find ways to cope. Our efforts to cope with these stressors can add more stress. Finding and using positive coping strategies to deal with minority stress is essential to our health and happiness as individuals and as a couple.

To help you begin to recognize and reflect on the minority stressors in your own lives, in each section of the book we describe common minority stress experiences that couples encounter in different social contexts. The contexts that we focus on are our family of origin, our family of creation, religious institutions, the workplace, our communities, and laws and policies that affect us. We suggest a variety of positive coping strategies that couples can use to overcome minority stress and strengthen their relationship in each of these contexts. The stories and activities in this book offer insights and practical ideas to empower couples with new understandings and new tools for dealing with stigma and the minority stress that it creates.

HOW WALKING THE DOG BECOMES MINORITY STRESS

Imagine Sean and Jake, a 30-something couple who live in a quiet, tree-lined neighborhood. One Saturday morning, while walking their dog, they hear someone yelling insulting remarks about gay people. Sean and Jake ask each other, "Did he intend for us to hear that?" They aren't sure. They seemingly forget about the incident and continue their day, going to a movie, having dinner with friends, and picking up groceries on the way home.

The next evening, as they walk their dog to the park, Sean and Jake find themselves avoiding touching. Later, they wonder out loud if they should take their rainbow bumper sticker off their car. Over the coming weeks, they start to pay close attention to the smallest indications that their neighbors might be politically or religiously conservative, assuming that this knowledge would tell them whether their neighbors accept them or not.

Sean and Jake become hypervigilant and preoccupied with concerns about their neighbors' perceptions of them. These thoughts trigger internalized stigma; specifically, they worry that perhaps they brought this incident on themselves somehow, by being "too gay." They find themselves fearing that other neighbors and people in their community may reject them if they are honest and open about their relationship.

Their anxiety starts to feed upon itself. The more they hide their relationship, the more isolated and alone they feel in their own community. The more isolated, alone, and shamed they feel, the more they fear rejection and the more they hide. Their isolation makes them feel even more unsafe and guarded. They increasingly perceive that disclosing their relationship is risky and dangerous.

Sean and Jake are experiencing the minority stress process. First, Sean and Jake experience *prejudice* (the loud, derogatory remarks). Second, they react by becoming self-conscious and hypervigilant as a way to *anticipate rejection* or other prejudicial events. Third, they start to *conceal* their relationship (they stop touching in public). Fourth, negative feelings about being gay that they learned as children are triggered (*internalized stigma*), which make them even more anxious and fearful. Finally, they *cope* by isolating themselves in their own neighborhood.

Many times same-sex couples fail to notice the extent to which they are caught in a cycle of minority stress. They become accustomed to these experiences and acclimated to the stress that they feel. Sean and Jake, for instance, may not realize how much effort they expend speculating about what their neighbors think of them. They may not realize that their isolation is harming their relationship as a couple. They may blame each other instead of focusing the blame on the real source of the problem—stigma. They need to interrupt this cycle.

HOW COUPLES CAN DEAL EFFECTIVELY WITH MINORITY STRESS AND THRIVE

Same-sex couples, such as Sean and Jake, can benefit enormously from learning how to recognize and positively cope with minority stress. Creating a positive identity as a same-sex couple involves actively thinking about social expectations and reimagining our lives in new, creative ways. Doing so can help us replace negative ideas with positive ones. Our thoughts are just thoughts, and it is entirely possible to replace unhelpful and problematic thoughts with more helpful and supportive ones.

Sean and Jake can also learn skills and strategies for building emotional closeness in their relationship. Using good communication skills with our partner helps us to recognize and identify minority stressors. Communicating effectively can also help us explore how our current coping strategies may be adaptive but ultimately unhelpful. This is the first step toward adopting new, more positive coping strategies that will be healthy and helpful over the long term.

Couples such as Sean and Jake can benefit from social support in their families and communities. Creating social support for our relationship is another important coping strategy. Cultivating a network of friends and allies around us helps us have a sense of belonging and a safe space where we can get support for our relationship as we deal with the outside pressures that create stress in our lives.

Couples need to practice prizing their relationship and asserting appropriate boundaries when others devalue them. They also need to learn ways to trust their partnership in the face of life's challenges. All of these strengths and skills take practice. Welcoming people into our lives who validate and celebrate our couple relationship can help us as we practice our skills. The good news is that same-sex couples can build enduring and satisfying relationships by recognizing and reframing minority stress experiences as opportunities for enhancing their relationship skills, for building their social support networks, and for taking positive action. In this book, we suggest specific activities that can help couples to better understand and manage the minority stress in their lives.

A satisfying relationship is good for our mental and physical health. A strong, loving relationship makes us more confident, more resilient, and better able to cope with life's challenges. Solidifying a loving partnership can make a positive difference in the physical and psychological health and well-being of couple members. To do this, we need the appropriate resources, tools, and skills to nurture our relationship.

HOW TO USE THIS BOOK

We have organized the book into six parts, each devoted to one important environmental context: our family of origin, our family of creation, our religious community, our workplace, our neighborhoods and local communities, and laws and policies. Each part of the book includes several chapters. Each chapter focuses on one minority stressor, which is illustrated with stories about real same-sex couples. These stories are composites of many similar stories that we have heard in our interviews. All of the names, of course, have been changed, and the details of the stories have been modified to obscure individual identities. So, if you think you recognize someone, that's probably because these minority stress stories are still all too common.

Although we focus on one minority stressor in each chapter, remember that all of the minority stressors are highly interrelated, as illustrated above with Sean and Jake. Internalized stigma, for instance, may make us anticipate rejection and thus hesitant to disclose our same-sex relationship. Because these minority stressors are related to each other, you will see overlap between the topics in the chapters. Life is often complicated, and so is minority stress.

In each chapter, we ask couples to do a Pause and Reflect activity in which they think about their own experiences. These activities are intended to increase couples' awareness of their own unique life experiences. Often, couples benefit from simply stopping, thinking, and talking together about their experiences and what these experiences mean for them.

Talking to each other about your experiences and how they impact your relationship can enhance the intimacy in your relationship and keep you strongly aligned as you collaborate to create a meaningful and joyful life together. Don't limit your conversations to just each other, though! It is very important that couples have meaningful connections outside their own relationship. Have some friends over for coffee and get their take on the challenges and opportunities they have experienced.

At the end of each chapter, we suggest a Guided Activity to help you turn your insights into action. We hope to give you some new ways of thinking about your relationship and some new tools for managing stress and promoting well-being. Ultimately, we want to help you to mobilize your strengths, resources, and skills and use these to protect your well-being and enhance your relationship.

We hope that these activities are helpful. Not everyone will need or want to do every activity. Pick the ones that seem most helpful to your situation and your relationship.

As we noted earlier, every same-sex couple is unique. Our experiences are shaped by age, personality traits, individual histories, class, ethnicity, race, religion, national origin, geographical location, economic resources, education, and many other individual characteristics and social factors. The exercises in this book are designed to allow couples to give voice to their own unique experiences and to devise their own unique action plans.

This book is not meant to be read in one sitting. Take a break. Go for a walk, play with the kids or the dog, listen to some relaxing music, or make dinner together. Come back when you are ready.

We recognize that the issues that we are asking you to think about and work on can be very challenging. They can evoke strong emotions. That's OK! If you are feeling overwhelmed by negative feelings, remember that they are only feelings. Take a deep breath and let it go. Our strong emotions come and go. Try not to get attached to them. Instead, be curious about your feelings and the important insights they may provide.

The Pause and Reflect and the Guided Activities have been adapted for same-sex couples from common techniques and exercises that counselors use to help people gain insight and then take action to improve their lives. We hope this book will be therapeutic in the sense that it will be helpful and supportive. However, this book is *not* a substitute for professional counseling or psychotherapy.

If you and your partner are struggling with basic communication and conflict resolution, you may need additional resources to improve these skills. There are many resources for couples that focus on the interpersonal skills that couples use to manage their relationship. Finding an affirmative and skilled therapist may be helpful if you are having difficulties communicating and negotiating with each other.

Ultimately, the cure for minority stress is ending all stigma and prejudice against same-sex relationships and individuals who identify as LGBTQ. We will accomplish this goal, together, by using our strengths and resources. Meanwhile, having a supportive and compassionate partner as we journey through life is a wonderful gift. We want to support you as a couple in transforming your minority stress experiences in ways that help you to create and maintain a happy, satisfying, and enduring relationship.

Guided Activity: What I Love About Us

Take some time together to share your responses to the following.

1. What do you appreciate about your partner? What do you appreciate about your relationship and your life together? Take a moment to reflect on the positive qualities of the relationship you are building together.
2. Make a list of the positive relationship qualities that you think may be at least partially due to being a same-sex couple. Remember to express confidence that you are both growing and learning together and will continue to do so by sharing your thoughts and feelings in this way.
3. Think about things you want to do and small actions that you want to take as a couple in response to the insights you gained from this time of reflection and sharing with each other. One action may be to read this book together and try some of the activities!

HAPPY TOGETHER

Same-sex couples deserve to thrive! We wrote this book to empower couples with new insights and new actions that can contribute to a happy and healthy relationship. Some people might argue that the tide has turned and same-sex couples are on their way to being treated just like different-sex couples. Some folks may think that same-sex couples are already treated equally and that there are no unique issues that same-sex couples face. Same-sex couples, on the other hand, know the reality of continuing minority stress. Same-sex couples, more than ever, need the tools, resources, and role models to pursue their relationships, happy together.

NOTES

1. We choose to use *different-sex* instead of *opposite-sex* as a more accurate label for couples who are perceived to be heterosexual. The term *opposite-sex* implies that only two sexes exist, which is not accurate. Furthermore, this term suggest that these two sexes are "in opposition," which plays into our cultural mythology about the "battle of the sexes." Changing our language opens up new ways of thinking. New ways of thinking open up new ways of being. We encourage our readers to experiment with using this term in their own everyday conversations to see what happens.
2. Meyer, I. H. (2003). Prejudice, social stress, and mental health in lesbian, gay, and bisexual populations: Conceptual issues and research evidence. *Psychological Bulletin, 129*, 674–697. doi:10.1037/0033-2909.129.5.674

Part I

FAMILY OF ORIGIN

When you think about your "family," who do you include? Most of us would think first about our partner, and our children if we have any, as our immediate family. Then we might add all or some of our parents and siblings, and their partners and children, to our family circle. We might also list close friends, former partners, and people we rely on for support.

Same-sex couples often have three parts to their family circle: family of creation, family of origin (FOO), and family of choice. Your *family of creation* is the family that you and your partner have formed together and any children that you might have. Your *FOO* is the family that raised you, including your biological or legal relatives. Your FOO may include parents, siblings, grandparents, aunts, uncles, cousins, and guardians. Your *family of choice* includes the people that you depend on and who depend on you for emotional, physical, and sometimes material support. Close friends, coworkers, and former partners and their family may be part of your family of choice. Same-sex couples have helped to lead the way in expanding our definitions of family, and that is a very positive thing! Modern families come in many configurations and express diverse values, strengths, and resources. Fundamentally, we idealize family as a place where we can be our true selves surrounded by people who love us unconditionally.

In this section, we focus on the relationship between same-sex couples and their respective FOOs. As most of us know, and as many television sitcoms and dramatic movies portray, our relationship with our FOOs can be complicated! When family interactions are tinged with prejudice or heterosexism, our already complicated relationships can become a painful source of minority stress.

Ideally, couples know they can rely on their FOO during a crisis, such as illness or job loss, or during a life transition such as the arrival of a child. Knowing this FOO support is available helps couples feel secure and confident. So, on the one hand, when FOO members reach out to same-sex couples for similar types of support, these couples experience a sense of belonging and inclusion that encourages them to participate and contribute in ways that benefit the entire family. On the other hand, our research has found that when couples don't have support from their FOO their well-being can suffer. For example, the FOO may hesitate to fully acknowledge and include the couple in holiday celebrations, family photo albums, or everyday conversations. These types of actions leave couples feeling excluded and damage relationships with the FOO. Couples must be careful not to let this type of minority stress negatively affect their own relationship.

Couples may also experience minority stress when family members believe negative stereotypes or hold other prejudicial attitudes. Many couples have told us, for instance, that members of their FOO express, directly or indirectly, negative and false beliefs about the stability and commitment of same-sex couples. Thus, even if FOO members are not outright rejecting, they may say or do things that unintentionally cause same-sex couples to feel unaccepted and not fully included in family life.

Even in generally supportive FOOs, same-sex couples may feel isolated. For example, most people share their racial or ethnic identity with other members of their FOO. Their FOO provides important emotional support and guidance when a couple encounters prejudice based on racial or ethnic identity. In these situations, the FOO can share experiences and advice, offer empathy, and instill pride in their shared racial or ethnic identity.

In contrast, most same-sex-partnered people grew up in homes with parents and other family members who are in different-sex relationships and do not share their lesbian, gay, bisexual, transgender, and/or queer (LGBTQ) identity. Their FOO most likely has no direct experience of minority stress based on their sexual or gender identity. Even when our heterosexual family members are our supportive allies, they do not experience the same level of stress that we do.[1] These complicated relationships and differences in experiences may make same-sex couples less likely to consider FOO members as role models and sources of support when they encounter challenges related to minority stress.

Hopefully your FOO is a source of support for you, your partner, and your families of creation and choice. Commonly, couples navigate FOO relationships that are not entirely rejecting and not entirely accepting. A couple may have some FOO members who are accepting and supportive, some who are rejecting, and others who are somewhere in between. These variations of support are also likely to evolve over time, making for interesting, stressful, and ever-shifting family dynamics.

It's been found that most FOOs, over time, become more welcoming and supportive, especially if the family values closeness and flexibility. Typically, these FOOs go through a process in which they rethink their beliefs and expectations. Hopefully, this process leads to acceptance and affirmation of the same-sex couple within the family. Unfortunately, not all FOOs fully achieve this transition.

Although interacting with FOO members who are in the middle of this process (not totally rejecting but not yet totally accepting) can increase same-sex couples' minority stress, there are many positive things that couples can do. For instance, couples can provide emotional support to each other. Our partners may need to share their anger, disappointment, and grief if their FOO members are behaving in unsupportive or disrespectful ways toward us and our partnership. Simply listening with compassion and validating our partner's feelings is helpful and supportive. Just remember to stay focused on understanding your partner's feelings rather than venting your own feelings or your judgments and advice about your partner's FOO!

It is important to remember that homophobia and heterosexism are the problems. FOO members may need time to discard long-held beliefs and expectations and adopt new understandings. Letting go of a worldview about sexuality and gender that is no longer useful can feel very scary.

To the extent that we can empathize and see ourselves and our FOO struggling against a common enemy (heterosexism), we can be more compassionate. This broader perspective can help us avoid blaming ourselves or them. We can also make a conscious effort to remember the positives about our families and the values and strengths that we still all share.

Remember that being patient does not mean being passive. Avoiding blame does not mean that we should avoid holding ourselves and our families accountable. We all need to act with mutual respect and compassion. No family is perfect.

Acceptance and affirmation may be hit or miss. Thus, we need to develop and practice good assertive communication skills as we navigate the ongoing relational journey between ourselves and our families. It is helpful to remember that we are all learning and growing. The good news is that FOO members who resolve their own conflicts about LGBTQ family members and same-sex couples in their families often come to prize the personal growth and closer family relationships that result.[2]

In this section, we illustrate and discuss some common issues that same-sex couples may experience as they interact with members of their FOO. The issues that we discuss have their roots in stigma and prejudice against same-sex couples and the minority stress that results. For example, same-sex couples may experience minority stress as they deliberate over whether or not to come out to members of their FOO. They may avoid talking about their relationship with FOO members who have made prejudicial statements. These common experiences can take a toll on a couple's relationship, as well as their relationship with their FOO. Therefore, couple members must work together and recognize and effectively address the minority stress they experience in their FOO interactions.

In Chapter 1, we focus on the minority stress that surrounds decisions about disclosure and concealment and illustrate how one couple found the courage to come out to a family member. In Chapter 2, we illustrate how couples can assess and address their stress related to family interactions that might be characterized by dysfunctional family rules, such as "don't ask, don't tell." In Chapter 3, we discuss how couples can assertively deal with FOO members' behaviors that are offensive, that are homophobic, or that otherwise express prejudice. In Chapter 4, we illustrate how traditional gender role socialization and expectations within FOOs can trigger a minority stressor called *internalized stigma*, or the distressing perception that we are not okay because of our same-sex attraction. We illustrate how couples can begin to transform the negative messages that they have internalized by practicing appropriate assertive responses in interactions with their family members. In Chapter 5, we discuss how families of choice provide an important source of emotional and psychological connection and a sense of belonging. Finally, in Chapter 6 we recognize the support that many FOOs provide and suggest ways to encourage and reinforce positive behaviors.

FOOs can be a source of support or a source of minority stress. Most likely, they are a mixture of both! When couples have the support of their FOO, they reap emotional, social, and material benefits. Acceptance and inclusion enables same-sex couples to be authentic. Affirmation provides a sense of belonging and connectedness. These qualities are important to the well-being of individuals and couples.

Same-sex couples can learn to capitalize on FOO support and minimize the effects of minority stress. Every couple's experiences with their FOO are unique. Hopefully, the couples in this section will inspire you to find strategies that will help you negotiate relationships with your FOOs that support your well-being as a couple.

NOTES

1. Horne, S. G., Rostosky, S. S., & Riggle, E. D. B. (2011). Impact of marriage restriction amendments on family members of lesbian, gay, and bisexual individuals: A mixed-method approach. *Journal of Social Issues, 67*, 358–375. doi:10.1111/j.1540-4560.2011.01702.x
2. Gonzalez, K. A., Rostosky, S. S., Odom, R. D., & Riggle, E. D. B. (2013). The positive aspects of being the parent of an LGBTQ child. *Family Process, 52*, 325–337. doi:10.1111/famp.12009

CHAPTER 1

COMING OUT TO GRANDMA

Are you out to all members of your family of origin? When we interviewed same-sex couples, many told us that before becoming a couple, one or both of them had not disclosed their sexual or gender identity to some or all of their parents, grandparents, or other close family members. As these couples moved in together and began a life together, it became increasingly challenging for them to conceal their couple relationship. Many couples wanted to affirm their relationship and their life together by being out to their families. Making decisions about disclosing or concealing one's relationship affects both members of the couple and affects their relationship.

Mark, age 35, and Kevin, age 27, have been a couple for about a year and a half. They met through a mutual friend, dated for several months, and recently bought a home together. They now have two terrier puppies. Mark works full time as a professor at the local college, and Kevin is in medical school.

Mark and Kevin realize that they enjoy many advantages in life. They both have advanced degrees, they are upper middle class, and they are White and male. Yet, they still experience stigma as gay men. They have experienced this stigma acutely in their own families. As they reflect on their family and relationship histories, they attribute some of the difficulties of their previous relationships to being closeted.

Because of their past experiences, being out as a couple is very important to both of them. In the medium-sized city where they live, they consider themselves out as a couple to their friends, neighbors, and coworkers. Nevertheless, when it comes to certain family members, both Kevin and Mark find themselves concealing their identities and their relationship.

Kevin, for instance, grew up going to his grandma's house every summer. She taught him to appreciate the arts. She was the only person who listened attentively to his fascination with airplanes. Yet, she was exacting and sometimes critical of others. Hearing these comments about others increased Kevin's insecurity about how she would react to his coming out to her. So he has avoided her.

Mark explained, "Kevin loves his grandmother dearly. He has distanced himself from her because he is afraid to tell her about us. She started calling a few months ago, though. She actually asked him if he was dating anyone."

Kevin continued the story:

> She asked me, "Do you have a girlfriend?" She's culturally liberal, but since I haven't really seen her much for the past couple of years, it would be really awkward to come out to her on the phone, like "Hey, Grandma, I'm gay." It just feels risky since some of my other family members have made obnoxious remarks about gay people.

Even though they don't feel particularly close to some of their family members, Kevin and Mark noted that this "secret" and their efforts to censor themselves when they talk to these relatives make them feel tense and anxious. Plus, the nagging sense that he is being dishonest makes Kevin feel disappointed in himself.

Mark explained the impact of this secret. "We'd like to have Kevin's grandmother over for dinner or take her to the theater with us, but that's not possible as long as we're still in the closet where she is concerned." They want to be honest about their lives, but it isn't easy to take the risk that they might be rejected.

Pause and Reflect

Who are your family members? For each partner, make a simple chart like the one below that lists your family members in each category.
   Parents (including stepparents)
   Grandparents
   Siblings
   Aunts and uncles
   Nieces and nephews
   Cousins (other family members)
On your lists, give each family member a percentage that designates how out you are, as a couple, to this person from 0% (*not out at all to that family member*) to 100% (*out to that family member*).

Mark and Kevin are like many of the couples we have interviewed. They anticipate rejection by one or more family members. Then, they try to cope with that fear by concealing their relationship. Yet, hiding makes them feel anxious and dishonest, worsening their minority stress.

We depend on our emotional connections to others for support. The thought of losing the love and approval of a family member is painful. Because of this fear, many same-sex couple members are willing to go to great lengths to conceal information. They try to create a sense of control over how their loved ones feel about them, even when doing so is harmful to their own well-being.

The irony of these situations is that we are never in control of how other people choose to respond to us. Our attachment to our families, the cultural values that support our vision of what an ideal family looks like, and the rules we have learned from our families all shape how we think, feel, and respond. Even after we have supposedly achieved independent adulthood, we are still influenced by social expectations and our human need for connection. Thus, our families can push our buttons, trigger our sense of vulnerability, and otherwise evoke powerful emotions in us, but we may still long for the approval and acceptance of our families. We still want to feel a sense of belonging and connection to them.

Many of us have long and complicated histories with our family of origin. Those histories may keep us emotionally vulnerable to their rejection. Recall that trying to anticipate rejection is one of the minority stress factors. The hiding and concealing that we do to try to ward off rejection is another minority stressor. We often internalize society's negative messages about our relationship and ourselves (still another minority stressor). In doing so, we may contribute to our own stress and the stress in our relationship. This vicious cycle of minority stress takes a toll on our individual well-being and the well-being of our relationship, as is illustrated in this conversation between Mark and Kevin.

> Mark: I try not to take it personally when you edit me out of your phone conversations with your grandma. I think I've been very patient and understanding. I certainly don't want to pressure you and then have it all backfire if your grandma doesn't take the news about our relationship very well.
>
> Kevin: Yes, you have been patient, and that makes me feel even more guilty for not being honest with her. Every time I avoid telling her, I know it is disrespectful to you and to

our relationship. But in my defense, I did promise that I am going to tell her as soon as the right time presents itself. I need you to trust me that I'm not going to keep our relationship a secret from her forever.

While they try to be sensitive, patient, and understanding with each other, like most couples, they are each very good at seeing the problematic behavior of the other. Kevin would like for Mark to be more understanding when he edits Mark out of his conversation with his grandmother. He wants Mark to trust in their love and commitment. Mark, on the other hand, can clearly see that Kevin's grandma has already dropped clues that she knows Kevin is gay. Yet, Kevin still tries to avoid a direct conversation with her about his relationship with Mark.

Mark and Kevin found it helpful to complete a cost–benefit analysis of continuing to conceal their relationship from Grandma. In this case, the cost–benefit analysis included the emotional and psychological costs and benefits of disclosing or concealing their relationship. They also listed the long-term relationship costs of not sharing this important part of their lives with her. Based on their experiences with family members who know about their relationship, they listed a number of benefits to being out to Grandma, regardless of how she might initially react.

Mark was able to help Kevin see the support that Grandma was trying to extend. Kevin's grandmother was already giving signals that she was not going to reject him. Kevin was so focused on anticipating rejection that he overlooked these signs. Sometimes our partners can offer a different perspective that helps us with our blind spots.

In this case, with Mark's encouragement and support, Kevin was able to reevaluate the costs of his avoidance. Kevin practiced coming out to Grandma. Mark played the role of "Grandma," and they enjoyed some stress-relieving laughter over possible reactions.

Kevin found courage and comfort in the process of practicing what he might say. He realized that with Mark's support, he could handle any reaction that he got from Grandma.

Kevin called Grandma to set up a dinner date and in that conversation shared with her that Mark was his partner. Grandma's reaction was one of relief that Kevin is neither alone nor lonely. The three of them now enjoy Sunday brunch together every few weeks. They have tickets to a play next month. Mark and Kevin now consider Grandma an important source of connection and emotional support for their couple relationship.

Guided Activity: Making Disclosure Decisions

With your partner, review the list of family members that you each created in the Pause and Reflect exercise in this chapter. Which family members are you 100% out to? For the family members that you are completely out to as a couple, answer the following questions:

a. What are the benefits of having shared our relationship with ___?
b. What are the losses that we have experienced as a result of sharing our relationship with ___?
c. On a scale from 1 to 10, how positive is our relationship with ___?

Now, move on to the family members that you are not completely out to as a couple. Answer the following questions about these family members.

a. What costs are there to hiding our relationship from ___?
b. The thoughts and feelings that arise when we consider being more honest, direct, or authentic in our relationship with ____ are _____?
c. How realistic are our fears? How would we cope if our imagined worst-case scenario happened?
d. What benefits might we gain from being more honest, direct and authentic in our relationship with ___?

CONCLUSION

Making decisions about coming out to family members can be a source of minority stress for same-sex couples. These decisions are shaped by many factors that are unique to each couple's family history, culture, and current situation. You can evaluate your disclosure decisions and practices by reflecting on your interactions with family members whose rejection you fear.

You can also evaluate your fears to see how realistic they are. The worst-case scenario that you might imagine is like a movie in your head and would rarely come to pass. Even if it does, you can find effective ways to handle it. When you take time to examine the costs and benefits of hiding and concealing your identity from family members, you will be better able to make conscious decisions that support your relationship.

CHAPTER 2

WHEN THE FAMILY RULE IS "DON'T ASK, DON'T TELL"

One variation on the experience of coming out to family is the explicit or implicit rule of "don't ask, don't tell" (DADT). For some people, this is a family rule that applies to many topics, not just sexual orientation or gender identity. For others, this is a rule that the couple may use as they try to balance being authentic with avoiding possible rejection. These couples may believe that they would be rejected by family members if they talked openly about their relationship.

In this chapter, we illustrate the DADT rule and how it can exacerbate minority stress for same-sex couples. We also illustrate how couples can recognize different manifestations of DADT. After recognizing this dynamic, couples can work on breaking the DADT rules of their family or rewrite their own DADT rules to benefit their relationship.

Trish, age 39, and Wanda, age 37, are an interracial couple who have been together for 6 years. Trish is from a small town, and although her parents know she is a lesbian, they have never directly talked about it. Wanda is out to her parents, who live in the suburbs of a large metropolitan area. The couple had been together for a couple of years before Wanda met Trish's parents. They recounted their history with Trish's family.

Trish: With my family it took a little bit longer to get you introduced in there. Race may have played a little part in that because you refused to go see them for a while because you didn't want to go to my small hometown "in the middle of nowhere" where everybody is White. You were afraid that might be a place where a Black person shouldn't go. But once you went, my parents accepted you right away.

Wanda: Yeah, but I was never introduced to them as your partner. I'm still just considered your "Black friend."

Trish: Well, that's true. But it's something that's understood without saying. It's something my family doesn't want to discuss. It's the big elephant in the room that nobody wants to talk about. You're just there. "Enough said," as far as they are concerned.

Trish is convinced that everyone in her family understands the nature of her relationship with Wanda. However, because no one ever asks about their relationship, she also believes that they don't want to talk about it. She is happy that her family treats Wanda well, even asking about her in conversations and including her in invitations to holiday gatherings. To sidestep upsetting her family and to escape their possible rejection of her relationship, Trish avoids calling Wanda her partner or talking directly about their relationship as a couple.

Many couples we interviewed have similar experiences. Together, they ponder who in their family knows they are a couple and who doesn't. They speculate about what different family members think about their relationship. They watch for the smallest signs or clues to interpret how family members are reacting to them. After interacting with these family members, they replay their conversations and behaviors to see whether something they said or did might have given away the true nature of their relationship.

Monitoring interactions and the nonverbal cues of others for signs of possible rejection or acceptance is a form of hypervigilance. A common strategy used to try to anticipate and prevent rejection, hypervigilance is part of the minority stress process.

Trish and Wanda actively look for clues about whether any member of Trish's family understands that they are a couple. They also spend a lot of time generating stories to explain their family members' behaviors, as illustrated here.

> Trish: My parents really like Wanda. They gave her Christmas presents last year! If I call and say I'm coming home, they want to know if Wanda is coming with me. They really try to make her feel comfortable and all that, but there is still a kind of tentative, uncomfortable feeling that I can't quite put my finger on.
>
> Wanda: I think they don't know how to interact with us. Or maybe it's because I'm Black. Trish's dad patted me on the back and gave me a big handshake the last time we were there. That shocked me, in a good way! We had a good laugh about that. Trish's sisters are always talkative, but sometimes her parents get quiet and strained-looking and don't seem to know what to say to me. Maybe they are afraid they will offend me by accidentally saying something racist.
>
> Trish: Yeah, but that's how they are with everyone. My parents are very reserved. They aren't expressive like Wanda's family.

Like Trish and Wanda, many couples puzzle over the sense of disconnection that they feel from their families. Is it just the different, sometimes difficult, personalities that are involved? Do they just not have anything in common? Would it be the same if they were a straight couple? Or is the difficulty because they are a same-sex couple and no one is talking about it?

Pause and Reflect

The first step in dealing with our fears of rejection is to acknowledge that they are there. Are there topics or issues related to your lesbian, gay, bisexual, transgender, and/or queer identity or relationship that you don't talk about when you are interacting with your family of origin because you are afraid of how they will respond? What do you fear will happen? List the thoughts that lead to feelings of anxiety, worry, fear, sadness, or anger. How strong is the evidence that these disturbing thoughts are true?

The code of silence that governs some families can lead to speculation and attempts to read the minds of others. It is not unusual for couples to report that they have never had a direct conversation with a parent about their sexual identity or their same-sex relationship. Some couple members explained to us that they were "waiting for the right time" to have a conversation with their family. In some cases, couples had already been waiting for more than a decade for that elusive right time. Meanwhile, they may censor their behaviors when they are with their family members, purge the house of any indicators that they are a couple when family members come to visit, sleep in separate bedrooms, or spend major holidays going their separate ways to visit their respective families.

Some of the couples who go to the greatest effort to pretend that their relationship is not an intimate, committed one strongly suspect that their family members already know this information. Yet, these couples continue to play by the often-unspoken rules of the family. They feel responsible for the potential discomfort or conflict that might arise if they violated these rules. These couples perceive that holding hands or interacting exactly like the straight couples in the family would be "rubbing it in our family's faces" or "insensitive to their discomfort." They collude in treating typical expressions of affection as somehow offensive or inappropriate.

The irony is that continuing to take part in DADT does not really help couples avoid the rejection that they fear. Instead, they participate in it. They still suffer from the anticipation that they will be rejected. Plus, they reinforce others', and possibly their own, negative beliefs about themselves and their relationship.

Couple members comfort themselves by thinking they are controlling their family members' perceptions and opinions of them. In these instances, couple members may be projecting their own discomfort and using their family members' discomfort as an excuse. In reality, some family members may feel relieved when the "secret" is no longer a secret and they can have an authentic relationship with the couple.

Under DADT, truth and authenticity are sacrificed to avoid possible conflict and rejection. Adhering to the code of silence is a strategy that may feel "normal" for some people because it has been practiced and perfected since early childhood. Sometimes, silence seems like the path of least resistance.

The problem is that following these rules and taking the path of least resistance also forecloses the possibility of authentic connection. Following these rules can significantly strain the couple's relationship. Their fears of rejection can cause couple members to interact with their family members in ways that hurt their partners. For example, Wanda sometimes feels aggravated by how Trish's behavior toward her changes when they are with Trish's family.

I used to fuss at Trish, and to be honest, I sometimes still do . . . like if we're down there at her parents' house, she will sometimes act like I'm not even there. Like, she stiffens up and doesn't react to me the same way she would if we were at home. I used to get on her about that. I usually say something like, "You get all uptight and act like I'm not there, and you don't laugh about things that we think are funny, or you don't come over and sit down next to me on the couch." Now, I try to just accept it because I don't want to cause more stress to our relationship by complaining about it all the time. But it still bugs me.

Trish admits that she thinks her family knows that she and Wanda are more than friends or roommates, even though no one talks about it directly. As a result, Wanda feels like she is "on pins and needles."

"It just wears me out to go visit them." Wanda continues, "As much as I want to go along with Trish, at the same time it's like a punishment! It's a lot of stress on both of us, because we are both on edge the whole time."

It takes a lot of energy for a couple to live in a DADT environment. They constantly monitor and censor. They check themselves. Yet, they convince themselves that everyone in the family really knows, but they just don't want to talk about it.

They also convince themselves that if they did talk about their relationship, family members would reject them. They convince themselves that DADT is the price they pay for peace in the family. As Trish says, "Family means a lot to me. It's hard to risk losing that."

Wanda took a risk and told her family about her relationship with Trish. Although at first they expressed surprise and were reluctant to include Trish in family gatherings, Wanda continued to express her love for Trish and the importance of their relationship. Eventually Wanda's family adjusted, and they now treat Trish like a part of the family.

This imbalance has caused tension between Trish and Wanda. They wonder to what extent race and the legacy of racism shape their feelings about being a couple and their fears of rejection by Trish's family. Interracial same-sex couples are often uncertain about the exact source of their minority stress. If they are uncertain whether they are dealing with racism, heterosexism, or both, they may be uncertain about the steps they need to take to reach a resolution.

Like many couples, Trish and Wanda realized that they were expending considerable time and energy closely monitoring how Trish's family reacted to them. Trish and Wanda recounted to each other specific instances in which they actively looked for clues about whether people in Trish's family know they are a couple and whether they are accepting or rejecting. They agreed that this is not how they want to spend their energy when they visit.

Trish and Wanda talked about the kind of relationship they want to have with each set of parents and what would have to happen to achieve that relationship. In the relationship they envision, Trish's and Wanda's parents would be able to show their love by acknowledging their relationship and supporting their desire to have a child. To get to this point, however, would require a direct conversation with Trish's parents.

The communication patterns that we learn as children in our family of origin (FOO) tend to be the same ones we use when we interact with them as adults. Many of us feel like we are 12 years old again as soon as we cross the threshold into our parents' home. Maybe the pattern includes anger and defensiveness, blaming and criticizing, or silence and withdrawal. These patterns are predictable and ineffective.

With our partner's FOO, we may feel like an outsider. We may worry that our relationship is on the line if our partner's family doesn't approve of us. No wonder we cave into the DADT rule if we think it will save us from unpleasant interactions and feelings.

What do you imagine would happen if you broke the "don't tell" part of the DADT rule in your family? Trish and Wanda imagined the worst-case scenario and how they would handle it. They recognized the possibility that they would get a negative reaction. They also acknowledged that their family's reactions would probably not be as bad as the worst-case scenario they created in their minds.

They decided that when a family member referred to one of them as "your friend" that they would correct them. They practiced saying, "She's my partner," and "Please refer to her as my partner" or "We're partners." To Trish, these seemed like very confrontational statements to make to family members.

Trish practiced using a friendly but clear and assertive tone. She decided to soften her statement a bit by leading in with "I would appreciate it if you would refer to Wanda as my partner." Wanda helped Trish practice repeating this phrase, over and over again. This technique is called the "broken record," harking back to the time when phonograph needles would get stuck on a vinyl record and play the same thing over and over again.

They also role-played the negative verbal reactions that Trish anticipated so that they could practice responding. For example, Wanda pretended to be an exaggerated version of Trish's dad, responding to Trish's assertive statement with a gruff, "Geez, you don't have to rub it in our faces." To this, Trish practiced calm, assertive responses such as, "Wanda is my partner; that is the appropriate way to refer to her."

CONCLUSION

Each couple must decide how to relate to their FOO and the role that these family members will play in their lives. Remember that you are not in control of the "don't ask" part of the DADT interaction. Your FOO may or may not choose to break that part of

---

Guided Activity: Breaking the "Don't Tell" Rule

What "don't tell" rules might you and your partner consider breaking? Perhaps you aren't even fully aware of the times that you censor yourself. Here is a step-by-step plan for changing the rule from "don't tell" to "tell the truth."

1. Start to notice when you censor information, fail to correct misinformation, or otherwise participate in "don't ask, don't tell" in your family of origin. Sometimes your partner can be the most astute and accurate observer because he/she is not as enmeshed in the family system. Enlist each other to observe and discuss what happens in family interactions.
2. Make a list of specific statements that would break the "don't tell" rule.
3. Pick the easiest statement on the list, the one you feel most confident that you can say.
4. Try out the statement with your family member or members and note what happens next.
5. Be prepared to use the broken-record technique if your family resists changing or honoring your request. When you meet resistance, just keep calmly repeating the assertive statements that you have practiced.
6. Be sure to also notice and positively reinforce any good behavior you observe in your family member or members. For example, you might say, "I appreciated it when you addressed the holiday card to both of us."

the rule. You are, however, in control of the "do tell" part of the interaction. The boundaries that you negotiate between your couple relationship and your FOO are influenced by your cultural values, generational patterns within your individual family systems, and the ideal relationship that you desire with your families. You can learn to interact with your FOO in ways that support healthy couple boundaries and positive family relationships.

CHAPTER 3

FAMILY GATHERINGS

Couples experience minority stress in interaction within their family of origin (FOO) if members of their family express prejudice instead of support and acceptance. Unfortunately, some family members are overtly rejecting of same-sex couples. They may behave in ways that show blatant prejudice or disapproval. Typically, these behaviors include treating same-sex couples as different from, and inferior to, different-sex couples in the family.

Even more commonly, family members engage in subtle forms of prejudice, called *microaggressions*. This type of prejudice includes comments that downplay or ignore the importance of same-sex couples' relationships. Experiences of prejudice within the FOO, whether blatant or subtle, cause stress and potential harm to couples.

Phyllis, age 35, and Helen, age 30, have been a couple for 4 years. They met through mutual friends and dated for 2 years before moving in together. Phyllis's family has made several remarks in front of them about opposing a local ordinance that would prohibit discrimination against gay men and lesbians. They also voiced their support for the constitutional amendment in their state that barred recognition of the civil marriages of same-sex couples.

Although Phyllis and Helen were not surprised by these comments, they still hurt.

A little more than a year ago, Phyllis and Helen got married in a neighboring state that had marriage equality. Their marriage and the accompanying wedding reception that they had in their local community publicly celebrated the commitment they had made to build a life together. Phyllis has always valued being close to her parents, but she knew they would not be happy about the wedding. In fact, when she first informed them about the wedding reception, her father immediately refused to attend. In response to the beautiful invitation she sent them, he told her that he saw her wedding as a "shameful" example of "flaunting" her "lifestyle." Although Phyllis's mother said she wanted to come to the reception, she tearfully decided not to attend to "keep the peace at home."

Phyllis described the stress leading up to the wedding:

> My mom was calling me and crying several times a day because they weren't coming to the party. She felt bad about it. At the same time, she felt caught between my dad and me. She felt she really had no choice even though she wanted to come.

Prejudice-related behaviors in the FOO hurt Phyllis and Helen, but they also affected other family members. At first, Phyllis felt responsible and guilty about her mother's anguish. It didn't help matters that her older sister frequently called to fret,

> I don't know what's wrong with Mom; it's like she's aged 10 years since you told her about this wedding. I've never seen her cry so much. Why couldn't you let well enough alone? Why do you have to put them through all this?

Phyllis felt immobilized by these accusations: "I really resented that my sister couldn't take my side and support me and

Helen. I already felt horrible. I kept thinking, 'I'm hurting my mother' and that's really how I felt. It was a hard time." Helen and Phyllis reflected together on what they learned from this experience.

Helen: It was a horrible experience at the time, but I think in the end it served as a real defining moment for us, because we really explored what we would and would not tolerate from our families. We sat down and really talked about where our boundaries were and how we would establish our own identity as a couple and what compromises we would and wouldn't make. I guess in some ways, as hurtful and painful as it was, it made us stronger because we communicated a lot about what was happening, how we felt, and what we would do every step of the way.

Phyllis: I guess my dad's disapproval of our marriage really was one of those pivotal moments that helped me turn a corner. I really wanted my parents to come. It mattered to me that they weren't going to be there to celebrate with us. I was deeply hurt and sad—underneath my fury! But I realized that there was a relationship that was more important to me than the size of their disapproval. I made the decision that their disapproval would not sway my decision or decrease my happiness. When you don't make the right decisions for yourself, you can't make anyone else happy in your life either. I had tried to make them happy, but when it comes down to it, I have to live my own life, and they'll have to find their own happiness in life. I have to stop being responsible for their happiness. It's not easy. I have to remind myself over and over that it's their decision whether they're happy or sad; it's their decision whether they're in misery or not. I have to do what's right for me and my wife.

Phyllis and Helen are describing a very important strategy for dealing with family members' negative and unsupportive behaviors. First, they each took time to acknowledge their feelings. Helen shared, "I really can't say that I felt angry at Phyllis's parents. I just thought they were making unfortunate decisions, but that was their deal, not mine." Phyllis, on the other hand, had to grieve the loss of her family's emotional support. Grief includes sadness but also anger, fear, and perhaps other intense emotions.

Helen and Phyllis were able to share their feelings with each other and accept them without judgment. Phyllis also recognized that she and her parents are autonomous adults who are each responsible for their own choices. She is responsible for neither her father's decision to skip the wedding reception nor her mother's decision to support her father instead of her. She and Helen are only responsible for their own behaviors and decisions. Because Phyllis and Helen were able to draw this boundary that appropriately prioritized the integrity of their couple relationship, they were able to give up trying to control Phyllis's parents' behaviors. Instead, they accepted Phyllis's parents' decisions and then focused on their own behaviors. This response is easier said than done, but it is a key to individual and couple well-being. When Phyllis chose not to spend her time and energy resisting her parents' decisions, she was able to refocus on celebrating her and Helen's marriage with supportive family and friends.

Instead of dwelling on her parents' absence, she tuned in to all of the people who came to support and celebrate with them. This support included Phyllis's brother and sister, their spouses and kids, and several cousins and their families. Helen's mother and father were proud parents for both brides. Phyllis and Helen recounted with delight how much time Helen's mom and dad spent on the dance floor and how much fun they had at the party.

It is interesting that in the year since their wedding, Phyllis's parents have shown more support for their relationship and occasionally visit their home. When Phyllis and Helen stopped resisting Phyllis's parents' decisions, there seemed to be some room for small movements toward change. For instance, Phyllis's mom made a Christmas stocking with Helen's name on it to hang on the mantel alongside the other family members' stockings.

Although Phyllis's father is still a bit standoffish, he has accepted that Phyllis is now a married woman, just like his other daughters. He expects to see Helen with Phyllis at all the family gatherings. Although he may still oppose marriage equality, he has stopped talking openly about it. Phyllis and Helen suspect that their allies in the family have confronted him about his unsupportive behaviors and he is responding to the pressure.

Drawing appropriate boundaries with family members feels risky. If we grew up in homes where boundaries were violated and we were taught to feel responsible for other people's feelings and behaviors, getting clear about the line between our own feelings and the feelings of our family members can be challenging. To the extent that family members are accustomed to overstepping the bounds and making inappropriate demands, they are likely to react negatively to our asserting our boundaries.

When we make any change in our behavior in relation to our family, the first reaction that we can anticipate is a countereffort to get us to change back. All of us tend to resist change. We like the status quo. We like our relationships to stay constant, predictable, and comfortable. Setting boundaries with family members may evoke strong feelings of sadness, anger, and loss in everyone involved. Recognizing and accepting those feelings in ourselves and our family members without giving in to them can be challenging but is an important part of the process.

So what does all of this discussion of boundaries have to do with overt prejudice? Prejudice leads to discrimination, which is behavior that is disrespectful of the basic integrity of others. When we are treated with disrespect, a boundary has been crossed. Our basic right to respectful treatment as human beings, and as a couple, has been violated.

The first step that you can take as a couple is to identify your FOO's inappropriate and disrespectful behaviors. Acknowledge when these behaviors cause stress, and identify your thoughts and feelings. Then, you can practice using assertiveness techniques such as the ones outlined at the end of this chapter to clarify boundaries and expectations for mutually respectful behaviors.

Pause and Reflect

Think about your families' reactions to your relationship and their actions toward you and your spouse/partner. Can you recall any times when a family member said something or did something that was stigmatizing or otherwise disrespectful of you, your partner, or same-sex couples more generally? Make a list. What were your thoughts and feelings in these moments? Did you talk together about these incidents? How did these incidents impact you as a couple? Make a second list of respectful behaviors that you would like to see (be very specific).

Like Phyllis and Helen, you and your partner may need to give yourself permission to take care of yourselves as individuals and as a couple. Sometimes setting healthy boundaries or limits with family members may be as simple as saying out loud to yourself and your partner, "That is their problem, not ours." Letting go of the responsibility for the prejudice of others establishes an important and healthy boundary.

Many of us grew up thinking we would be rejected and abandoned if we said no to a family member who imposed or took advantage of us in some way. Some of us take care of others' needs at the expense of our own. Ignoring our own needs may have become a way of life. Taking responsibility for our own lives rather than the feelings of our family members (over which we have no control anyway) is a sign of self-respect. Establishing these psychological boundaries is important for healthy relationships.

In our culture, it's a big deal when a parent refuses to celebrate a child's marriage. There is nothing subtle about the message of disapproval that is communicated. Much more frequently, however, we have interactions with family members that leave us scratching our heads and asking ourselves, "What did they mean by that?" We might question ourselves, "Am I being overly sensitive or was that comment really as offensive as I interpreted it to be?"

These more subtle expressions of prejudice are microaggressions. The ambiguity in some interactions can make them just as stressful as blatant forms of discrimination. Microaggressions can quickly add up and take a toll on a couple's well-being.

For example, for the 11 years they have been together, Jim, age 44, and Blake, age 43, have coped with occasional small acts of prejudice or microaggressions that communicate their second-class status relative to the different-sex couples in their respective FOO. Jim's parents, who live in a neighboring state, are very supportive when Jim and Blake come to visit them. However, when it came time to make plans for a reunion of their extended family, Jim's mother asked Jim to attend the reunion, without mentioning Blake. It didn't feel right to Jim or Blake, who knew that Jim's brother and sister-in-law were going. Jim recounts his conversation with his mother.

> Jim: I asked her if she meant me and Blake when she asked if "I" was going? She said, "Don't you think that it would just be easier on everyone, including you two, if you came alone? Don't you need someone to stay home and take care of the farm?" I said, "Would you ask Jason [Jim's brother] to go without his wife? Doesn't someone need to stay home and

take care of their farm?" She just had it in her head that it would be weird if Jason went without his wife, but it was okay for me to go without Blake. I told her I wouldn't go without Blake.

Jim's assertiveness about an unreasonable request is very difficult for some couples. Sometimes we allow our family members to make us feel responsible for their choices. Clearly, Jim has chosen Blake to be his partner. They have chosen to make a life together. Jim's mother is fully responsible for choosing her response to her son, his partner, and the extended family.

What if Jim had caved in to the pressure and attended the family reunion alone to "make it easier on everyone"? Sometimes sacrificing our own integrity and well-being seems like the most expedient thing to do. It may represent the path of least resistance.

However, compromising our integrity in these "small" ways or "just this one time" reinforces others' discriminatory behavior and makes it even harder the next time to assert the right to be respected as a couple. The habit of compromising our integrity can damage our own self-esteem, that of our partner, and our relationship as a whole.

To deal with the discrimination in their FOO, Blake and Jim draw on their sense of resilience, their commitment to each other, and their determination to succeed in their relationship. They are learning to appropriately assert themselves and their decisions in relation to their families. They know that all relationships, including their own relationship and their relationships with their FOO, take energy.

Having compassion and empathy for our family members is laudable. We often hear couples offer excuses for their family members: "Well, he grew up that way," or "She doesn't know any better." We can have compassion for others and at the same time maintain our integrity. It is reasonable to expect our family members to treat our relationship with respect.

We need to practice the skill of knowing when and how to be assertive. Assertiveness, as opposed to passivity or aggression, allows us to address interpersonal problems in ways that are mutually respectful. When we clearly communicate with family members how their behaviors affect us, without blaming or attacking, we are being appropriately assertive. When we clearly communicate the specific behaviors we want to see and the likely consequences of these positive behaviors, we are also being appropriately assertive.

Assertiveness may be particularly effective with family members who are already generally supportive and perhaps are not aware that they are being offensive or unreasonable in their requests. The central skill is to determine and describe (as if you were looking through the lens of a video camera) the specific behavior that you are requesting. Dredging up a lifetime of hurts and offenses is not an effective change strategy. Making a very specific request and then rewarding that behavior when you see it is much more likely to produce results and improve relationships.

To handle Jim's mom's request that he attend the family reunion without Blake, Jim used the LADDER technique[1] to compose an appropriately assertive response (see the Guided Activity for more on LADDER). First, Jim and Blake reminded themselves that they are a couple who deserves the same respectful treatment as the other couples in their families. They are clear in their decision to not participate in unfair and disrespectful treatment by agreeing to attend family events alone.

Second, when Jim's mother originally brought up the subject of the reunion, Jim was taken off guard. He wanted to process the issue with Blake rather than react angrily in the moment. He told his mom he would get back to her in a day or two.

Third, Jim and Blake stated the problem objectively using the facts. When he and Blake sat down to talk to Jim's mother a couple of days later, Jim recounted that she had asked him to attend the reunion without Blake and a similar request had not been made of his siblings.

Fourth, Jim shared his feelings using an "I" message. Specifically, he stated, "I was angry when you asked me to go without my partner. I feel hurt and rejected when our relationship is treated like it is something to hide."

Next, Jim made a clear statement of their decision and the specific behavior they wanted from his mom. He said, "If we are not welcome at the reunion as a couple, then neither one of us will attend. In the future, please do not ask me to attend any event to which my partner is not also welcome."

Jim and Blake ended the conversation on a positive note by sharing something that they appreciated about Jim's mom: "We really enjoyed that weekend trip that we all took last year. We felt close to you and included. When you treat our relationship with respect, we feel supported and happy that you are in our lives."

CONCLUSION

Remember that it is important to follow through on your assertive communications. No doubt Jim's mother, like all people, will resist changing her behavior. She may protest, rationalize, or blame Jim as a way to maintain the comfortable status quo. Jim and Blake must stay the course. If Jim gives in to the pressure and attends the family event by himself, he has effectively reinforced the very behavior that he wants to change. It is important to remember to follow through and be consistent.

At the same time, you can be compassionate with your parents' and family members' mistakes. Remember to be on the lookout for positive, inclusive behaviors that you can reinforce. They, like all of us, need encouragement and reinforcement to learn and grow.

Guided Activity: Practicing Assertiveness Using the LADDER Technique

Is there a microaggression or overtly discriminatory behavior that you need to address in your family? (You might consider using an incident you thought of in the Pause and Reflect exercise in this chapter.) Take a piece of paper and write *LADDER* in bold letters down the left hand side. Work together using the guide below, and Jim and Blake's example, to create a similar plan for assertive communication about the incident or behavior that you identified.

L: Look at your rights and your wants. You have the right to be treated with respect and dignity as a couple.

A: Arrange a meeting to discuss the situation with your family member(s).

D: Define the problem. State the facts objectively. Describe the problematic behavior as if you are looking through the lens of a camera. What do you observe specifically? (Example: "You asked me to attend the family reunion without my husband" instead of vague statements such as "You were disrespectful.")

D: Describe your feelings. Use "I" statements. Do not place blame or label. (Example: "I feel hurt and angry" instead of "Your severe character flaws are making me miserable.")

E: Express what you want concisely and clearly. Be polite, be precise, and be direct. (Example: "I want you to ask 'How is Blake' just like I ask how your husband is.")

R: Reinforce the positive. Behavior that is reinforced is repeated. Paint the picture of the positive consequences of complying with the request. (Example: "When you acknowledge my relationship in our conversations, I feel valued.")

Note. Davis, M., Eshelman, E. R., & McKay, M. (2008). *The relaxation & stress reduction workbook* (6th ed.). Oakland, CA: New Harbinger.

Many resources and workshops are devoted to assertiveness skills training and you may want to take advantage of one or more of them. Meanwhile, remember the following:

1. You have the right to be authentic.
2. You have the right to choose your partner/spouse.
3. You have the right to maintain your integrity as a couple.

Creating and maintaining healthy boundaries that protect you from the destructive effects of prejudice while maintaining a mutually respectful and compassionate relationship with your FOO is an important task for same-sex couples. Couples need the skills to make and then reinforce their decisions about appropriate boundaries with their FOO. Practicing assertiveness skills can help couples to respond to overt or more subtle instances of prejudice that they experience in their families.

NOTE

1. Davis, M., Eshelman, E. R., & McKay, M. (2008). *The relaxation & stress reduction workbook* (6th ed.). Oakland, CA: New Harbinger.

CHAPTER 4

OUR FAMILIES, OURSELVES

We are all initially socialized into our culture by family members and primary caretakers. During our formative years, we are taught the characteristics and behaviors that are valued (and devalued) in our society. Our own behaviors are shaped through a process of reinforcement and role modeling. In this way, we learn the rules and the "should's" about gender, sexuality, and relationships.

In much of American culture, people are taught to value heterosexuality and traditional gender roles and to devalue any behavior that does not conform to these roles. These lessons are consistently and pervasively reinforced by families and by most other social, educational, political, and religious institutions. As a result, most people have internalized negative messages about any sexual identity, gender expression, or relationship that breaks the rules established by a Eurocentric and heterosexist society.

Many people who identify as lesbian, gay, bisexual, transgender, and/or queer (LGBTQ) and are a member of a same-sex couple find the courage to embrace their authentic sexual and gender identities even if that means breaking these rigid societal rules. Their tenacity deserves acknowledgement and admiration. Even so, it is still likely that the negative messages about their identities that are learned very early in childhood can be triggered by certain inter-actions or events. Interacting with their families of origin may easily trigger these internalized negative messages.

Cathy, 27, came out to her father 3 years ago when she and Anna, 28, became a couple. Until then, Cathy had only dated men and had never told her father about her attraction to women. Cathy's father is politically, religiously, and socially conservative; he refuses to acknowledge the couple's relationship. In fact, her father told Cathy that she is "going through a phase" and that he expects this "fling" to run its course. He is sure that she will soon realize that she is not a lesbian, go back to dating men, and resume her role as Daddy's little girl.

Her father's rejection of her and her relationship with Anna can easily trigger Cathy's negative view of herself. Her relationship with Anna violates the traditional gender role and sexual identity expectations that she internalized during her childhood. Breaking these rules has broken the relationship between Cathy and her dad, and she finds herself taking responsibility for that rift. She catches herself thinking that she is not being a good daughter.

> Cathy: I'm being honest with my dad now about who I am and about my relationship with Anna. He just can't get past that I love Anna, a woman! And Anna looks pretty masculine, butch, so he thinks . . . well, he just can't figure out how to talk to any strong, independent woman. He wants to treat all women like they are helpless and needy. I get hooked by all this when I get to feeling bad about myself for breaking the unwritten "Thou shalt be heterosexual" rules of my family.
>
> Anna: I try to be supportive, but it's hard to see him as any-thing but a sexist, bigoted old man. I see what it does to Cathy. It scares me that she has so bought in to all that stuff that she acts reluctant about our relationship sometimes.

Cathy: I'm not reluctant. I'm just fighting these feelings that I'm being a "bad girl" by falling in love with a woman.

Cathy needs to unhook herself from the internalized stigma that interacting with her father triggers. Intellectually she understands that the problem is her dad's rigidity, not her relationship with Anna. Anna and Cathy need to negotiate how they will interact with Cathy's father as a couple while dealing with Cathy's self-blame.

Negative messages that we have internalized can hook us unexpectedly and trigger self-judgments that we are somehow not acceptable or worthy. We may react to these thoughts with anger, sadness, or fear. Or we may experience depression, anxiety, or defensiveness. We may also become aggressive, or engage in avoidance or escapism.

You can begin to deal more effectively with internalized stigma by slowing down enough to become aware of the negative messages that you have internalized. That means getting quiet long enough to actually pay attention to these messages that may be so automatic that you don't even realize they are there. Your partner or a close friend can help by listening carefully without judgment or criticism as you work to identify and label the negative messages that you have been taught about your identity and relationship.

Pause and Reflect

What were the messages that you learned from your family about lesbian, gay, bisexual, transgender, and/or queer identities and same-sex relationships? Make a list of these messages. Then put a + or − next to each depending on whether they were positive/affirming or negative/rejecting messages. Share your list with your partner/spouse. For each message you listed, how do you feel when you hear it or think it? How do you typically react when this message triggers negative feelings about your identity or relationship?

As we work to become more aware of how internalized stigma triggers negative feelings and reactions, we need to have compassion for ourselves. Many of us have a habit of being hard on ourselves. We expect to quickly get over it or to just stop it once we realize what is going on. Be patient! Most of us have spent many years in this automatic and largely unconscious negative cycle and it will take some time, effort, and courage to try something new!

While you are changing this negative cycle, remember that the negative messages that you have learned are not who you are. They are just a story you have been told. Once you can accept, with compassion rather than judgment, that these messages are there, they will begin to lose their power over you.

You can actively choose to detach from these negative messages and choose new positive ones instead. This process takes practice. Once you have the awareness, you still have to act on it. Keep in mind that you had to learn how to "do" stigma. Learning how to do pride and self-acceptance also takes some time and effort.

Many couples struggle with how to respond (rather than knee-jerk react) when their internalized stigma gets triggered by family members. Remember Jim and Blake from Chapter 3? They manage a 500-acre farm. They have faced serious economic and physical challenges related to their family business. Blake's family lives on a neighboring farm, and in many ways the shared struggle of managing farms in uncertain economic times has kept them bonded. Yet, the couple still struggles with how to respond to family members when they say or do things that trigger their internalized stigma. Jim and Blake believe that their family's behaviors toward them are at least partially based on the negative (and false) stereotype that gay men's relationships are superficial and unstable. Same-sex couples are painfully aware of these negative stereotypes. Their own self-doubts drive them to react defensively or work extra hard to disprove the low or negative expectations held by their families. They are hurt by the lack of support from family members who don't consider their relationship to be important. They think that their family members don't expect them to stay together and weather inevitable ups and downs. These negative messages trigger Blake and Jim's own self-doubts, especially when they get into the inevitable conflicts and disagreements that couples experience.

> Blake: As a same-sex couple, we don't have family members that we can count on to encourage us when things get tough. They aren't going to say, "Ah, come on, you guys got problems, but you can work it out!" We don't have that, that's for sure. If Jim and I broke up, there are members of my family that would say, "Oh well, what did you expect? It's for the best. You'll get over it." They wouldn't support the relationship and our trying to hang on to it . . . they wouldn't. And that's the biggest difference in the way we're treated and the way my straight sisters' relationships are treated.
>
> Jim: Yeah. And it's not like they are mean to us. In fact, they rely on us when they need an extra hand with something. I think they actually care about us, but our relationship certainly is not equated with a "real" marriage in either of our families. And I have to confess that it sometimes raises doubts in my own mind, like I occasionally ask myself, "Could they be right?" I know it's not rational, but that doesn't keep the nagging thought from entering my mind, especially when Blake and I get really stressed or exhausted or get into an argument.

Family members' hurtful comments and behaviors can trigger our own internalized stigma. We can quickly become caught up in a cycle of minority stress. That is, when we hear negative messages about our identities and relationships, these reinforce lingering self-doubts or negative self-views that we have absorbed through the powerful forces of socialization. When this negative self-view is activated, it is less likely that we will assert our right to be treated respectfully.

We can break this cycle by changing our self-view and practicing assertive communication skills. First, we need to recognize how our families trigger our negative self-views about ourselves and our relationship. Then we need to respond effectively to our family members from a place of positive self-regard. Practicing these skills will improve our well-being and our relationships.

Guided Activity: Generating Assertive Responses

When people stop doing stigma and start doing pride and self-acceptance, they have the confidence to draw boundaries and make appropriate requests of others. Try these activities to practice your pride as a couple.

a. Write an advice column or how-to instructions for couples to use to overcome their internalized stigma and live with pride.

b. Look at the negative messages that you listed in the Pause and Reflect exercise. Rewrite each negative message into a positive affirmation. Remember that you and your partner are worthy of respectful treatment from your families. You can learn to interact with your families from a place of pride and self-acceptance.

c. For each couple discussed in this chapter, brainstorm some verbal responses and requests that each could make. For example, what might Cathy say to her dad? What request could she make? What might Blake say to his mom? What request might he make?

d. Keep in mind that people are more likely to get what they want when they are assertive rather than aggressive. Assertive responses follow two basic rules:

1. Use "I" messages. For example, "I feel hurt when you refer to Jim as my roommate."

2. Ask for a concrete behavioral change rather than something vague and abstract. For example, "Please refer to Jim as my partner or spouse."

Now think of a pattern of communication in your own family that triggers your internalized stigma or somehow makes you feel bad about your identity or relationship. With your partner, brainstorm a two-step assertive communication that you could use to address it.

CONCLUSION

When you buy into or participate in interactions that support negative beliefs about same-sex relationships, a process that you may not be fully conscious of, you are less likely to question discriminatory treatment by your family. People act out of their own internalized stigma. Allowing your internalized stigma to drive how you interact with your family and with your partner can undermine your individual and couple well-being.

Living a life that is characterized by a positive identity is the ultimate antidote to internalized stigma and the foundation for successful relationships (with your partner, family members, children, and friends). Once you are aware of your residual negative beliefs that get triggered by your family members, you can choose more positive (and accurate!) beliefs about yourselves. As Dr. James Croteau, counseling psychologist and expert on LGBTQ issues, has eloquently stated, eradicating internalized stigma is "ultimately about liberating the human capacity to love" (p. 652)[1]. The good news is that you can reexamine the negative beliefs you have been taught and choose more positive beliefs. You can learn to appropriately assert your needs when family members behave in ways that are disrespectful. These two actions will help eradicate internalized stigma and increase your well-being.

NOTE

1. Croteau, J. M. (2008). Reflections on understanding and ameliorating internalized heterosexism. *The Counseling Psychologist, 36*, 645–653. doi:10.1177/0011000008319285

CHAPTER 5

WE *CAN* CHOOSE OUR FAMILY!

You may have heard the saying that we don't get to choose our family. However, most couples, same-sex or different-sex, do create a family of choice. The family of choice provides a support network that is important to the well-being of the couple. This support network may include friends, other couples, former partners and their children, childhood friends, and other people that we rely on. A family of choice may also include some members of the family of origin (FOO) and extended family.

Support from the FOO is important. However, it is not always available, consistent, or strong. For most same-sex couples, actively creating and maintaining a family of choice is important. Even though family of choice, like any family, is still composed of imperfect human beings, active participation in a family of choice can fill needs for support and belonging that might otherwise be unmet.

Remember Blake and Jim from Chapters 3 and 4? Blake and Jim live and work very long hours on their 500-acre farm in a rural part of their state. They have many strengths as a couple, yet the nature of their work and their lives in a rural county keep them socially isolated much of the time. They do not get a lot of support for their relationship from their FOO.

To fill this need in their life, Blake and Jim have created a family of choice that consists of people who can be counted on to support them as a couple. Their family of choice includes a lesbian couple that lives about an hour from their farm. About eight years ago, this couple invited another gay male couple to a dinner party that included Blake and Jim. All three couples have since become chosen family for each other. They spend time together on a regular basis and vacation together once a year. Other family-of-choice members include the straight woman that Jim took to the prom in high school and her husband. Additionally, Jim's 22-year-old niece and Blake's 24-year-old nephew and his girlfriend are included.

One important aspect of this family of choice is that all of the members know each other. Each summer, Jim and Blake hold a gathering for their family of choice at their farm. Their family of choice comes to ride horses; fish in the pond; hang out playing games and cards on the deck; fire up the barbeque; and spend hours talking, laughing, and sharing stories. These reunions are deeply satisfying and very important to Jim and Blake. These are times when they feel supported and validated as a couple, without question.

Pause and Reflect

With your partner, list the people that you consider your family of choice.

Connections to a family of choice enable same-sex couples to develop long-term relationships with others with whom they can share a history and a set of meaningful rituals. Family rituals are important for providing a sense of continuity, meaning, and belonging that supports individual and couple identity. Couples therapy experts note that rituals that create a shared history and positive emotional connections can be informal, like meeting at the movie theater for a Sunday matinee, or more formal, like birthday and holiday celebrations. Building a support network of people who recognize and respect the couple's relationship is important to individual and relational health. Building this kind of network, however, does not happen overnight or automatically. Like all close families, members of a family of choice need to interact, share experiences, and build a history together.

Dee, 50, and Eliza, 53, have created a family of choice that is composed of a core group of three same-sex female couples; a straight couple; and several single friends who identify as lesbian, gay, bisexual, transgender, and/or queer or are straight allies. This family grows and contracts as people move in or out of the community. Over the years, their family of choice has established a calendar of annual events that everyone looks forward to with anticipation. These happy occasions create rituals of connection that everyone enjoys. For example, one couple hosts an annual brunch that includes the members of Dee and Eliza's family of choice as well as other friends of the host couple. The group also travels together occasionally.

Many humorous stories about the adventures of this family are repeatedly told (and often embellished) until they have become a part of the family lore. One member of the family is an avid photographer and documents every event and shares the pictures on a website. Storytelling and picture sharing help to create and document the history of the family group.

For the past decade, Dee and Eliza have hosted an annual holiday party in December. This party revolves around a unique theme or activities, such as playing bingo, solving a holiday murder mystery, or decorating holiday stockings. These parties have become a ritual that provides an important touchstone for the family around the holidays. All of these celebrations have become ritualized and provide a sense of continuity, stability, and celebration to the family of choice.

Family of choice is especially important during times of crisis. These close networks provide tangible and intangible support. At one Thanksgiving dinner, someone observed that in the previous decade, almost everyone at the table had suffered a crisis to which family of choice members had responded with physical help and emotional support. Family members also help each other routinely by giving advice on topics ranging from gardening to child rearing and by sharing tools, trucks, and heavy lifting.

Guided Activity: A Family of Choice Circle

To do this exercise, each partner will need a blank piece of paper and a pen. Draw your own picture following the steps below. Then, share your picture with your partner.

1. Draw a small circle in the middle of a blank piece of paper and put you and your partner (and your children if applicable) in the middle of this circle.
2. Draw another circle around the first. Place the names of two to six of the closest or most important people in your life as a couple/family. Focus on people that provide the two of you with emotional, financial, mental, spiritual, or physical support.
3. Draw another circle around the first two. In this circle, add the names of other close and supportive friends and family members.
4. Draw another circle around the others. Place in this circle the names of acquaintances and family members with whom you have ties but are not particularly close.
5. Finally, draw an outer circle that encloses all the others. In this outer circle, put the names of those who are more distant or peripheral to your family life.
6. Now draw lines to show which people in your picture are also connected to each other. Use solid lines to indicate close connections between people and dotted lines to indicate a looser connection.

(continues)

Guided Activity: A Family of Choice Circle (*Continued*)

7. When you are finished with your picture of support, share it with your partner. What similarities and differences do you notice?

8. Looking at the pictures that you drew, make a note of activities that you engage in with the people you placed in your inner three circles. Are there any rituals of connection that you all engage in? Do you spend regularly scheduled times with your family of choice? Do you celebrate birthdays or holidays together?

9. Now make a list of activities that you might enjoy doing with your family of choice. Are there activities that you would like to add to the things you already do with this group? If so, add those to the list and circle them. How can you schedule time with members of your family of choice, both individually and as a larger group? What type of record or history can you create for the group that honors the importance of these times together? What additional "rituals of connection" can you establish?

10. Finally, is there anyone that the two of you would like to add to your family of choice? If so, write down a plan for how to include this person in the activities you describe above. How can you expand your family of choice?

Note. Green, R. J., & Mitchell, V. (2008). Gay and lesbian couples in therapy: Minority stress, relational ambiguity, and families of choice. In A. S. Gurman (Ed.), *Clinical handbook of couple therapy* (4th ed., pp. 662–680). New York, NY: Guilford Press.

Family therapists suggest that every couple needs a minimum of six people in their lives who provide ongoing and accessible support.[1] The Guided Activity will guide you in building your own family of choice.

CONCLUSION

By examining the solid lines in the family of choice portrait you created in the Guided Activity, you will have a good idea of the density of your family of choice, as well as your larger social support network. When your friends are also friends with each other, the network is stronger. Imagine a safety net with many strong ties and very few gaps. The more dense or integrated your network, the stronger your social support system. Forging strong, reciprocal relationships with the individuals (family and friends) in your inner circle and then connecting these individuals together into a family of choice is very important to a couples' well-being.

A dense social network or family of choice can provide the validation and emotional support that same-sex couples need. Be patient. If you are starting from scratch, building a mutually supportive family of choice will take a while, and the maintenance of these relationships will continue for years to come. The payoff in terms of your well-being and life satisfaction will be lifelong.

NOTE

1.   Green, R. J., & Mitchell, V. (2008). Gay and lesbian couples in therapy: Minority stress, relational ambiguity, and families of choice. In A. S. Gurman (Ed.), *Clinical handbook of couple therapy* (4th ed., pp. 662–680). New York, NY: Guilford Press.

CHAPTER 6

WARM WELCOMES AND FAMILY ALLIES

Our heterosexual family members often must go through their own process of education and self-reflection as they evolve into our allies and sources of social support for people who identify as lesbian, gay, bisexual, transgender, and/or queer (LGBTQ). In the beginning, this process may require some patience and encouragement. Strengthening family bonds and creating a supportive environment takes time and effort. The good news is that many family members do become our supportive allies.

It is important to recognize and reinforce the positive support that we get from our family of origin (FOO). Sharing our experiences with our family members can help in this process. Talking about what is positive about being a same-sex couple can, over time, help to change old negative beliefs, attitudes, and behaviors while creating or reinforcing affirming beliefs, attitudes, and behaviors.

Keisha, age 31, and Amy, age 30, have been together for almost 5 years. Both FOOs have been supportive of the couple. Amy and Keisha recognize and appreciate that support. Amy noted:

> Keisha's mom is so embracing that it just motivates us and inspires us to continue to do our best. We can always count on

her. I think it would crush her if we didn't stay together and make our relationship work.

Amy and Keisha also recognize that their families have worked hard to become allies who speak out on their behalf. Amy and Keisha recalled when one of Amy's cousins posted an antigay remark online. Amy described the incident:

> While we were sitting around talking and worrying over how to respond, or whether to respond at all, my straight brother posted a reply that said he was offended by the comment and called it what it was—an expression of prejudice. Our cousin ended up apologizing to everyone. We realized that we are not the only ones hurt by that kind of prejudice, and it felt really good to know that we aren't the only ones who will say something about it!

Amy and Keisha focus on the positive and supportive relationships that they can count on. They thanked Amy's brother the next time they saw him and shared with him how important his support was to them. Finally, at the next family gathering, they thanked Amy's cousin for posting the apology, and now that cousin is an ally as well.

Pause and Reflect

Who are the family members that you can count on to be supportive of your relationship? Are there times that they have acted as an ally for your relationship?

Family support is important for all couples. For many same-sex couples, this source of support is neither assumed nor taken for granted. Although different-sex couples may expect family support for their relationship, same-sex couples often do not.

Same-sex couples sometimes talk about how "lucky" they feel when their family is supportive. This feeling is often a reaction to witnessing the lack of support that other same-sex couples or friends who identify as LGBTQ have experienced. Amy shared her insights about this:

> We both feel very lucky that our families have been as open as they have. We consider ourselves lucky instead of assuming this is the way it should be. It's interesting that we don't take for granted that we will automatically have the support that all loving couples like us deserve!

Amy and Keisha reminisced about telling their families about their commitment to each other and how their families responded.

> Amy: When we decided to move in together, the first thing we did was tell our families because they're such a vital part of our relationship, and we got resounding support. It's kind of astonishing because we are an interracial couple and I know that in society that is still another problem for some people. I thought for sure my family would have some reservations, but just the opposite; they accepted Keisha with open arms. They consider her part of the family. I don't know, I guess we've been very fortunate.
>
> Keisha: I remember how nervous I was about meeting Amy's family for the first time. When we walked in everyone was so nice to me. Amy's mom hugged me and kissed me, and her dad hugged me. That was when I knew that I was accepted because her dad really isn't a huggy person, and when he hugged me I was like, "Whoa!" I stuck my hand out and he grabbed my hand and pulled me in and gave me a hug and that was, to me, like he was saying, "Welcome

to the family." And on my side of the family, I know that Amy had to endure some family tension, especially when my brother insisted that marriage was between a man and a woman and we got into a big argument. On the other hand, my mom and dad loved Amy from Day 1. I tell you, I think my mom loves Amy more than she does me!

Amy: I know that Keisha's parents' reaction has really played a huge part in my confidence about our relationship and our commitment to each other. It also affects my feelings about myself. Their acceptance and support have gone a long way toward me feeling better about being gay, and I think that goes hand in hand with me feeling stable and secure in our relationship.

Many same-sex couples find that family members, over time, do evolve into solid and reliable sources of support. As family members go through their own growth process, it is important to focus on and reinforce even the smallest positive behaviors. Remember that behaviors that are reinforced are more likely to be repeated. We need to catch our family members behaving supportively and be vocal in our appreciation.

We can sometimes get caught up in a cycle of mentally replaying remarks and behaviors that are unsupportive or critical. We need to practice noticing and commenting when family members say or do small things that are supportive of our identities and our relationship. When we remember to take the time to reinforce the supportive behaviors of our family members, they are more likely to continue to grow and respond in supportive ways.

Sam and TJ's families are still in the process of accepting and celebrating their relationship. Sam, age 25, and TJ, age 24, met 2 years ago at a conference on transgender health. They share a downtown apartment that is close to work. They each came out to their respective families in high school. Their couple relationship, however, has forced each of their families to become more visibly accepting of the couple.

Sam and TJ have watched their families struggle in different ways with the couple's gender and sexual identities. They both want to be supportive of their families' process. As TJ said, "We know they are trying. They don't always get it right. They still slip up with pronouns sometimes but they try and they are making a lot of progress toward really being there for us." Sam added,

> We make it clear that we are a couple. At first my parents would act very nervous when we'd go to visit them and awkwardly put TJ's things in my old bedroom and my things on the sofa in the living room. The last time we were there, though, my mom told us that she had put clean sheets on the bed for the two of us. I hugged her. That was a huge sign to me that she was making progress in accepting our relationship.

Sam and TJ have made a conscious decision to recognize and celebrate the small signs of progress that their parents make. When TJ's parents invited them both, as a couple, to join them on the family camping trip, TJ and Sam both thanked them for explicitly extending the invitation. During the vacation, TJ's little sister responded to a song that was playing on the radio by whining "that's so gay" and changing the station. TJ's mom told her she shouldn't say "that's so gay." TJ immediately smiled and gave her a grateful nod.

Noticing small acts of support and taking time to express gratitude to our supportive family members fosters positive family connections and enhances our own positive well-being. Sometimes we forget to stop and think about the positive support that our families offer us. We must work to be mindful and express our gratitude.

The Guided Activity can help you to practice noticing positive actions that you can reinforce in the moment. You can also use the

---

**Guided Activity: Noticing Supportive Behaviors
and Expressing Gratitude**

1. As a couple, generate a list of ways (big and small) that your family members have been supportive of your relationship. Use this list to help you become more aware of the positive actions of your family members. (In this exercise, don't question their motives! Just take their positive actions at face value and accept them.) For each supportive behavior, brainstorm ways that you might have verbally or nonverbally reinforced the supportive behavior in the moment.

2. Next time you and your partner go to a family gathering, watch for any small thing that a family member says or does that is supportive of your relationship. Find a way to immediately give positive reinforcement. It may be as simple as a smile, a hug, or a thank you.

3. As a couple, look back at the list from the Pause and Reflect. What are your happy memories of times that a member of your family communicated support and acceptance? Write a short note to that family member expressing gratitude for their support. Deliver the letter in person, if possible. If sending the letter is not possible, save it in a special place to read when you need to be reminded of the support you have received.

activity to reinforce the positive support of your family members in letters of gratitude.

CONCLUSION

A positive, healthy relationship with your partner will benefit your own health and well-being and can also have positive effects on your family members' attitudes, beliefs, and behaviors. Many people have become powerful allies as a result of knowing and loving the same-sex couples in their family. Couple members can help their family members and themselves along the path to acceptance by discussing and sharing the many positive aspects of their lives.

Likewise, having positive family support in your life can contribute to the health and well-being of your couple relationship. You can make a point to notice and express your gratitude for even small expressions of support. Verbal or nonverbal expressions of appreciation are powerful reinforcements for behaviors that you want your families to continue. It is easy to get caught in the habit of only noticing and responding to the negative things that you witness. Noticing and responding to positive things you witness is an important habit to cultivate for your own and your family members' benefit.

Relationships with family members present opportunities for personal growth and for developing skills of compassion and caring about others. When couples feel good about themselves and their relationship, they project the kind of strength, resilience and equanimity that family members are likely to respond to in kind. From a place of strength and acceptance, it is easier to notice the positive things that family members do to support us. When couples focus on the positive aspects of their identities and their relationships and express gratitude to others for their support, they experience a greater sense of well-being.

Part II

FAMILY OF CREATION

Many same-sex couples raise children.[1] Same-sex couples may become parents by having biological children, through surrogacy or adopting children, by becoming foster parents or guardians, or by partnering with someone who is already a parent. Every parenting couple has a unique story about their family of creation.

Regardless of how or when same-sex couples become parents, they may face parenting challenges that are related to minority stress. Public debates about the ability of same-sex couples to raise children have taken place in legislatures, courts, government and private agencies, educational institutions, and medical and mental health professions. Most of these social institutions have come to agree that same-sex couples are capable of raising healthy, happy children. Most of these entities conclude that the problems children may face are not due to having parents that are the same sex; the problem is prejudice against same-sex couples.

However, significant pockets of resistance still maintain false negative stereotypes and prejudice about the families of same-sex couples. When same-sex couples have to deal with the prejudice and discrimination of individuals and institutions, they may feel like they are under a social microscope. They may worry about whether they are good parents and whether they are raising healthy kids. Same-sex couples need to remember that every loving parent has moments of self-doubt; these may prompt healthy introspection. Sometimes parents deal with the prejudice against them by trying too hard to be perfect. Reacting to stigma by trying to overcompensate for being a same-sex–parented family can increase stress on the family. Children easily pick up on the unwritten rules of their family. If one of these unspoken rules is "We must appear to be perfect," the pressure to comply can become a burden that undermines family health and well-being. It is important for parents and children to learn to recognize that they are reacting to stigma and prejudice. Naming this aspect of minority stress and finding social support within and outside of the family is an important step toward deliberately and consciously responding rather than unconsciously reacting to or internalizing negative messages about our parenting.

Parenting is challenging! Parenting has a way of pushing our buttons and triggering our own fears and vulnerabilities. Thousands of parenting books, workshops, and other resources are available to support parents in raising their children. A growing number of resources are specifically written for parents who identify as LGBTQ. However, surprisingly few resources directly address the minority stress that same-sex couples may encounter in their role as parents and grandparents.

Learning to be an effective parent, or grandparent, requires on-the-job training. The learning never ends because the job constantly changes as children grow and develop. Parenting a 4-year-old is very different from parenting a 14-year-old. And, of course, every child is unique, so effective parenting must take into account a child's temperament and individual needs.

Developmental stages and the needs of a child factor into minority stress experiences within the family. For instance, it is important for same-sex couples to be honest and open with their children about their couple relationship and their family structure. However, decisions about disclosure to people outside of the family may vary markedly depending on the specific situation and the developmental stage of the child. Parents may feel like they are in a "revolving closet" as they strive to be appropriately responsive to the needs of their child.[2]

For example, the young child who outs us at unexpected moments may want to shove us back in the closet while she navigates middle school. Regardless of the specifics of the situation and the ever-changing needs of the child, parents can facilitate their children's healthy development by consistently modeling and reinforcing positive identity and family pride. Decades of research have shown that same-sex couples raise healthy, happy kids. There may even be some distinct advantages to being raised by same-sex partnered parents! For example, same-sex couples may share parenting roles more equally because they are not bound by the traditional gender roles of different-sex couples. This freedom from gendered parenting scripts allows same-sex couples to create their parenting roles in ways that capitalize on their individual strengths and their family values and goals.

These family values often include egalitarian ideals that provide strong internal support for everyone in the family. Same-sex couples may be more likely to involve their children in family decisions, teach their children respect for differing perspectives, and reinforce empathy and compassion for others' feelings. These family strengths promote well-being in the parents and children, alike.

Same-sex couples cultivate these strengths as parents in response to their own life experiences with stigma and discrimination. However, these experiences may also prompt same-sex couples to think extra hard about becoming parents because they worry that their children will have to deal with discrimination and stigma because of their parents' identities. Voicing these concerns and talking with other same-sex couples who have children can be very helpful.

Couples who desire to be parents may benefit from spending time together critically examining their own family histories. They can examine the ideas and beliefs that they have learned about what being a good parent looks like. Although it is freeing to let go of old ideas that do not fit and are not useful, it can also be anxiety provoking.

The broad consensus from research on child development is that there are three important ingredients associated with healthy outcomes for children. Those ingredients are (a) the quality of the relationship between the parents, (b) the quality of the relationship between the parent and the child, and (c) the availability of economic and social resources. Parents who focus on creating and sustaining high-quality familial relationships characterized by warmth, commitment, emotional support, and appropriate limit-setting can be assured that they are providing the security and stability that is needed for the well-being of their child.

In the current environment, however, the stability and security of same-sex couples and their child are often threatened by the lack of legal recognition. When one parent has a legally recognized relationship to a child and the other does not, strains and insecurities in the couple and family relationship can be the inevitable result. (We specifically address the minority stress that results from discriminatory legal policy later in Part VI.)

Same-sex couples need to find or actively create social and institutional support for their families. Communities vary widely in acceptance, affirmation, and resources for same-sex couples and their families. Same-sex couples may feel isolated from the general community of parents. They may also lack support from the family of origin. Same-sex couples may have to deal with and help their children deal with expressions of prejudice from outsiders, as well as from members of their own extended family.

One of the most important things that same-sex couples can do is build a strong support network in the LGBTQ community and among community allies. These allies may include our child's teachers, coaches, religious or spiritual leaders, and the parents of our child's friends. In addition to their parents, experts suggest that children benefit from having access to at least one unrelated, supportive, and LGBTQ-affirmative adult that they can talk to about their family relationships and their own minority stress experiences.

In this section, we share the stories of couples with children of various ages to illustrate common challenges that may arise. In Chapter 7, we illustrate how the family of origin can be the source of minority stress for same-sex couples who are parents or grandparents. We suggest positive ways to cultivate support. In Chapter 8, we discuss ways to deal with experiences of prejudice in the child's world of school, peers, and neighborhoods. In Chapter 9, we show how parents can manage the revolving closet of disclosure and concealment as their child grows and develops. In Chapter 10, we illustrate how our fears that our children or our entire family will be rejected can lead to hypervigilance and the pressure to be the perfect family with perfect kids. We urge parents to release themselves from the impossible task of having to be the model family. Chapter 11 discusses how internalized stigma can affect same-sex couples' decision to become parents and how they can positively address this challenge. In Chapter 12, we conclude this section with additional positive actions that same-sex couples can take to strengthen their families.

Parenting is a challenge under any circumstance. Same-sex couples who are parents have the added challenge of dealing with minority stress from discrimination and prejudice that impacts them and their children. Nevertheless, same-sex couples who are parents and grandparents can develop their coping skills, resources, and support for dealing with minority stress. They can help their children and grandchildren develop effective coping strategies as well. Same-sex couples who do so will enjoy the deep satisfaction and personal growth that accompanies the adventures of parenting and grandparenting.

NOTES

1. The focus of this section is on same-sex couples and the minority stress these couples experience in their roles as parents. We recognize that many individuals who identify as lesbian, gay, bisexual, transgender, and/or queer (LGBTQ) are raising children as single or unpartnered parents. We also recognize that many families involve more than two parents. The issues that we discuss in this section may also apply to those families.

2. Lynch, J., & McMahon-Klosterman, K. (2012). The gay and lesbian stepfamily. In J. J. Bigner & J. L. Wetchler (Eds.), *Handbook of LGBT-affirmative couple and family therapy* (pp. 233–248). New York, NY: Routledge.

CHAPTER 7

"YOU AREN'T THE 'REAL' PARENT"

Children are magical. They transform the lives of their parents. They bring smiles to faces of family. They inspire joy, protectiveness, love, and attachment. Children can also transform relationships, especially between same-sex couples and their family of origin (FOO). As one couple shared,

> We were amazed that once we adopted our daughter, our parents did a big 180 in terms of their acceptance of us as a family. Of course she has them wrapped around her tiny finger. That's no surprise, but we can still hardly believe the difference she has made in how our parents treat us!

It is unfortunate, however, that for some couples, the FOO is not supportive and does not celebrate their couple relationship and family of creation. One of the most challenging minority stressors that same-sex couples experience is prejudice from members of their own FOO. Recall that in Part I of this book, we defined our FOO as the people who raised us. Our FOO may include our parents, grandparents, siblings, aunts, uncles and cousins. When a same-sex couple relationship is not supported by the FOO, the relationship bond with a child or grandchild may also be disrespected. Same-sex couples have shared stories about members of their FOO who refuse to recognize or participate in a relationship with the couple's child or grandchild. For many of these couples, the message they receive from other relatives is that a nonbiological parent is not a "real" parent. Their FOO refuses to extend the same support and respect that "blood" relatives receive.

Robin, 34, and Janet, 31, have been a couple for 3 years. They just completed all of the necessary paperwork for Janet to officially adopt Robin's biological son, Patrick, who just celebrated his seventh birthday. Janet, Robin, and Patrick consider themselves a family, and they are taking every step possible to legally protect their family. The problem is that Janet's parents do not consider Patrick to be their grandchild because their daughter is not the biological parent, as Janet and Robin discuss below.

> Janet: My parents treat Patrick very differently than they do my sister's kids. They invite her kids to visit in the summer for a week, but Patrick is not included even though he is about the same age. My parents travel to my sister's house for all of her kids' birthday parties and bring lavish gifts. They don't even bother to send Patrick a birthday card!
>
> Robin: It's heartbreaking. We really want Janet's parents to step up and be positive and supportive grandparents to Patrick. It's really important to me because my parents are deceased, so they are the only grandparents left. We keep hoping that if they would just have some quality time together the three of them would bond.
>
> Janet: Yes, we really want that for Patrick.

Robin and Janet speculate about whether the problem is blended families, or attachment, or whether their same-sex relationship is the real issue for Janet's parents. Robin summarized the situation as follows:

> The bottom line is, Janet is not acknowledged as Patrick's "real" mom and thus Janet's parents do not consider him their grandchild. They even told Janet that I'm Patrick's real mom and that she should not invest too much in raising him!

Robin and Janet keep trying to bring the family together by inviting the grandparents to visit and participate in the life of their family. So far, Janet's parents keep their distance. They would like to come up with a strategy for communicating with Janet's parents about this issue.

Pause and Reflect

Which members of your family of origin (FOO) give full support to your family of creation? Which members of your FOO have trouble supporting your family of creation? Do you think prejudice plays a role in the lack of support? Share your perceptions with your partner.

Support for your family is very important. Denying and disrespecting the bonds between children and their parents is one of the most painful and personally upsetting expressions of prejudice that couples experience from their FOO. If your FOO chooses to not be supportive, then you as a couple have steps you can take to empower yourselves.

Robin described how they perceive the situation: "We are banging our heads against a wall in efforts to get Janet's parents to come around and act like real grandparents." They decide that they will be better off spending this energy finding the support they need from others in their social network and community. They look to their friends, including older people in their friendship circle who identify as lesbian, gay, bisexual, transgender, and/or queer, to include in their family events. This strategy has helped them to create much-needed positive social support for their family.

Many same-sex couples are also grandparents. Sometimes it is grandparents whose bonds with grandchildren are ignored. Nathan and Roberto, both in their 60s, have been together for 20 years and married for 11 years. They have a grandson, Jimmy, who is 10. Jimmy's mom is Roberto's daughter from a previous marriage. Since Jimmy was a baby, Nathan and Roberto have spent a lot of time with him. They have taken him on trips with them, babysat while his mom worked, and contributed financially to help Jimmy's mom make ends meet. There is a strong emotional attachment between Jimmy and both grandparents.

About two years ago, Jimmy's mom remarried and moved with her new husband to a neighboring state. Nathan and Roberto have missed having their grandson close by, and they have gone to great lengths to travel to his new home to spend time with him. They also arrange for Jimmy to visit them during summer breaks and holidays.

Jimmy's paternal grandmother, however, does not consider Nathan and Roberto to be real grandparents. Because she also lives in the same town as Nathan and Roberto, there is a lot of tension between them when it comes to deciding how Jimmy's time will be shared during his visits. Roberto gave an example:

> Last summer while Jimmy was in town for a visit, we planned an overnight camping trip and bought tickets for the waterpark. The night before we were scheduled to leave, our daughter called and said that Jimmy would not be able to go because his Nana wanted him to come to her house to visit with her relatives. Of course we want him to know his Nana's family, but there was no respect for our plans. We know that Nana knew about our plans, and we think that she probably did this intentionally.

At times they get frustrated with their daughter for not being more assertive and for allowing Nana to treat them with disrespect. They are not sure of the extent to which their status as a same-sex couple accounts for this disrespectful treatment, but it does raise questions in their minds. As a result, they worry that their time with Jimmy will continue to be a low priority, even as they work harder and harder to maintain their special relationship with their grandson.

What can Nathan and Roberto do in this situation? First, Nathan and Roberto can fully claim their relationship with their grandson as legitimate and important. They can insist that their relationship with Jimmy is just as important as his relationship with his other grandparents. Nathan and Roberto can also confidently assert that Jimmy's positive growth and development is enhanced by having his grandparents' consistent presence, love, and support.

Same-sex couples may hesitate to assert the importance and legitimacy of their relationships when they are not recognized by other family members. Naming the prejudice and discrimination against same-sex couple relationships that creates this situation is important. By labeling the situation as discriminatory and unfair, same-sex couples are less likely to internalize the prejudice and passively accept it.

Sometimes couples accept a second-class status in their families and inadvertently reinforce it. Nathan and Roberto, for instance, may convince themselves to take what they can get and not rock the boat instead of asserting their desire to have their relationship with their grandson respected and supported. They may fear that asserting the importance of the relationship and directly asking for what they want could make the situation even worse instead of better.

It is important for Nathan and Roberto to join together in asserting their desire for other family members to support and respect their time with their grandson. To be effective in getting what they want—a commitment to respect time and plans made with Jimmy—Nathan and Roberto can join together with Jimmy's parents and the other grandparents to pursue a common goal. After all, everyone is invested in providing emotional support and love so that Jimmy thrives. Joining together around their common values and intentions will help everyone focus on Jimmy and hopefully lead to positive solutions.

Nathan and Roberto decided to initiate a family meeting with Jimmy's parents to generate a plan for sharing Jimmy's time and to negotiate ground rules about the circumstances under which the

---

Guided Activity: Communicating With Families of Origin To Accomplish a Specific Goal

Start this activity by writing a short mission statement for your family. What are you and your partner's goals for your relationship between you, your children or grandchildren, and other members of your family of origin (FOO)?

Choose a goal related to your mission statement. State this goal clearly, and describe the specific actions you would like for your FOO to take in support of your goal. Also include a statement of the actions that you will take to accomplish this goal and reinforce positive FOO behaviors.

Now, write a letter to your FOO stating in a positive way your family relationship goal and your right to respectful treatment. End the letter by asking for specific actions. State clearly how these actions will support your positive goal and foster a positive relationship for everyone.

Set a time to meet with the FOO to deliver the letter. If a face-to-face meeting is not feasible, then send the letter with a request for a response within a certain period of time. Write down the date so that you remember when you need to follow up. Invite positive dialogue.

Remember that communication with your FOO should focus on goals (specific actions that people want) rather than problems (actions people don't want). If a dialogue starts to focus on who is to blame, families get stuck in the problem. Family therapists suggest that family communication is more effective when people focus on positive strengths and motives. Remaining positive in all communication with a FOO member is important.

---

plan can be altered. The immediate goal was to assert the importance of the bond between Jimmy and Nathan and Roberto. Later they may include the other grandparents in a family meeting, as well. The ultimate goal is to support Jimmy's well-being and the well-being of the entire family by valuing, supporting, and protecting these important bonds. If you experience a challenge to your family bonds, consider using the Guided Activity to help you communicate clearly and assertively with members of your FOO.

CONCLUSION

Asserting the legitimacy and importance of your couple relationship and your relationship to children and grandchildren can be a big challenge. It is very easy to get caught up in long-standing family dynamics and patterns of interaction that are negative and unproductive. Changing the way you think about yourselves and how you interact with other family members is hard work, but the benefits are great.

In some cases, same-sex couples may benefit from coaching from a professional counselor or family therapist. These professionals can help couples to develop and practice effective assertiveness skills that are tailored to their specific situation. Other same-sex couples may simply need to be reminded that their couple relationship and their family relationships are important and deserving of respectful treatment.

CHAPTER 8

WHEN BAD THINGS HAPPEN TO OUR KIDS

When we experience discrimination and prejudice because of our sexual or gender identities, it is stressful. When our children are the targets of other people's prejudice against our families, the stress is compounded. We want all children to thrive—thus we have every right to be protective and proactive.

When our children are being affected by the bigotry of others, we feel angry. We may even want to lash out. In this chapter, we focus on positive and effective ways for us to cope, and to help children cope, with the prejudice that they may encounter in their daily lives.

Madison, 36, and Jackie, 35, have been a couple for 10 years. They were married in California. Together, Madison and Jackie are raising three daughters. Two of them, now young teens, are Madison's biological children with her ex-husband. Jackie gave birth to their youngest daughter, Nikki, 6 years ago.

Their family has recently moved back home to a more socially and politically conservative region because they want to be near their families of origin. "We wanted the girls to have grandparents in their lives. That was more important to us than anything else," stated Jackie. "We knew it would come with a price, though. We were just hoping to make the best of it."

Nikki came home from school one afternoon in May very distraught because her teacher would not allow her to make two Mother's Day cards. The teacher told Nikki that the other children were only allowed to make one card and that it would be unfair to allow her to make two cards. Nikki was upset that she didn't have a card to give each of her moms. Madison and Jackie were upset by the insensitivity of their child's teacher.

After getting out the crayons and construction paper so that Nikki could make another card, Jackie contacted the teacher to request an appointment. At the parent–teacher meeting, Madison and Jackie calmly related the facts of the Mother's Day card incident. They described exactly what Nikki had shared with them, sticking to the facts that they observed. Then, they asked the teacher what she had seen and observed.

By sticking to the facts, or what someone might see through the lens of a camera, Madison and Jackie were able to take a more objective, problem-solving stance. They were not accusing or blaming the teacher. They made it clear that they just wanted to discuss what had happened and its impact on Nikki.

In this instance, Nikki's teacher was unaware of the impact of her one-card rule. Madison and Jackie's feedback, delivered without accusation or incrimination, led to a change in the rule about cards and a new sensitivity to their family. At the meeting, Jackie and Madison offered to donate some age-appropriate books on diverse families. They even volunteered to come and read the stories to the children during story time. Nikki's teacher referred them to the school principal to discuss the suggested resources.

Parents who identify as lesbian, gay, bisexual, transgender, and/or queer (LGBTQ) are more likely than other parents to volunteer at their child's school and to participate in parent–school organizations.[1] Before enrolling their child, many parents who identify as LGBTQ make a point to meet the principal of the school to ask her or him questions about diversity and how families like theirs are included in the curriculum. Many parents proactively meet their child's teachers to tell them about their family rather than waiting for an issue to arise.

As children leave elementary school and enter middle school, same-sex couples may find themselves limiting their engagement with the school. Sometimes this change in their school engagement is at the request of their young adolescents, who are busy individuating from their parents. (Let's face it: Adolescents often go through a period of time where they don't want their parents around unless absolutely necessary!) Figuring out the extent to which young teens are being developmentally appropriate versus trying to avoid disclosing information about their family composition can be challenging. Same-sex couples may feel like they are between a rock and a hard place at times. They have to decide when it is appropriate and helpful to be involved in their child's school and when it is more important to respect their adolescent's needs for independence and autonomy.

When same-sex couples feel excluded by the school, they may be less likely to attend parent organization meetings or chaperone school events. Although it may be easier to keep a low profile, research has shown that parent involvement at school enhances student learning and well-being. Negotiating parental involvement is an important family conversation that shows respect for adolescents' competence and independence while not abdicating responsibility for providing support for their education.

In addition to interactions at school, children may encounter prejudice in their own neighborhoods. One of Nikki's neighborhood friends, for instance, told her that she was not allowed to come over to Nikki's house to play because she had two moms. When Nikki tearfully relayed this message to Madison and Jackie, they were furious.

Jackie's impulse was to suggest to Nikki that she end that friendship so they could help her find other friends to play with instead.

> **Pause and Reflect**
>
> A wealth of resources for assessing the school climate and advocating for all children's safety and well-being at school is available at the Gay, Lesbian, & Straight Education Network (www.glsen.org) and the Family Equality Council (www.familyequality.org). Take some time right now to check out these websites and others for some ideas and inspiration!

As Madison and Jackie talked it over, they decided that this was an important opportunity for teaching their daughters how to deal constructively with this kind of prejudice. Taking a time out to determine a response rather than reacting to our distress in the moment is an important skill to develop and to teach our children. Ultimately, we want our children to be empowered to confront prejudice, whether it is directed at them or someone else. So we must develop this skill ourselves if we want to model it for our children!

Same-sex couples must be willing to talk to their children about prejudice and label acts that are disrespectful, unkind, or uninformed. These kinds of conversations help to inoculate children against the discriminatory behaviors and prejudicial attitudes of others.

Madison and Jackie made a commitment to openly and compassionately discuss these kinds of incidents with all of their children. They name the negative attitudes that are behind them and counter these attitudes with messages of pride in their family. They also empower their children with new assertive responses, such as, "My family does not believe in calling people names" or "Difference is a good thing."

The goal is to help their children externalize, rather than internalize, prejudice. This message must be communicated to children clearly and repeatedly. Their family is not the problem. The problem is the misinformation that people have about families with same-sex parents.

Madison and Jackie also explicitly tell their children that they do not need to protect their parents from the things that other children or adults say or do. Madison explained: "We tell them we are the adults here. We can handle this. The only thing that really hurts us is secrets. So we all have to have faith in each other."

Jackie continued:

> We have said it so much that our older daughters just roll their eyes at us now when we say it, but they get the point. We have encouraged them to talk to Nikki, too. Nikki looks up to her older sisters, and they reinforce that we have to talk about the things that hurt our feelings or make us uncomfortable.

In return, they have promised their daughters that they will not take any action without talking with them first. Showing our children that we can respond appropriately and thoughtfully rather than react in haste and anger builds their trust and confidence in our ability to deal effectively with this kind of stress. As Jackie described,

> Sometimes our children will not want to tell us things that happen because they are afraid that whatever we decide to do will make things worse instead of better. We kind of have that fear too. People always fear the bully, but in the end you have to come up with some kind of strategy for dealing with these things or they will just continue. Prejudice doesn't just go away. We have to be brave and take action. We know we are in the right.

In their talk with Nikki, Madison and Jackie helped her to express how she felt when her friend could not come over to play. She drew a picture of her moms and her sisters all holding hands under a bright smiling sun with their cheery home in the background. She then drew a picture of herself with a big sad face and tears, reaching out for another small figure that was also sad and mournful. The family pets were also weeping in the picture.

Madison and Jackie asked Nikki questions about her picture that allowed her to verbally express her feelings of hurt and sadness. They validated her feelings and asked her if she would like to share her picture with her friend's mom. This idea pleased Nikki.

Madison told Nikki that with her permission, she would deliver the picture and talk with her friend's mom about this situation that was making Nikki so sad. Then, Madison called to invite the friend's mom, Laura, to meet her for coffee at the local coffee shop. At first Laura was hesitant, but she eventually agreed to a meeting where the conversation unfolded.

> Madison: Is it true that your daughter is not allowed to come over to our house to play because Jackie and I are Nikki's moms?
>
> Laura: No offense, but I don't want my daughter exposed to that lifestyle. We're Christians and live by the Bible's teachings.
>
> Madison: I, too, believe that it's important to teach about love and compassion and peace. These are important lessons in the Bible. We teach these values to our children. Especially the Golden Rule: "Do unto others as you would have others do unto you." Jackie and I are doing our best to teach this rule to our three girls. Everyone deserves to be treated as we would want to be treated. So, that is our "lifestyle" and the values that we are trying to live by and teach our kids.
>
> Laura: You seem like nice people, but I still don't want my daughter to think it's okay to be gay. I don't want her to

grow up thinking that is acceptable to me because it's not what I want for her. I want her to grow up normal, get married to a man, and have children.

Madison: So, you're afraid that if your daughter plays with Nikki at our house, she will get the idea that it is okay to be a lesbian and will decide to become one?

Laura: Yes. I do believe it's a choice . . . a sinful choice, according to the Bible. I do everything that I can to protect my child from seeing inappropriate things on TV. How can I turn around and be a hypocrite by letting her be exposed to a lifestyle that the Bible says is immoral?

Madison: Yes, I think I can see your dilemma. She might come to our house and see that we're a family just like your family. We provide for the physical and emotional needs of our three children. What is it, exactly, that you object to?

Laura: I object to my daughter seeing two women together.

Madison: I want to say clearly that your daughter playing with Nikki at our house is not going to have any effect on your daughter's sexuality. Whatever it turns out to be, she won't get to choose it, any more than you chose to be straight. She could, however, see that our house and our family is pretty much the same as every other friend's house and family and pretty much like her own house and family. And I could see how that might be threatening to your belief that same-sex couples are sinful. What I need you to know, however, is that while you are preventing your daughter from seeing that our family is just like yours, you are hurting both of our daughters by not allowing the girls to play together. Here is the picture that Nikki drew expressing her hurt that you won't allow your daughter to come over to play. I am here today to convey Nikki's feelings about your rejection of her family and to ask you to have compassion and respect for our daughters' friendship and allow them to play together.

Laura: I'll discuss it with my husband. Don't get me wrong. Nikki is a sweet kid. I don't have anything against an innocent child.

After this conversation, Madison and Laura found themselves feeling uneasy about risking Nikki's exposure to Laura's "Christian" lifestyle. Eventually, however, Madison and Laura agreed to a schedule that would allow their daughters to play at each home for 1 hour a week during the school year and perhaps a little more during the summer vacation. Madison is not under the impression that she has changed Laura's attitudes, but she is happy that she at least negotiated a small change in Laura's behavior toward the friendship between their daughters.

Madison and Jackie took a number of positive steps to help Nikki with this situation. First, they gave Nikki tools appropriate to her age (markers and paper) to express her feelings about the situation. Then Madison and Jackie validated the feelings that Nikki expressed to them, reinforcing her ability to articulate her emotions appropriately. Older children might be encouraged to write a letter. Teenagers might benefit from role playing a conversation.

Madison and Jackie also gave Nicki an active role in the decision to talk to her friend's parent. They used the conversation to reinforce pride in their family and respectful treatment of others. In the end, they reported back to Nikki and made sure she felt okay about the situation and understood the actions that they had taken to empower her. Parents can use the following activity to similarly guide them in turning a negative incident into a teachable moment that reinforces important values and skills.

Guided Activity: Validating and Empowering Our Child(ren)

Think of a situation involving your child(ren) that you are currently dealing with or an incident that you have dealt with in the past. Talk together about how you could use this situation as an opportunity to reinforce important values and skills. Answer the following questions about the incident.

1. How can you help your child(ren) express their feelings?
2. How can you validate your child's feelings and experience?
3. How can you help your child externalize (instead of internalize) the problem of prejudice?
4. How can you empower your child to use appropriate assertiveness and other problem-solving skills to address the problem?

CONCLUSION

We want to make it clear that we do not believe that it is the responsibility of same-sex couples to educate straight people about heterosexual privilege or diverse families. However, there are times when you will decide that it is important to your children's well-being to take the time and energy to give feedback and positively assert the needs of your family to others. Organizations such as the Family Equality Council recommend that parents volunteer in the classroom and introduce themselves to the other parents and children. You can also show appreciation for teachers and other school personnel who show support for your family. Reinforcing positive ally behaviors is important and effective!

When children experience discrimination or prejudice from others, they need to have an opportunity to express their feelings of hurt, anger, and sadness. They also need to be empowered to take positive action on their own behalf. Likewise, parents need to have a chance to express their feelings, at least to each other, and then model positive action for their children.

Be a role model for your children by showing that disrespectful treatment of others is never okay. It requires a lot of energy and effort to assertively address these types of situations. Sometimes the temptation is to avoid the problem rather than confront it head-on. Sometimes in your effort to solve the problem quickly, you may leave your children out of the loop. Slow down and include your children in the problem-solving process. Including them in the process gives your children the opportunity to develop important life skills for addressing the prejudice and discrimination expressed by others. Children need to feel confident that they, and you, have the tools to respond appropriately and effectively. So use those teachable moments!

NOTE

1. Kosciw, J. G., & Diaz, E. M. (2008). *Involved, invisible, ignored: The experiences of lesbian, gay, bisexual and transgender parents and their children in our nation's K–12 schools.* New York, NY: Gay, Lesbian & Straight Education Network.

CHAPTER 9

"INS AND OUTS" OF PARENTING

Deciding whether to disclose or conceal one's sexual identity to specific people or in specific situations is a minority stressor that takes more energy than couples often realize. In many instances, couples get to decide whether or not to come out. When couples have children, they may find themselves having very little control over whether they are out.

Young children are naturally truthful about their two dads or two moms. They naturally out their parents because they are comfortable talking honestly and truthfully about their family members. To them, their parents are simply the people who love and care for them.

In contrast, self-conscious, image-conscious older children or teens may fear that their peers will reject or ostracize them if they know about their two moms or two dads. These kids may pressure their parents to go back into the closet. Same-sex couples may find it challenging to negotiate disclosure, especially when they have children of different ages and developmental needs. Imagine a family in which one child routinely outs his parents and the other wants to lock them in the closet, metaphorically speaking.

Mike, 40, and Howard, 33, adopted their 3-year-old son, Eric, when he was an infant. Eric is the biological son of one of Howard's cousins. Therefore, Howard is the legally recognized parent, and because of state laws, Mike has no legally recognized connection to Eric. (This issue is discussed further in Part VI of this book.) Of course, as far as Eric is concerned, he has two daddies and that is a very good thing.

One beautiful Saturday morning in the spring, Mike took Eric with him to the local garden center. As they waited in a very long line to pay for their purchases, Eric lost his patience and began to howl. As Mike picked him up to try to calm him, Eric screamed, "I want my other daddy!" The man in line behind Mike frowned, and Mike started to feel uncomfortable. The man asked Eric, "How many daddies do you have?" Eric stopped crying immediately and began to inform the man that he had two daddies and he wanted the daddy who was at home with the cat and not this daddy who was making him stand in a long line. The man responded with a short grunt and then looked away.

Mike was relieved to finally check out and go home. He worried that Eric might have sensed the tension and discomfort that he, himself, felt in that situation. He didn't want Eric to get the wrong message. Mike and Howard want Eric to be proud of his two daddies and their family. Thus, they needed to be ready for these kinds of "outings."

Mike and Howard talked about this incident for a long time. They discussed how their fears of rejection or discrimination caused them to conceal their relationship in certain situations. They decided that in future "outings" they needed to respond to their son and not to their fear of what others might do or say. They realized that sometimes they focus more on others' reactions rather than their son's needs and behaviors.

Pause and Reflect

Think about a time that you were outed by your child (or any child).

- How did you feel at that moment?
- How did you react in that situation?
- In hindsight, is there anything you would do differently?
- What would you advise other parents to do in similar situations?

Mike and Howard visualized how they would redo the situation in the checkout line with a focus on calming Eric. They thought of giving him a task that would help them get home to his other daddy faster. Mike suggested that they might help Eric count the number of items that they would need to pay for or distract him by asking him to name all of the members of his family, including the cat. Howard was helpful in recalling other occasions when they had been unexpectedly outed. They talked about positive ways they might have handled those incidents.

Together, Mike and Howard generated a list of things they could say and do in these moments. Their goal, or mission, is to keep their focus on Eric instead of thinking about the actions of others. They practiced these responses until they felt more prepared and empowered for the inevitable next "outing."

Elise, 44, and Andrea, 40, have a different challenge when it comes to disclosure and concealment. Elise's biological daughter, Michelle, is 14 years old. A couple of years ago, Elise divorced Michelle's dad and began a committed relationship with Andrea. Michelle is very vocal about not wanting anyone to know about her mom's new relationship.

Elise recognizes that Michelle is experiencing her own form of minority stress—fear of being rejected by her peers and others.

All of this comes at a time when Michelle, like all teens at this developmental stage, is focused on individuating from her parents and being accepted by her peers. Elise explained:

> I know the divorce is tough on Michelle. It's a lot of change to adjust to. Sometimes I feel guilty about that. But she has to get used to it, and if she gives it a chance, I think we can all move forward together.

Elise feels like she is being shoved back in the closet by her angry and unhappy teenager. She is unsure how patient she should be with Michelle's developmental process and how firmly she should enforce limits and expectations for Michelle's behaviors toward her and Andrea. Negotiating agreements about disclosure can be a lot of work, but the process is important for everyone's well-being. For instance, a few months ago, Michelle requested that only Elise attend her dance recital. Michelle did not want Andrea to attend because she was afraid someone would figure out that Elise and Andrea are a couple. As Andrea, laughing, said:

> It's a good thing I have a thick skin! Elise and I discussed it, and we decided that since this was Michelle's event, not ours, we would let her call the shots. So I didn't attend the recital. On the other hand, we were clear with Michelle that we were not going to tiptoe around her and her friends when they are hanging out in our living room and eating everything in the kitchen pantry. That's where we draw the line! I thought that might cut down on the number of teens underfoot, but strangely enough, Elise and I can usually count on having to share the sofa with Michelle and a couple of her friends on family movie night! Go figure!

Same-sex couples who have children from a different-sex relationship often have the complications of establishing new identities and roles in the context of preexisting parent–child relationships.

The same-sex partner who becomes a stepparent has to figure out his or her role in the family. For Elise and Andrea, as parents of adolescents, the process is complicated by the normal developmental tasks of adolescent individuation and desire for independence. Then, surround all of these challenges with an environment that stigmatizes same-sex couples and their families. Parents must figure out how to navigate all of these family relationship challenges in an authentic way that supports their child and the integrity of their family relationships.

Elise and Andrea found it helpful to give Michelle a safe place to talk about her feelings about all the changes in her family life, including her fears of peer rejection. Michelle's desire to keep her family in the closet needed to be heard and validated. To facilitate this process, Elise and Andrea looked for opportunities to allow Michelle to raise questions with them or with another caring and supportive adult.

Elise and Andrea also knew that it was important that Michelle develop her own positive identity and a sense of pride in her family. They knew that over time most adolescents in same-sex–parented families choose to come out to their closest friends, who frequently become a strong source of positive support. Elise and Andrea have made a point to get to know Michelle's closest friends, who seem to actually enjoy their company, much to Michelle's surprise and relief. These positive interactions are helping to alleviate Michelle's fear of rejection.

An important part of growing up is learning and practicing new sets of skills. Learning to recognize and constructively confront prejudice and deal with fears of possible rejection is an important lesson for us all! Developing skills will help children build their confidence in managing their own relationships with integrity and authenticity. Feel free to adapt the following two activities to the age and developmental needs of your child.

Guided Activities: Discussion Questions and Role-Play for Children and Teens

An important part of growing up is learning and practicing new sets of skills. Learning to recognize and constructively confront prejudice and deal with fears of possible rejection is an important lesson for us all! Developing skills will help children build their confidence in managing their own relationships with integrity and authenticity. Feel free to adapt the following two activities (Gianino & Novelle, 2012) to the age and developmental needs of your child.

Structured Discussion Questions

Some version of the following questions may be useful in talking with your child. If your child does not want to talk with you about these issues (which may be a normal response that parents get from their teens), then find a trusted friend or family member to help out.

- Who is it safe to tell about my family?
- How do I decide when to tell or how to tell?
- What do I do if they freak out?
- Why is it important to be honest about my family?

Role-Plays

Teens may welcome the opportunity to practice how they might tell close friends about their family. Then they can practice responding to the reactions that they anticipate. In a role-play, teens can act out their worst fears of how a friend might react. These over-the-top performances can be fun as well as skill-building. If teens are equipped with skills to handle the reactions they most fear, then they will feel empowered to handle the milder and often supportive reactions that they are more likely to receive.

Note. Gianino, M., & Novelle, M. (2012). Considerations for assessment and intervention with lesbian and gay adoptive parents and their children. In J. J. Bigner & J. L. Wetchler (Eds.), *Handbook of LGBT-affirmative couple and family therapy* (pp. 215–231). New York, NY: Taylor & Francis.

CONCLUSION

You may be accustomed to controlling your disclosure decisions. When you have children, however, your control over these disclosures may change. Your focus shifts from the impact of your decisions on yourself to the impact on your child's well-being. Experts on same-sex parents and their children note that parents who model pride and acceptance of their identities find that this pride and acceptance takes root as their children consolidate their own identities and move through adolescence into young adulthood.

Children need acceptance and support from you, their parents. Just like you, children may experience prejudice and fear rejection. These experiences are stressful. You need to recognize the stress your children may experience, validate their feelings about these experiences, and help them learn positive skills and strategies for coping. Additionally, you need to externalize the source of the stress: Externalizing the problem means that you need to help your children clearly identify that prejudice is the problem, not their family! By reframing the problem in this way, you reinforce the integrity of their family.

CHAPTER 10

ON THE LOOKOUT

Same-sex couples who are parents may experience anxiety and fear of rejection for many reasons. When parents come out, they may fear that their child or children will reject them. Same-sex couples may fear discrimination and rejection by their children's schools or in their communities. Sometimes they feel self-conscious, like people are judging them or watching to see how their children behave. Unfortunately, research suggests that the parenting skills of same-sex couples are indeed often judged more harshly than those of different-sex couples.[1]

As a result, same-sex couples often feel pressure to be the perfect parents with perfect children. This pressure comes from a fear that our families will be treated badly or that our children will be rejected in some way if we are less than perfect. Parents who try to anticipate rejection can become hypervigilant, watching for the smallest sign that someone is disapproving of them or their children.

Connie, 53, and Luce, 50, have been together for a little more than a decade. When they first became a couple, Connie's children from a different-sex relationship were 12 and 15. Looking back, Connie and Luce are not sure how much of the anger and unhappiness that Connie's kids expressed was due to the divorce, to Connie's coming out and beginning a new relationship with Luce, or to the normal edginess that seems to accompany adolescence. The kids often blamed Luce for their parents' divorce and their mother's coming out. They got plenty of reinforcement for this position from their father and even from Connie's own parents.

> Connie: I remember how anxious and scared I was during that time. I was terrified that my children would hate me. I was terrified that a judge would side with their dad if we went to court over custody. I was terrified that the kids would want to go live with their dad full time so that they wouldn't have to live with us.
>
> Luce: It was a tough time. I admit that I sometimes got frustrated when Connie overindulged the kids or avoided setting limits with them because she was so afraid they would reject her. It was hard on our relationship, too. There seemed to be very little energy left over for us.

Looking back on those years, Connie realizes how much her fear of rejection affected her parenting skills and her relationship with Luce. In many ways, these challenges are typical of families adjusting to divorce and new relationships. Compounding this typical stress, however, was the stress of social stigma directed at Connie and Luce's relationship. Although Luce's family was supportive of their relationship, few of Connie's extended family and friends offered the couple support during this time. This rejection, added to the fears of the kids' rejection, exacerbated Connie's internalized stigma and further affected the quality of the couple's relationship.

> Connie: I wish I had been able to set aside my fears of what might happen and focus instead on what was going on in the moment. I was so focused on my anxiety about the kids that I really neglected mine and Luce's relationship. I was

proud of the authentic life that Luce and I were creating for ourselves and the kids. I wanted that for my kids. I wish I had reminded myself that my intention was to live each day with courage and authenticity. Instead, I let my self-doubt and my fears of what might happen get the best of me and cloud my judgment. That negativity and preoccupation with the kids was not good for mine and Luce's day-to-day relationship. It kept both of us stressed out and on edge.

Luce: The good news is that we didn't give up. And we certainly got lots of opportunities to practice communicating about difficult issues. I had to keep pointing out that what the kids were going through was normal. The kids adjusted, and over time we have become a close family. But we spent a lot of time talking about things that might happen and anticipating things that never did happen. We definitely can look back and see things that we could have done differently to better manage the stress, but overall I think we handled things okay. Even the kids think so!

Connie and Luce remember to give themselves credit for their perseverance during those challenging years. They also focus on how much they have learned and the positive, mutually supportive relationship that they have built with each other and with the kids, who are now young adults.

Connie and Luce's story illustrates how social stigma can cause parents to fear that their children will reject them. Mike and Howard, a couple from the previous chapter, shared their story about hypervigilance and fear of rejection from other parents.

Mike and Howard like to take their 3-year-old, Eric, camping: "We love to camp, so we are starting him early in hopes that this becomes a regular family activity that we can all enjoy together." Last weekend, the three of them went camping with a female couple

---

Pause and Reflect

Have you ever feared that your children would reject you because of the cultural stigma directed toward same-sex couples? To what extent do you focus on past experiences of rejection or fears of rejection in the future? How would your parenting behaviors change if you focused only on what is happening in the present?

---

who have a son about the same age as Eric. The first evening at the campground they met another (straight) family and all three families hung out together talking, watching the kids collect rocks, and making s'mores around the campfire.

Howard imagined that he could see the wheels turning in the minds of their new acquaintances. He imagined that they were trying to figure out who was with whom and who the kids belonged to. Mike observed the straight couple's dawning realization that he and Howard were a couple and that one of the little boys belonged to them. Just like at the garden center, Mike held his breath momentarily, afraid for what might happen next, but according to Howard, "That couple didn't miss a beat," and all three families had an enjoyable evening together.

The next day, when Eric threw a rock that hit their new friends' tent, Mike and Howard were mortified. Even though their friends' child was also throwing rocks, Mike and Howard felt responsible for Eric acting "properly" and quickly put him in time out. Their friends assured them that this is what 3-year-olds do—they throw things. Mike and Howard relaxed.

Fears and anxieties like these are often worsened by any vestiges of internalized stigma that parents may carry around with them. It is important for parents like Mike and Howard to recognize how negative self-views may be triggering some of their anxieties about being "perfect" parents. When they are able to manage their own anxieties, their child is less likely to absorb it.

For example, children can absorb parents' expectations that they be "perfect." Children of same-sex couples may feel pressure to demonstrate to the world that they are not being negatively affected by having same-sex parents. This responsibility for being the "perfect family" can be a big burden for a child to carry.

Letting our children be normal, perfectly imperfect human beings is a gift that same-sex parents can give their children. Sometimes they, too, need to be relieved of too much responsibility for being exemplars of our good parenting! Remember that children thrive from having our nonanxious presence, attention, and positive engagement with them.

Instead of placing unrealistic expectations on their children in hopes that they will never experience prejudice or be rejected, couples can put their hypervigilance to good use by training their highly developed skills of observation on the positive things that are happening during the course of their daily lives. For example, the next time that Mike was in the hardware store with Eric, he noticed that one of the salesclerks smiled in recognition. He and Howard began to keep track of all of the small gestures of kindness and support that they encountered during the day.

Mike and Howard spent time talking with Eric about all of the good and kind people that they had in their lives and what they could do to be kind and caring to others who may be sad or scared. This shift in focus did not, of course, mean that Mike and Howard never experienced prejudice from others. It did, however, train them to see that there were many more positive events than negative events in their lives. They did not want to miss the positives that their family experienced because they were so focused on anticipating negatives! This shift in focus helped them to feel much less anxious about how others were responding to their family.

Guided Activity: Acts of Kindness

At the dinner table, or during your family meeting time, share the acts of kindness that you have witnessed during the day (or week). Name acts of kindness you witnessed or experienced within the family. Name other acts of kindness that family members witnessed or performed during the week. If we know that we will be reporting on our own acts of kindness or observed acts of kindness, it is amazing how many examples we begin to accumulate! Focusing on the kindness and compassion that we witness enhances our individual and family well-being.

CONCLUSION

Experiences of discrimination and prejudice are an unfortunate reality in the lives of some same-sex couples and their families. The point of this chapter is not to gloss over that fact. Rather, it is to offer same-sex couples and their children effective ways to respond that will energize them rather than drain them.

Sometimes you find what you look for. Your expectations may often be confirmed. Therefore, it is important to train yourself to have positive expectations and to model these for your children. Then, when negative events happen, you will have the energy and resources to address them without letting them disturb your otherwise positive sense of well-being.

NOTE

1. Massey, S. G., Merriwether, A. M., & Garcia, J. R. (2013). Modern prejudice and same-sex parenting: Shifting judgments in positive and negative parenting situations. *Journal of GLBT Family Studies, 9,* 129–151. doi:10.1080/1550428X.2013.765257

CHAPTER 11

"ARE WE BEING SELFISH?"

Many same-sex couples have a desire to have children. For some of these couples, minority stress can trigger doubts. They may ask themselves, "Is it fair for us to bring children into a family like ours?" Other times, children from previous relationships are part of the package deal when same-sex couples form their relationship. Whether a partner brings children with them into a relationship or partners in a same-sex couple decide to expand their family, many same-sex couples worry that their children will face stigma, discrimination, and prejudice from others.

In these circumstances, couple members may struggle with their own internalized negative messages about lesbian, gay, bisexual, transgender, and/or queer (LGBTQ) identities or same-sex relationships. To a greater or lesser extent, because of their stigmatized status, same-sex couples may question whether they "should" be parents. They may have internalized doubts about their ability to effectively raise healthy, high-functioning children.

Camila, 41, and Zoe, 35, are two Latina women who have been together for 4 years. They recently began the process of adopting.

> Camila: We really want to adopt a child! I would mourn if we
> never had a child. When I was growing up and figuring out I

was gay, I thought that meant I would never have children. In my experience growing up, being a mother was not an option unless you got married to a man. People also gossiped that gay people shouldn't be around children. So, I resigned myself to the idea that I might not have a family, until I met Zoe.

Zoe: I want kids, too. We've worked really hard to become more financially secure, and we've actually begun the process, but we also want to feel confident that we are doing the right thing. Some of my family members have warned me that it's selfish to raise kids without a father because all children need a father and a mother.

Camila: So, we have spent way too much time talking about whether we "should" have kids. We know that we want them, and we are going to make it happen. It's just everyone else in our families says bad things about gay parents and that makes us doubt ourselves.

Camila and Zoe have a lot of love to give a child, and they look forward to being parents. Yet, because of the negative messages they were taught, they have fears about their own adequacy and ability to be good parents as a female couple. Their feelings are not uncommon. Most of us have grown up in a society that teaches us to idealize a rather rare version of "the perfect family." The middle-class mother–father–son–daughter (+ the family dog) family is not the composition of the majority of families in the United States. Yet, many of us have been socialized to use this ideal as a yardstick by which to measure the adequacy of our own families.

Breaking the rules by creating another kind of family may feel risky. To the extent that we have internalized rigid gender roles and definitions of family, we may have difficulty giving ourselves permission to create our own unique families. We may have difficulty believing that our own families of creation are just as good as the mythical ideals.

The truth, however, is that same-sex couples have many strengths to bring to their roles as parents. Same-sex couples are more likely to contribute equally to the nurture and care of their children and to model egalitarian relationships and social engagement. Our research findings[1] suggest that people who identify as LGBTQ have highly developed skills of empathy and compassion that are vital to effective parenting. Parents also need a sense of humor, a strength that many same-sex couples have honed in the face of challenging circumstances. Lucky are the children and adults who have had this kind of parenting!

Pause and Reflect

If you are parents (or prospective parents), set aside some couple time to think about and share your answers to the following:

1. What negative messages have you been taught about same-sex–parented families?
2. What qualities do you have that you want to pass along to your child or children?
3. How might your child benefit from being nurtured in a same-sex parented family?
4. What is your purpose as parents? (You may want to write out a Parent Mission Statement.)

As you reflected on the Pause and Reflect questions, you may have talked about the importance of teaching children self-respect, self-acceptance, and authenticity. If we want these things for our children (and of course we do!), then we need to model them. Children benefit from parents who model strengths such as courage, compassion, and commitment and who live lives that are characterized by positive relationships, meaningful contributions, love, and joy. These gifts, plus support and nurture, provide children with the resources they need to thrive and flourish.

Children don't always express gratitude for their parents' support, however. "You've ruined my life!" was the angry vindictive that could make Drew's knees buckle, and his two kids knew it. Drew and Martin, both in their early 40s, have been together for a little over a decade. When they first became a couple, Drew's children from a previous different-sex relationship were 2 years old and 5 years old. Drew and Martin shared custody with the children's mother. For Drew, angry pronouncements like these triggered residual feelings of shame for coming out before his kids were grown and out of the house. His internalized stigma was further exacerbated by his nagging belief that his decision to come out may have led to his younger child's learning disability and his older child's low self-esteem.

Drew and Martin both grew up in houses where their unhappy parents made it clear that they had "stayed together for the sake of the children." Their own fathers modeled very traditional gender roles, in which being a "real" man meant bringing home a paycheck but doing little in terms of hands-on parenting. They were both taught that being gay was antithetical to being a "real" man according to the rules of patriarchy that governed both families.

Although Drew and Martin love being fathers, each of them sometimes struggles with internalized stigma. In many conversations with each other, they have shared their insights and self-awareness.

> Drew: I feel guilty sometimes about the kids' problems. I find myself wondering if their problems are at least partly because I'm gay and they have been forced to deal with that fact. I know that isn't exactly rational, but I can't seem to help wondering if they would have had it easier if I hadn't come out when I did.
>
> Martin: Of course it's not your fault, or mine, that the kids have challenges to deal with. We've created a good, structured environment for the kids. That is important for them.

They may not appreciate it now, but one day they will. But I know what you mean. It can feel bad, like somehow we're the cause of their struggles.

Drew: It doesn't help that I feel like everyone is judging us and thinking that we are bad people and bad fathers because the kids aren't doing great in school. I end up feeling guilty every time we go to a parent–teacher conference, like I'm failing our kids.

Martin: Yeah, I sometimes wonder if people think we're bad parents because we are gay. At times I start to doubt myself as a father. Then I remind myself all we've done for our kids.

Drew: It's just complicated!

Drew and Martin are struggling with their own minority stress while trying to be good parents. It's important for them to

---

Guided Activity: Assessing and Appreciating Our Strengths

Our lesbian, gay, bisexual, transgender, and/or queer (LGBTQ) identities can contribute to rather than detract from our strengths as parents. Considering how our children benefit from our LGBTQ identities helps us to let go of our fearful thoughts that our identities are a disadvantage. The following discussion questions will help you refocus on the positives and the strengths that you bring to your roles as parents.

1. What strengths, skills, and resources do you bring to your roles as parents?
2. Are there things you have learned as a person who identifies as LGBTQ or as same-sex couple that has made you a better parent than you might otherwise have been?
3. What parenting behaviors do you feel good about?
4. As you reflect on the past week, what has gone well? What positive interactions or moments have you shared as a family?

separate their internalized stigma from their evaluation of themselves as parents. The reality is that child rearing is challenging for every parent! We just do the best that we can and hope that all will be well in the end.

All children and parents have challenges of one sort or another along the way. Normal developmental challenges can be stressful for the entire family as young children transition to adolescence and then to young adulthood. During these transitions, the whole family may struggle with forging their unique identities while still staying connected. During challenging times, it is easy to forget all of the good things that are happening in the family and all of the strengths and resources that parents provide to their children.

CONCLUSION

Internalized stigma can show up when couples begin to make decisions about creating their own families and as their family grows and develops. It is important for you as a same-sex couple to examine the messages that you have been taught about who should and who should not become parents, which kinds of families are acceptable, and what it means to be a good parent. You should also examine negative messages that you may have absorbed about same-sex parenting and challenge these messages by reading summaries of research showing that same-sex couples are raising happy and healthy children!

NOTE

1. Riggle, E. D. B., & Rostosky, S. S. (2012). *A positive view of LBGTQ: Embracing identity and cultivating well-being.* New York, NY: Rowman & Littlefield.

CHAPTER 12

IT TAKES A VILLAGE, PEOPLE!

Same-sex couples find creative ways to cultivate pride in their family and mobilize the support of their allies. Every family has a unique set of strengths and resources. Think about your family and the strengths and resources you have. Naming these strengths is a good start toward cultivating pride as a family unit.

Strengths and resources come from within the family as well as the surrounding environment. The family activities illustrated in this chapter provide examples of ways to recognize and build family strengths and resources. These types of positive activities can enhance the well-being of both parents and their children.

When Mike and Howard (from Chapter 9) became parents, they said that they "looked high and low for other families in our same situation."

> Mike: The unexpected problem was that our children were in different developmental stages so we couldn't really hang out together as families. Don't get me wrong, it's wonderful to know these other couples, and we love to go out to dinner with them and get their advice since they've already gone through more of the developmental stages than we have. They are terrific sources of information and support. But our child's age, not our sexual

identity, has turned out to be the factor that determines our social life.

Howard: Who would have predicted that our closest friends would be a straight couple with 3-year-old twins? We know them from daycare and spend more time with them than with any of our gay friends!

To make sure that they, and their son, Eric, have the opportunity to interact with other parents in similar families, Mike and Howard made a commitment to go on a family vacation every year with other same-sex parents and their children. They realize that seeing other families like his is an important part of helping Eric to feel proud of his family. Mike and Howard report, for instance, that Eric loves to read stories about other families with two dads or two moms. Howard reported, "Those are his go-to books at bedtime. And he gives the dads in the stories our names or the names of our friends. He is obviously using these stories to create a place for his family."

Open communication is a strength commonly found in same-sex–parented families.[1] Providing a safe place for children to ask questions, share feelings, and learn coping skills is an important way to capitalize on this strength. Whatever the age of your child or children, having a set routine that includes time for all family members to be together is important to well-being. As children grow and develop, it is important to include time for all family members to talk about their hopes, dreams, wishes, and goals for their family. These conversations provide opportunities to develop communication skills, problem-solving skills, and feelings of connection.

Some families use family meetings to plan outings and vacations, review the weekly activities, or have a discussion about a current event. Same-sex couples with young children can use this and other special time as opportunities for their children to practice talking about their family. The Pause and Reflect activity suggests questions that parents can use to facilitate this type of conversation. (Additional ideas can be found at www.familyequality.org.)

Pause and Reflect

Take some quiet time to reflect with your young children:

1. Who are the people who make up our family?
2. What makes our family special?
3. How is our family different from other families we know?
4. How is our family similar to other families we know?

Using questions such as the ones in the Pause and Reflect exercise can help children develop important communication skills as they solidify their sense of belonging and security in their family. In these kinds of conversations, parents can share with their child illustrations of many different kinds of families. Parents can use age-appropriate books to facilitate discussions with their child about diverse families. Families can discuss their support team with their child so that their child is clear about the people who are available to them outside of the immediate family for support, caring, and help.

Children need opportunities to practice articulating the strengths of their family and their family's values. Older children can begin to reflect on what it means to live by family values such as respect, compassion, and commitment. They can make connections between their values and actions. Some families even create a family motto that represents their values or sense of connection. All of these positive activities help to strengthen family well-being so that these strengths can be mobilized when family members experience minority stress as a result of the prejudice of others.

Many same-sex couples are raising children from one partner's previous relationship. Finding family activities for all ages to enjoy together can help create a positive, inclusive, and supportive environment. We introduced Elise and Andrea and Elise's adolescent daughter Michelle in Chapter 9. Although the relationships in this new family have been challenging at times, Andrea and Elise have looked for opportunities to create positive, shared memories. For instance, Andrea enjoys snowboarding and offered to teach Michelle. As Elise stated,

> Michelle couldn't help herself. She wanted to snowboard, and that meant spending time with Andrea. So of course they bonded, in part by laughing every time I fell! Michelle even invited a friend along on our last ski vacation. That was an important step.

Parents also need to remember to take time to engage in activities that support their couple relationship. Psychologists have found that one of the most important ingredients for child well-being is the quality of the relationship between the parents. Date nights, time with close friends, a shared hobby, volunteering, or social activism in the community can help same-sex couples strengthen their bond with each other, reduce minority stress, and connect to their communities. Happy, empowered parents are better equipped to cope (and help their children cope) with minority stress.

Madison and Jackie, for instance, volunteer at the local food bank. Often, they take the kids with them. They feel enriched and energized by the friends they have made. They feel good about volunteering and teaching their daughters to give back to their community.

Camila and Zoe, who we introduced in Chapter 11, have now adopted 6- and 8-year-old siblings. Camila and Zoe want the children to have lots of good role models, so they have enlisted the help of their chosen family. They have family holiday meals and special game nights so that the kids feel a part of a larger family with many different people, including gay, straight, bisexual, transgender, Latino, White, younger, and older. Camila and Zoe are happy to have the support of this diverse and dynamic family of choice.

Guided Activity: What Can We Do for Fun?

The following questions can be used to guide your discussion about activities that support your family's well-being.

1. When does your family have fun together? At your next family meeting, brainstorm some fun activities that you can do together in the coming 4 to 6 months. Plan and schedule one family activity for the coming month.
2. What fun or rewarding activities do you and your partner do together? Make a list of activities that would be rejuvenating and empowering. Remember that spending quality time with your partner is an important part of being a good parent!
3. What group activities support your parenting efforts? Same-sex couples who are parenting need strong social connections that affirm and support them when they experience minority stress as a result of stigma and discrimination.

CONCLUSION

Effective parenting is a challenging task! Minority stress compounds the challenge. Focus on your goals and what you want as a family rather than on the negative attitudes of others. Positive activities that increase positive emotions will give you the positive energy you need to model effective coping strategies for your child and to transform minority stress into opportunities for building skills.

Family well-being is enhanced when parents and children have strong, positive relationships with each other. Researchers have found that the quality of the relationship between the parents and the quality of the relationship between the parents and the children are instrumental in promoting the development and well-being of children. These strong family connections will bolster your abilities to cope effectively with minority stress when you need to.

NOTE

1. Goldberg, A. E. (2010). *Lesbian and gay parents and their children: Research on the family life cycle.* Washington, DC: American Psychological Association.

Part III

RELIGION

Religious beliefs, institutions, and communities may be a source of minority stress or a source of support for same-sex couples. Sometimes religion is both. *Religion*, as we use the term in this book, refers to the institutionalized or organized practices that sustain and express a set of beliefs about the relationship between humanity and a higher power or being. The official policies of many traditional religious institutions are less than fully supportive of (and sometimes overtly hostile to) same-sex couples' relationships.

Religion has been and continues to play an important role in American cultural and political life. Although only one in five people attend religious services weekly, a majority of people in the United States report that they were raised in a specific religion and have some affiliation with a denomination.[1]

Thus, religious beliefs may have *direct* influences on the lives of same-sex couples through their own religious affiliations and beliefs or *indirect* influences through religiously affiliated family members, coworkers, and neighbors.

Even if they are not members of a religious community themselves, same-sex couples will encounter and interact with people who are part of a religious community. For some, the religious community they indirectly encounter will be welcoming and affirming. Other couples will interact with people who hold religion-based beliefs that are prejudicial and rejecting. Whether the prejudicial belief is punitive or more passive, religion-based prejudice creates stressful interactions for same-sex couples.

Many people are socialized from early childhood into a specific set of religious values and beliefs. Religious doctrine and teachings may include negative messages about lesbian, gay, bisexual, transgender, and/or queer identities or same-sex sexual attraction.[2] This socialization shapes their worldview. If they perceive that their sexual identity conflicts with their religious identity, they may experience some internal tensions, making them vulnerable to internalized stigma, one of the minority stress factors.

Unfortunately, many same-sex-couple members have had very painful experiences as a result of prejudice and discrimination rooted in religious beliefs. It is common for these couple members to go through a process of reexamining and disputing negative messages about sexual identity that they were taught in the context of religion. They work to claim new interpretations, insights, and understandings that allow them to integrate both identities.

Same-sex-couple members can begin this process by making clear distinctions among the beliefs and practices of various religious groups. Religious groups that label themselves Baptist, for instance, vary widely in how they interpret the Bible and how they treat same-sex relationships. Although the Catholic

Church (Vatican) teaches that same-sex relationships are incompatible with doctrine, many Catholics are supportive of same-sex marriage and same-sex couples. Understanding the spectrum that exists, even within one denomination, offers a new perspective and new possibilities. Reevaluating one's religious background and experiences may increase conflict with one's family of origin (FOO). The FOO may feel threatened and fearful. Same-sex couples may perceive that their FOO's lack of acceptance has been reinforced and supported by religious institutions and communities. Navigating this complex interchange between the FOO's religious belief system and the same-sex couple's relationship can challenge couples as they strive to make their own healthy decisions about faith and family.

As we have noted, minority stress factors are interconnected, forming a circular process with no clear beginning or end. For example, when we experience stigma that is rooted in religious beliefs (prejudice), we may react by keeping our sexual identities hidden (concealment) from people we know to be religious (anticipating rejection). This secrecy may increase our negative feelings about ourselves (internalized stigma). The worse we feel about ourselves, the more we may anticipate rejection when we are around religious people, creating even more anxiety and stress. It is a vicious cycle.

Not uncommonly, one member of a same-sex couple has experienced religion as a source of strength and support, whereas the other couple member has experienced religion as a source of psychological abuse and rejection. When couples have very divergent experiences with religion and very divergent spiritual worldviews, it is important that they spend time listening to and understanding each other's experiences. Forging a shared spiritual worldview that honors each couple member's experiences can be challenging, but it is also an opportunity for individual and relational growth. In our research, couples have told us that sharing their different perspectives and negotiating individual and shared activities that express their spirituality are enriching learning experiences that help them to stay in tune with each other.

Many same-sex couples experience their sexual identities and their religious identities as deeply connected to each other. In interviews, for instance, couples have told us that they considered their relationship to be "a gift from God." They experience their spiritual or religious community as a source of strength and support for their relationship. One couple told us that the love, prayers, and material support they received from their church during a health crisis sustained them through a long recovery period. Another couple found motivation for their social justice work in the priest's homilies and the engagement of the congregation with the needs of the surrounding community.

Many same-sex-couple members identify as spiritual rather than religious and make a sharp distinction between the two terms. We use the term *spirituality* to mean a broader set of beliefs and values that may or may not be expressed within an organized religion. Spirituality is a contemplation and practice that allows us to transcend ourselves, experience awe and wonder, and find meaning and purpose in our lives. Spirituality is sometimes understood as more private, subjective, and relational than religion, which is considered to be more public, formal, and ritualized.

Although many same-sex couples express their spirituality by participating in an organized religious community, others do so through other kinds of meaningful activities such as contemplative practices, inspirational reading, artistic expression, and social/environmental activism. Any area of life, including work, parenting, the couple relationship, or social activism, can be imbued with positive spiritual meaning and purpose. Researchers have found that a shared spiritual worldview that is expressed in meaningful activities can strengthen a couple's relationship.

In Part III, we explore common challenges couples face in finding support from religious beliefs and institutions. In Chapter 13, we discuss the religion-based stigma that couples can encounter from their FOO. We make suggestions for how couples can define healthy boundaries that reinforce the couple relationship while having compassion for conservatively religious family members. In Chapter 14, we describe how same-sex couples can cope with both blatant and more subtle forms of discrimination and prejudice that they experience in religious communities. In Chapter 15, a couple who conceals their relationship to avoid rejection in a religious community works to overcome their fears. Likewise, in Chapter 16, we share the story of a couple who carefully self-monitor their behaviors so that even though they are out at church, they expend enormous energy trying not to appear to be "too gay." In Chapter 17, we illustrate how the effects of religion-based internalized stigma can blindside couple members even outside of a religious setting. In each of these chapters, we suggest strategies for empowering the couple to respond to stigmatizing religious beliefs expressed by their family members, religious institutions, or others in the couple's community. Finally, in Chapter 18, we focus on positive religion and spirituality as a resource for same-sex couples' well-being. We illustrate the positive support that couples can find in a religious community that fully accepts and affirms them, and we suggest ways that couples can cultivate positive religion and spirituality as a resource that can help them transcend and transform the effects of minority stress.

Religion-based stigma can generate minority stress for same-sex couples. Couples must find positive, productive ways to deal with the minority stress that they experience in relation to religion. Integrating our religious identity/spirituality and our identity as a same-sex couple in ways that affirm both is important. Living in sync with each other and with transcendent values, such as compassion, generosity, forgiveness, and with a sense of connection to all living things enhances our well-being.

NOTES

1. Hartford Institute for Religion Research. (n.d.) *The church attendance gap*. Retrieved from http://hirr.hartsem.edu/about/news_and_notes_vol4no1.html
2. The interpretation of religious texts such as the Bible is beyond the scope of this book and has been covered extensively by others.

CHAPTER 13

"MY FAMILY THINKS OUR RELATIONSHIP IS AN ABOMINATION"

Our family members often facilitate our first contact with religion or spirituality. In our families we may learn values and rituals that form a shared religious or spiritual identity. They may mold our religious and spiritual beliefs and behaviors from the time we are born.

Many families socialize their children into specific religious traditions that may have been part of the family heritage for generations. If our families believe that lesbian, gay, bisexual, transgender, and/or queer identities are incompatible with the family's religious identity or beliefs, they may attempt to get us to deny, renounce, or change our identities. Their fears of divine punishment or community ostracism may lead them to use tactics that include guilt, shame, manipulation, or rejection. This type of interaction is based on prejudicial beliefs and causes minority stress for couples.

Ron, 53, and Seth, 48, have been a committed couple for 21 years. Both are the only sons of parents who are Orthodox Jews. Ron's parents live across town, and Seth's parents are about three hours away. They are devoted sons, and they each make time to visit their respective parents every few weeks to observe Shabbat. When they are not at their parents' houses, Ron and Seth attend a Reform Temple in the large city where they live. They have tried for years to "logically and rationally" explain their relationship to their families but to no avail. No amount of sound argument has convinced their families to reconsider their belief that the Torah "is clear in its condemnation of homosexuality." In fact, the more effectively Ron and Seth provide counterarguments to this prejudicial view, the more upset their parents become.

Ron and Seth have been very patient and understanding over the past two decades. They understand their parents' vulnerability to being rejected themselves if they were to disclose their sons' same-sex relationship to their tight-knit Orthodox community. For years, Seth went back into the closet when he went home (by himself) to visit: "I even went with them to synagogue and participated for my parents' sake, letting everyone assume I was their devoted [straight] son. My father would be disgraced if his son were found to be gay."

On the other side of the family, Ron's mother has been particularly unrelenting in her antagonism toward his and Seth's committed relationship. As Ron described,

> My mother is the kind of person who would do absolutely anything in this world to break us up because she disapproves of our relationship and is convinced that we have rebelled against G-d. In her view, our relationship is wrong in the same way that adultery and incest are wrong, and as long as I live this kind of "lifestyle," I am bringing shame to our family and community. She is still waiting for me to end my "rebellion" and find the right girl and settle down and get married like a good, observant son should. If I loved her, she tells me, I would have married one of the two dozen nice Jewish girls she has found for me in the last 25 years. In her mind, she is justified in doing anything that she can think of to break us up. My father isn't any help. He just tells me to listen to my mother. My mother has taken religion to the point that it has become evil. I hate to say that, because I am proud of my Jewish heritage. It is an important part of my identity.

Ironically, it is Ron and Seth's religious values that will not let them abandon their aging parents. Even after 21 years of blatant rejection from Ron's parents, they look to the important teachings of Jewish law (Halakhah) that require loyalty and honor for one's mother and father. Seth still feels an obligation to go home to visit his parents and help them with chores around their house.

This arrangement, however, is difficult to maintain. Ron and Seth sometimes question their obligations and responsibilities to their parents. Sometimes they disagree about where the boundary is between maintaining their sense of self-respect and integrity as a couple and their evolving roles as caretakers for increasingly dependent parents. Understandably, this situation is a source of sadness and stress for the couple.

Ron and Seth have sought the counsel of their rabbi many times. Their rabbi seeks to help them honor their parents and honor their relationship equally. In one meeting with the couple, the rabbi gave Ron and Seth some homework.

First, the rabbi instructed Ron and Seth to list all of the positive values that they had learned from their Orthodox Jewish heritage. Included in their long list were values such as self-discipline, a respect for ritual and tradition, and love of family. Using this list, the rabbi then asked Ron and Seth to make a list of short, simple responses, based on these positive values, that they could use when their parents made negative comments. For example, Seth reported that his father had said that Seth needs to "get married before it's too late." Seth used his positive value of love and honor of family to generate the following response: "I love Ron and he is my husband and family. Our religious values support our loving relationship."

Seth and Ron helped each other practice their short, positive phrases. They also made sure that they noticed and reinforced each other whenever one of them used one of the positive phrases to assert their integrity as a couple. By focusing on the positive things that they were doing, they were less focused on the negative statements and attitudes of their parents. This shift in their attention from the negative behaviors of their parents to their own positive behaviors helped them feel good about themselves and about their relationship.

Pause and Reflect

What are your family's religious or spiritual traditions? Has a family member or a member of your religious tradition ever made a prejudicial remark about your sexual or gender identity and used a "religious" justification for the remark? How did you feel about the remark? Did it have an effect on how you felt about yourself or your relationship? How did you respond to the person who made the remark?

Whereas Ron and Seth's parents pose a challenge for them, it's Bev and Carolyn's son and daughter-in-law that have brought religion-based prejudice into their lives. When they became a couple 22 years ago, Bev had a 10-year-old son, Josh. Although things weren't always easy during the teenage years, Josh and Carolyn bonded over a shared interest in college basketball and antique train sets. Two years ago, Josh married Maria, a young woman who is very involved and committed to a conservative form of Catholicism. Josh invested a lot of time and energy converting to Catholicism so they could be married in the Catholic church.

Maria has a 6-year-old daughter, Paz, from a previous marriage. She has made clear that she does not want Paz "exposed" to Josh's parents' "sinful lifestyle." As a result, Bev and Carolyn are not allowed to spend the night in Josh and Maria's home. At first, Carolyn was angry and boycotted any further visits. Eventually, however, they decided that they would stay at a nearby hotel and let it go. Bev states, "It's their problem, really, and we can work around it."

The couple is not happy with this arrangement. Paz is starting to question why Bev and Carolyn can't stay at her house when they come to see her. Josh and Maria are expecting a baby next month. Maria has made it clear that Bev and Carolyn are not welcomed at the hospital and are not invited to the house to see their new grandchild.

Like Ron and Seth, Carolyn and Bev are struggling over where to draw the line. They fear that if they take a firm stand and insist that Josh and Maria show respect for their couple relationship, they will lose contact with Josh and Paz. They fear that in a battle against Maria's religion-based prejudice about their relationship, they will lose. Even their son is not willing to challenge his wife's prejudice on their behalf.

Carolyn and Bev fear losing their relationship with the grandchildren. Understandably, they feel hurt and angry and even bereft, at times. How do they cope with this difficult situation in their family? They take time to talk together and express their feelings to each other. They have decided to limit how much time and energy they give to all of these negative feelings, however. Once they have clearly expressed to each other how they feel about Maria and Josh and their behavior, they decide to let go or release these feelings so that they can use their energies in more positive and productive ways. This is a basic technique in mindfulness-based approaches to mental health and stress reduction.

Next, Bev and Carolyn take time to focus on their own attitudes and behaviors. They spend some time together identifying and naming the "unenforceable rules" that they subconsciously have for Maria and Josh. For example, Bev stated that "Maria should honor and respect us like she does her own parents." Carolyn states, "Josh should stand up for us and insist that Maria welcome us into their home." By naming these *should*s, Bev and Carolyn are able to let go of their expectations and accept what *is* rather than focus on what *should* be (but clearly is not).

By accepting the reality of the situation rather than focusing on the way things should be, Carolyn and Bev are able to make decisions about what they *can* do. They turn their focus to their own behaviors, which are the only behaviors they have control over. They cannot control Maria's and Josh's behavior. They *can* make decisions about how they want to respond.

Bev and Carolyn decide to use their energy for problem solving rather than ruminating about their negative feelings. They can state their own positive values. They can ask for what they want. They can assert their limits. They can state what they want the future of the relationship to look like on the basis of their positive values.

One of the things that Bev and Carolyn want from their son and daughter-in-law is more understanding and empathy. They believe that these are important values in any family. Because they tend to blame Maria for the problem, Carolyn and Bev decide to spend some time discussing how they could bring more compassion and empathy to their relationship with Maria.

> Bev: I realize that Maria grew up in a very strict, very conservative religious home. I can see that she is anxious and scared and insecure.
> Carolyn: Yes, I understand that her background has shaped her attitudes toward us. But I also know that she, like us, wants Paz and the new baby to be healthy and happy and to feel loved and supported. Those are family values we all share.
> Bev: I just want her to see that we want to help provide some of that love and support!
> Carolyn: Have we ever actually told Maria that we appreciate her devotion to Josh and Paz?

With these positive feelings in mind, Bev and Carolyn decide to write a letter to Josh and Maria to express their appreciation for the strengths that they see in each of them and in their roles as parents. They also express their support for them and their wishes for a mutually supportive and positive relationship. They invite Josh and Maria to come and visit them to discuss how they can have a mutually satisfying relationship with the couple and their grandchildren.

While waiting for Josh and Maria's response, Bev and Carolyn make a short list of specific items that would improve their relationship with their son and daughter-in-law. This list included allowing them to babysit the grandchildren one Friday night each month while Josh and Maria go out. They also decide that if Maria and Josh do not want to treat them like a couple when they go to visit,

---

Guided Activity: Making Requests of Family Members

Instead of focusing on your family members' religion-based negative beliefs, focus on your own positive religious or spiritual beliefs. Think of the positive values that your religious or spiritual background has taught you. Make a list of those values.

Turn those values and beliefs into positive responses to people who make religion-based prejudicial statements. Model a new perspective based on positive values. Don't hesitate to use positive, assertive statements (starting with "I" or "We") to request specific behaviors based on these positive values.

State your own positive values clearly, and then make a specific request. Here are a couple of examples that Bev and Carolyn generated:

- "We believe that acknowledging family connections is important. We would appreciate it if you would introduce us to your friends as the children's grandparents."
- "We value spending time with our family. We need your help making a plan for spending time with the kids during the holidays."
- "We value the loving relationship that God has given us. We need your help to figure out how to honor the relationship that God has given to us and at the same time to show respect for the differences between us."

---

then Bev and Carolyn will ask Maria, Josh, and the grandchildren to come visit them at their home instead.

Bev and Carolyn don't know exactly how this conversation will go, so they are understandably nervous about it. However, they feel confident that their requests are reasonable and that the boundaries they are drawing with Josh and Maria are healthy. They feel good that they are being positively assertive rather than angrily aggressive or passively compliant in response to Josh and Maria's disrespectful treatment.

CONCLUSION

As a member of a same-sex couple, you might sometimes feel powerless when dealing with discrimination and prejudice that are associated with religious beliefs. Experiences of religion-based discrimination enacted by family members can be particularly stressful. Religious identities are often identities and histories that you share with your family members, making it particularly challenging to subject religion-based prejudice to the same degree of critical thinking, confrontation, and limit setting that you use to address prejudicial attitudes in other contexts. Confronting family members' bigotry and disrespect that are based in religious belief can be effective if it is done with compassion and skillful assertiveness.

CHAPTER 14

LOOKING FOR GOD IN ALL THE WRONG PLACES

Some religious communities are blatantly hostile toward same-sex relationships. Clergy and members of these congregations may label same-sex relationships as "sinful." They may urge same-sex couples to change their sexual identities through discredited and harmful forms of religion-based counseling or so-called reparative therapies. Identifying these forms of overt prejudice toward same-sex couples' relationships is not difficult, even when it is cloaked in claims to "love the sinner, hate the sin." Coping with this prejudice, however, can be challenging for couples.

More subtle expressions of prejudice, called *microaggressions*, are also potent sources of minority stress. Religion-based micro-aggressions can be more difficult to identify, and these more subtle behaviors can have a cumulative effect on our stress level. We may be so accustomed to absorbing negative religion-based messages about our relationship that we don't make the connection to the stress that we feel. This chapter illustrates these two types of minority stressors (overt discrimination and more subtle microaggressions) and how couples can recognize and cope with them when they happen in religious settings.

Dan, age 49, and Roger, age 54, have been a couple for 18 years. They met at church and consider their spiritual identities to be as important to them as their sexual identities. Roger is a professional church musician and has served in the music ministry of several conservative Christian churches. For the first 10 years of their life together, Roger and Dan were closeted because Roger was the full-time music minister for a very large and prominent evangelical Christian church.

Roger was inspired to come out to the senior pastor of the church after watching the Reverend Gene Robinson become the first openly gay bishop in the Episcopal Church. In response, the senior pastor asked Roger to continue to conceal his relationship from the congregation. The couple spent a long weekend weighing the pros and cons before Roger decided to resign his position. He and Dan recounted the financial and emotional stress that they felt during this time and the strategies they used to cope with it.

> Roger: Resigning from that full-time position was depressing for me, and financially and emotionally stressful for both of us. Dan came up with the idea that we should study the history of other groups of people who had been oppressed. We started by reading books out loud to each other in the evenings and watching documentaries about the history of African Americans, Jewish people, and Native Americans. We paid attention to how religion was used to discriminate and even justify horrible violence against these groups. It really helped us to keep a perspective on the discrimination that we experienced. It's weird. There was a sense of solidarity with this long history of oppression, and yet, we recognize that as White men we have also been privileged in ways that past generations and groups were not.
>
> Dan: We realize that being out and having the economic means to resign from a job that demeans our relationship are results of the privilege that we enjoy and others do not.

Somehow discussing all of this helped us be strong and resilient and helped us realize that no one could deny us our spiritual identities or our sexual identities. We have a collection of documentaries and books about religious gay people. We especially appreciate gay Christian couples like Reverend Mel White and his husband, Gary Nixon, who have been together for 30 years. Reverend Mel White was from a fundamentalist Christian background like us and went on to found Soulforce, an organization that confronts religious leaders and groups that are antigay. Their story inspires us to use our voices and our privilege well.

Dan and Roger are glad to be more out in their community; however, Roger still misses being a church musician and hopes to resume this role soon, even as a volunteer. Meanwhile, they found a positive way to cope with the discrimination that they experienced. They looked for spiritual role models who had faced discrimination in historical and contemporary times.

The following Pause and Reflect questions can be used as the starting point to help you identify the people who serve as your spiritual role models and the people who might look to you for support and guidance. Answer the questions first on your own, then share your answers with your partner.

Pause and Reflect

Who are your spiritual role models? Are there same-sex couples who are spiritual role models for you? What do you admire about them?

What spiritual qualities, behaviors, and values do you recognize in your partner? How is your partner a spiritual role model for you and others? How might you both be role models for others in your lives?

135

Keep in mind that the strengths that we admire in others are often qualities and values that we, too, possess. In other words, we might not recognize these strengths in others if they didn't also exist to some degree within ourselves. We can use our spiritual strengths to help us cope during times of adversity.

When we look at the lives of our spiritual role models, we can be reassured that we have what it takes to face our fears and act with courage in the face of discrimination. Dan and Roger's act of courage involved taking a financial risk to live more honestly and openly. To help them take this risk, they drew support and encouragement from their role models and from each other.

Dan and Roger experienced direct discrimination in a religious setting that resulted in Roger deciding to quit his job. These kinds of events produce acute stress. More subtle or unintentional acts of discrimination and prejudice sometimes catch us off guard. Something may feel off, but we are uncertain about the source of our upset.

Microaggressions often leave us feeling confused. We may doubt our perceptions or our interpretations of an interaction or an event. We may scratch our heads and wonder whether we are being too sensitive or whether we have the right to be offended. We may be particularly confused when these negative interactions take place in a religious setting where we thought we were accepted.

In most cases, we should trust our gut or our intuitive sense. If an incident, no matter how subtle or ambiguous, leaves us feeling confused or uncertain, we need to acknowledge it rather than ignore it. Holly and Tiana's story illustrate the unexpected, confusing, and stressful nature of a microaggression in a religious community that was officially affirming of same-sex couples.

Holly, 26 and Tiana, 28, moved to a university town a couple of years ago so that Tiana could attend veterinary school. They have an 18-month-old daughter named Jayda. They grew up with very different cultural and religious backgrounds. Holly is the daughter of a Methodist minister and "pretty much refused to have anything to do with religion until Tiana and I got together." Tiana is from Hungary and grew up as a member of the Salvation Army. It was extremely important to her that she and Holly find an affirming Christian community. Tiana said, "I felt very sorry that her church experiences had caused Holly so much pain and grief. Mine was not much better, but I still value what I learned about giving generously to others."

When they moved to their new home, they immediately started looking for a church that they could join. After investigating different possibilities, they visited a church that advertised "All are welcome" on their website. During the service, however, the minister asked Holly whether she wanted to introduce her "friend." Tiana recounts, "Obviously we are a family! At least, it seems obvious to us that we are both Jayda's parents!" "I was really caught off guard and a little stunned," added Holly.

Tiana stood up and nervously faced the congregation and said, "My name is Tiana. This is my wife, Holly, and our daughter, Jayda." As she scanned the faces looking back at her, she thought she saw a few raised eyebrows, but she wasn't sure. She wondered, "Didn't this congregation mean it when they said, 'All are welcome'"?

Social support from a spiritual community is very important to many couples. Although Holly and Tiana have since learned that they can count on the support of many of the congregants, they sometimes feel burdened with the task of educating the church about what it really means to be welcoming to same-sex couples like themselves. For example, Holly and Tiana's wedding anniversary was not included in the bulletin with the anniversaries of the different-sex married couples. Was this just an innocent oversight? Why are they overlooked for leadership or teaching positions despite their expressed interest and experience? "All are welcome" seems to have its limits when it comes to full participation in the congregation.

Experiences like this can leave same-sex couples feeling like second-class citizens in the congregations that they look to for spiritual, emotional, and social support. Talking about experiences of prejudice and discrimination, whether they are blatant or subtle, can help to raise awareness, validate one's experience, and lead to effective coping and problem solving. Perhaps you and your

---

Guided Activity: Assessing and Addressing Microaggressions

Use the following discussion questions to guide you in becoming more aware of experiences of subtle forms of prejudice in your religious community or in interactions with religious people. Once you are aware of microaggressions, you can decide on appropriate positive actions that you can take in response.

1. *Become aware of microaggressions you have experienced in the past.* Have you experienced interactions or events in your religious community that have made you question whether you were accepted and supported as a same-sex couple? Describe what happened and how you felt about these events or interactions. In hindsight, are there responses you would have liked to have made in the moment?
2. *Brainstorm changes that would need to occur to prevent these kinds of microaggressions.* What would have to change in your religious community for same-sex couples to experience full acceptance and support?
3. *Make an action plan.* What steps are the two of you willing to take to help promote full acceptance and support in your religious community? (Remember that small actions can make a big difference if enacted consistently and repeatedly.)

Couples may decide to share their experiences of microaggressions with other same-sex couples and their allies. For example, Holly and Tiana facilitated a larger discussion of this topic in their Sunday School class. This discussion brought new awareness and sensitivity to members of the congregation. With their allies, they have provided the church leadership with a list of suggestions for welcoming and affirming actions that the church can adopt.

---

partner might benefit from having a direct discussion about religion-based discrimination you have experienced and your options for responding.

CONCLUSION

Overt discrimination and more subtle microaggressions may be common experiences for you if you are seeking a spiritual community. The ultimate solution, of course, is the eradication of religion-based discrimination and prejudice that prevents same-sex couples from fully accessing an important source of social support for their relationship and their families. In the meantime, you can take steps to recognize rather than internalize these experiences.

Recognizing feelings of discomfort or confusion can be an important first step in becoming aware of microaggressions. Once you are aware of a microaggression, you can make choices about how to respond. You may often feel that you are alone, and you may be hesitant to be the squeaky wheel when it comes to confronting experiences of microaggressions. You may wonder whether you should just ignore these confusing and uncomfortable interactions. These microaggressions, however, add up, and the cumulative stress can take a toll on your sense of support and belonging in your spiritual community. Finding positive ways to address these microaggressions can ultimately benefit your well-being as a couple and your entire religious or spiritual community.

CHAPTER 15

TRUE CONFESSIONS

Disclosure of a same-sex relationship in a religious or spiritual community is an issue for many couples. Some couples may face challenges in making decisions about when, how, and to whom they will disclose their relationship. Decisions about disclosing or concealing our identities and relationships are part of the minority stress process that same-sex couples experience. Couples take a variety of approaches to these decisions when it comes to their religious communities.

Karen, 26, and Cicely, 27, have been together for 4 years. Karen grew up in middle-class suburb of a city in the Midwest. She earned a college degree in human resources and is now employed at a manufacturing facility in a smaller town. Cicely also grew up in a middle-class family in a Midwestern city and earned her college degree in fine arts. She is now a freelance graphic designer and works at home, allowing her to easily relocate to where Karen works. Karen and Cicely are an interracial couple; Karen is White and Cicely is African American.

Both grew up going to church and wanted to find a church community. They described their difficulty in finding a church that met their spiritual needs. As Cicely said,

> We wanted to become members of a church, and we were both raised Baptist, so it wasn't an issue about our religious beliefs

being in conflict. Our dilemma was, do we go to a Black church? Do we go to a White church? Do we go to a nondenominational church, which seems to be more racially diverse but not accepting of gay people? Where can we go to church where we will be accepted as a couple? Wherever we went, we were afraid of backlash either because we're a gay couple or because we're an interracial couple.

Shortly after they moved to their new home 2 years ago, Karen and Cicely visited almost all of the Protestant churches within 25 miles of their home. They visited one church from a denomination that is officially Open and Affirming. There were a few people of color in the congregation, but the rituals and the style of worship were very different from what they were used to. "Frankly," said Karen, laughing apologetically, "it was boring. I want to be inspired when I go to church, not put to sleep."

In the end, they chose to attend a predominantly African American church that was similar to the churches they each attended as children. They look forward to the worship services each week. The gospel music, the expressive and informal style, and the down-to-earth, generous, and joyful people make the couple feel at home.

Karen and Cicely have never heard the preacher attack gay men and lesbians from the pulpit. However, the sermon illustrations are always about husbands and wives, and the focus is always on marriage. People in the church assume that Cicely and Karen are friends and roommates. As Karen explained,

> Several of the older women in the church seem determined to find us husbands. Everyone seems to assume that we are just a couple of straight gals in need of husbands so we can get married and settle down. We make jokes to get out of it, but we don't really try to correct their assumption. We figure that would make everyone very uncomfortable.

Although they doubt they would be outright shunned if their relationship was revealed, they do have anxiety about the potential impact on their relationships with others in the church community. "Most likely," says Cicely, "they would 'love the sinner and hate the sin.'" Cicely and Karen are not eager to see what that stance might actually look like in practice.

On one level, Karen and Cicely are able to laugh about their situation. They love the church and the people. They particularly love the older women who worry so much about them. To them, concealing their relationship is preferable to leaving a church that feels comfortable and familiar. "I know that it's not ideal," says Karen, "but this way we can both share our spirituality and enjoy the services together." They have accepted this limitation in favor of being in a church that otherwise seems to be a good fit for them.

Karen and Cicely have a lot to talk about. They decide that they need to actively make a decision about their level of disclosure rather than continue to passively let people make false assumptions about them. They decide that it is important for their couple relationship to be acknowledged by people with whom they spend so much of their time.

Pause and Reflect

How do you define your spiritual/religious community?
How out are you as a couple in your spiritual/religious community?

Karen and Cicely feel anxious because, on the one hand, the nature of their relationship could come to light at any time and then they would have to deal with the repercussions. On the other hand, if they come out, they are afraid that they might be subjected to negative reactions. Then they would need to find another church community. They are wrestling with what might seem like a no-win situation.

Karen and Cicely are aware that they are making a big compromise in joining a church where they cannot be honest about their relationship. They have mostly tried to ignore the issue, but they are starting to realize that they are going to have to face their dilemma. They plan to have children someday, and it is very important to them to have a religious community that is safe and supportive of their family.

Karen and Cicely sit down and first identify the positives and negatives about their church involvement. They note that a big reason for joining the church is that they want the social support. At church they also find inspiration and strength for living each day according to their deeply held values.

> Karen: For us, going to church together is a part of the week where we get to share something important to us. We get to experience this feeling together. But we pay a price for that.
>
> Cicely: I think that being so involved at church has been good for us for the past couple of years as we made our home here. It has given us a place to meet a lot of people and get connected, in a good way. We do things with the church that makes it feel like we are giving to a community and getting support.
>
> Karen: But we've realized that it's not support for the real us. And we've started to feel like we are not being honest with people we care about. That's hard. That's not our values. God made us this way. We should be able to share that with people we love and care about.
>
> Cicely: I think part of this may be from my growing up in a Black church where it was all "don't ask, don't tell." We all knew who was gay, but no one asked and no one told. So I have these assumptions about the people here and how they will react to us if we broadcast that we are a couple. I guess I need to let go of some of that. I don't think all Black churches are like the one I grew up in. We both need to give

our church family a chance to know us. I want to hope for the best, but I have to admit it is scary.

Coming out at church feels like a big risk to Karen and Cicely. They wonder whether they are prepared to risk rejection. How will they cope if they are rejected? In the end, they remind each other that they are strong enough to handle whatever happens. They name sources of support and their own histories of successfully

---

Guided Activity: Discussing Disclosure and Concealment

If you are dealing with disclosure issues in the context of your religious community, you might benefit from having the following structured discussion about coming out versus concealing your couple identity. Find a comfortable and quiet place and allow at least an hour (or more) to discuss the following questions together.

1. What is challenging about being out in our religious/spiritual community? What are the advantages and disadvantages of being out in our religious/spiritual community? What do we imagine would happen if we were more out as a couple?
2. What challenges arise from concealing our relationship from others in our spiritual/religious community? What are the advantages/disadvantages of concealing our relationship?
3. What would need to change for us to feel comfortable in being more open about our relationship in our spiritual/religious community?
4. How might we go about being more open about our relationship in our religious/spiritual community? What actions might we consider? What are the advantages/disadvantages of each option?

Note. Crooks-Yared, M. M. (2003). The experiential ecomap exercise: Creating client-based narratives of the influence of ecosystemic environments on the coming-out process. In J. S. Whitman & C. J. Boyd (Eds.), *The therapist's notebook for lesbian, gay, and bisexual clients: Homework, handouts, and activities for use in psychotherapy* (pp. 44–49). New York, NY: Haworth Clinical Practice Press.

---

dealing with discrimination. Then they pick one influential and kind elder in the church to come out to next time they go over to rake leaves in her yard.

CONCLUSION

Some couples find it challenging to integrate their sexual identities and their religious identities. In some religious communities, couples may passively allow other people to make false assumptions about them. They may let others assume that they are just roommates when it feels risky to be honest.

Internalized stigma, especially lingering and perhaps unconscious doubts that being a same-sex couple is good and worthy of affirmation, can keep you from disclosing your relationship in a religious setting. The longer you conceal your relationship, the more stress you may experience and the more difficult it may be to come out.

Coming out in your religious community may be difficult; yet, this expression of authenticity is important to your health and well-being as a couple. Positive religious/spiritual identities and positive sexual identities are complementary. Therefore, linking your positive religious-based values to your positive sexual identities can help you to be more comfortable expressing both identities.

CHAPTER 16

GOOD RELIGION GONE BAD

Churches and religious communities can be, on the one hand, wonderfully supportive places for same-sex couples to express their spiritual beliefs and values. On the other hand, some churches and religious communities can be very unfriendly places for same-sex couples. Some of us have had experiences that confirm this unfortunate reality. As a result of our experiences of discrimination in religious contexts, we may learn to anticipate rejection in these settings. Likewise, we may anticipate rejection from people we perceive to be religious, even when we are in nonreligious settings.

Anticipating rejection is one of the minority stress factors that keep us hypervigilant. Although *hypervigilance*, or scanning the environment and looking for clues that we are not safe, can be an effective coping strategy, it also has a downside. While we are busy trying to avoid the pain of rejection, we may be increasing our stress.

Rae, 22, and Brooke, 21, are college students who have recently decided to make their relationship monogamous and committed. They love each other and want to get married when they graduate. Neither of them had a particularly religious upbringing, but both of them have been exposed to negative religion-based messages condemning same-sex relationships and people who identify as lesbian, gay, bisexual, transgender, and/or queer (LGBTQ). Rae identifies as bisexual and had relationships with men before falling in love with Brooke, whereas Brooke has identified as a lesbian since coming out at age 16. The couple has been having safe sex, but now they want to get tested for sexually transmitted infections (STIs) so they can make decisions about their sexual behaviors.

Rae made an appointment at the university health clinic. As she sat on the examination table waiting for the physician, naked except for a sheet wrapped around her body, she felt very vulnerable. To distract herself, she began to read the posters and signs on the walls of the examination room. Most were about health and self-care, but one item was a beautifully embroidered and framed Bible verse. The message in the Bible verse was positive, but as Rae explained, "I freaked out! I figured that any doctor who would put a Bible verse on his wall was not going to approve of my sexuality and help me with my sexual health." Rae asked for the STI screening but did not disclose her sexuality or her same-sex relationship to the doctor.

Couples like Rae and Brooke can help each other recognize their fearful thoughts and reactions. First, Brooke can help by listening with empathy and compassion as Rae shares what happened at the clinic and how she felt. This is a bit challenging for Brooke, because it is *their* sexual health that is at stake. Rae and Brooke acknowledge that what happened, at its roots, is due to the discrimination and stigma that they perceive to be supported by some forms of religion and by some types of religious people. From there, they use Aaron Beck's ABC technique (i.e., activating event, belief, consequence) from cognitive behavior therapy[1] to articulate how this event affected Rae.

A: The *activating event* was seeing the Bible verse on the wall of the doctor's examination room.

B: The *belief* (fearful expectation) was that this doctor would discriminate against her if she told him the truth about her sexuality and sexual relationships, and she thought, "I can't handle that."

C: The emotional *consequence* was that Rae felt anxiety, fear, and shame. The behavioral *consequence* was that she withheld important information from her doctor.

By using the ABC technique, Rae and Brooke were able to talk about the assumptions that they both make about religion as a source of rejection. They were able to articulate the fear and the beliefs that supported that fear and to distinguish these thoughts and feelings from what was actually happening. In this case, because of the religious saying on the wall, Rae was telling herself things that had not actually happened. Even if the doctor did reject her, Rae can handle it. She is not powerless, and Brooke is there to support her.

Pause and Reflect

(A) Can you think of a time when a religious symbol or saying <u>activated</u> a fear of rejection?

(B) What was the fear or <u>belief</u> that you had about that situation?

(C) What were the emotional and behavioral <u>consequences</u>? How did this incident make you feel at the time and what did you *do* in response to these feelings?

It is important not to blame ourselves for the very real discrimination and stigma that we face. The ABC technique can help us to evaluate the source and the consequences of our fears. When religion and religious institutions are used to support prejudice, we need to empower ourselves and take positive action on our own behalf. Instead of scaring ourselves with thoughts that all religious persons will reject us, we need to empower ourselves by recognizing that we can choose to tell our truth and we can handle the consequences. If a religious person does reject us for our honesty, it is a reflection on their character, not ours. Everyone is entitled to their religious beliefs, but they are not entitled to treat us with a lack of respect. In situations like Rae's, health professionals have an ethical responsibility to be professionally competent to treat people with diverse background and diverse needs.

Unfortunately, many couples have stories of anticipating rejection within their own religious community. Marcus, 53, and Nathan, 44, are out as a couple at church. They are both active and serve as leaders in the church, giving generously of their time and their money. They volunteer many hours each month, serving on committees and helping with various projects. In general, they feel appreciated for all the work they do and the contributions they make.

Nevertheless, they are very aware that some members of the church (both LGBTQ and straight) have expressed concern about becoming known in the local community as a "gay church." These church members fear that being known as a gay church would limit the church's appeal to straight people. As a result, Marcus and Nathan, as well as other same-sex couples in the church, are very careful to monitor their behavior so that they don't appear to be "too gay." Marcus explained, "We're pretty careful not to be 'in your face' about our relationship. We are careful to not hold hands or touch each other in church." "We don't walk in with rainbow flags draped around our shoulders—that's for sure," laughed Nathan. "In fact, all of the gay couples are pretty low-key."

They believe their self-monitoring behaviors are necessary to be respectful and understanding of a few of the straight people in the church who seem to be tolerant but not really accepting. However, Marcus marvels that he is able to be openly gay and with his partner in church:

> It is very meaningful to me because I didn't think I would ever be in a place where we could be as open as we are. I never

expected to feel comfortable going to church with a partner. I never expected I could be with the man that I love in a church setting and feel OK about it, although I admit I still have a bit further to go before I feel totally comfortable.

Marcus admitted, "We do walk on eggshells a bit. We don't want to offend the straight church members. We just want to be accepted and included." This story, however, may reflect the couple's internalized stigma and fears of rejection more than the actual attitudes of the other congregants. However, to test their fears of rejection by holding hands and acting just like the straight couples in their church feels too risky and makes them very anxious.

To some same-sex couples, churches are important places of spiritual support and expression. Yet, because of the negative messages that some religious institutions and religious-affiliated people have promoted, same-sex couples may fear rejection in religious settings more than in other settings. Some couples have experienced rejection firsthand from the religious institutions to which they belonged, so their fears seem very reasonable. These couples may go to great lengths to monitor their behaviors in religious settings. Self-monitoring and hypervigilance are protective behaviors that they learn in response to discrimination and prejudice.

Some couples may not be consciously aware that they are self-monitoring their behaviors when they are at church. Like Marcus and Nathan, couples may be devoting a lot of energy to keeping a low profile to ward off possible rejection from others in the church without even realizing it. They may rationalize their behaviors as simply being considerate of others. This kind of hypervigilance can be habitual and automatic.

For same-sex couples who want to be part of a religious community, the first step in addressing our fear of rejection is to start to pay attention to how much self-monitoring we do in religious settings. Many of us have cultivated self-monitoring skills that protected us in early stages of our lives when we were more vulnerable and dependent on others. These same skills, however, may be overused out of habit and may, in fact, be holding us back in some way. It is important that we not blame or shame ourselves for behaviors that have been adaptive and protective. Rather, it is important to recognize these skills that protected us at other times and places and then make more conscious choices about when and where we use them.

Sometimes it is helpful to personify a behavior that has become problematic to create distance from it. Nathan and Marcus, for instance, named their hypervigilance "Mr. Vig." Therapists call this technique *externalizing the problem.* The purpose is to use humor to distance ourselves from our anxious thoughts and feelings so that we can see that they are not unchangeable parts of our character or personality.

Nathan and Marcus describe Mr. Vig as a well-meaning and protective old man who is perhaps a little too intense at times. This humorous approach allows them to get some emotional distance from their thoughts rather than giving them power. With this distance, they can make realistic evaluations of and decisions about their fears and anxieties.

Marcus and Nathan started to pay attention to when they were feeling uneasy at church. They noted when they were self-conscious about their behaviors, when they were expending mental energy trying to figure out how they were being perceived, and how often they anticipated that they might be rejected. They also discussed what they each did to try to control how others perceived them. After several weeks of noting and discussing their experiences, they went out to lunch with several of the other same-sex couples from church to share their experiences and concerns. In this discussion, they used the questions in the Guided Activity.

Guided Activity: Assessing Our Fear of Rejection in Our Religious/Spiritual Community

Use the following questions to guide your discussion with your partner and others in your religious/spiritual community. You may want to think about the questions for a few days and then talk together about your individual perceptions.

1. How comfortable are we being ourselves in our religious community? What makes it easy for us to be ourselves? What makes it difficult? What kinds of behaviors do we do or avoid doing to ward off rejection?

2. Who is most accepting of us in our religious community? What would this person say is the reason that he/she is supportive? What does this person do or say that tells us he/she is supportive of us? Who is the least accepting of us? What would this person say is the reason? What does this person do or say that tells us he/she is not supportive?

3. When we are in our religious community, how does the fear of rejection creep in and influence our feelings about ourselves or others? When are we most vulnerable to our fear of rejection? When are we least bothered by fear of rejection? What would need to change for us to no longer fear rejection? When do we think we will be free of our fear of rejection? What is the first thing that we would notice that would indicate to us that there was no longer any fear of rejection? What small positive action step can we take to lessen our fear of rejection in our religious community? What would keep us from taking this step? What will we think/feel/experience when we take this step? What will change when we take this positive action?

Note. Crooks-Yared, M. M. (2003). The experiential ecomap exercise: Creating client-based narrative of the influence of ecosystemic environments on the coming-out process. In J. S. Whitman & C. J. Boyd (Eds.), *The therapist's notebook for lesbian, gay, and bisexual clients: Homework, handouts, and activities for use in psychotherapy* (pp. 44–49). New York, NY: Haworth Clinical Practice Press.

CONCLUSION

The positive support that you want to experience in your religious or spiritual communities can be negated by your fears of rejection. Monitoring your own behaviors in an attempt to ward off rejection takes enormous energy that can drain you rather than revitalize you. You may need to carefully evaluate how much self-monitoring you are doing and how this hypervigilance is affecting you.

Sometimes it may be hard to know how much of your anticipation of rejection is helpful to you and how much is a habit left over from your past experiences. It is important to discern when your coping strategies are helpful and when they are not. Risking rejection may give you opportunities to decide that you need to find a different community or that you need to set aside some old coping strategies that are not serving you well.

NOTE

1. ABC worksheets, references, and materials are readily available online if you would like additional instructions and examples of how to use this cognitive behavioral technique.

CHAPTER 17

LETTING OUR LIGHT SHINE

Many of us grew up in religious communities that taught us that attractions and romantic and intimate relationships between people of the same sex were "sinful." As young people, we may absorb and accept these types of messages because they come from religious authority figures and are regularly reinforced by other authorities in our lives, including our families, our communities, and the media. As we become aware of our own same-sex attractions, these negative messages using religion-based language can lead to feelings of shame and beliefs that we are unworthy of love and acceptance.

As we discussed in the Part I introduction, the perception that we are not okay because of our same-sex attraction is called *internalized stigma*. When we grow up hearing these messages in our religious institutions and from religious authority figures that we are told to respect, they become deeply ingrained in our thinking and take on a lot of power. These thoughts may stay with us even if we adopt more affirmative religious or spiritual practices.

Unless we stop and pay attention, we may not even recognize that these negative thoughts are still there. Thus, we may not be aware of when and how they are influencing our behaviors and our feelings about ourselves. These negative thoughts and feelings interfere with our psychological and spiritual growth and well-being.

Internalized stigma can also affect couples' interactions, as Susan and Liz discovered.

Susan, age 33, is a technology specialist. She has always lived in the South and as a child went to a conservative Southern Baptist church with her family. She can remember hearing comments at church, even from her youth pastor, about the "sin of homosexuality." Susan has a great deal of insight, so she recognizes that hearing hostile messages using religion-based language throughout her childhood created a burdensome piece of psychological baggage. She has worked hard to overcome the negative view of herself as a "sinner."

Susan has recently traded in her childhood conceptions of "the angry, male god" for a more benevolent Higher Power. However, Susan describes the continuing impact of her conservative religious upbringing on her feelings about herself: "The whole religious dogma I was raised in has such a hold on me. At times I still find that I'm not really completely free of the 'shameful sinner' mentality, even though I supposedly threw all that baggage away."

Susan met her partner, Liz, 37, at an outdoor music concert about three summers after Liz's company transferred her to the area. Liz's early socialization was very different from Susan's. Unlike Susan's childhood, Liz's did not revolve around religion and church. Susan thinks Liz has benefited psychologically from growing up in a home where she was spared the rejecting and shaming messages of conservative religion. Nevertheless, when Susan's internalized stigma is triggered by the prejudiced comments and actions of her family members or other conservatively religious people, Liz finds that she, too, is affected by the influence of these negative religious messages. Susan shared the following example to illustrate how these negative messages affect their relationship:

> I was driving along a main road headed to work one morning.
> I remember it was a typical morning commute, until I saw this

big billboard that must have been put up overnight. I thought I must be seeing things, but it was a big sign that said "Homosexuality is an Abomination" and then cited a Bible verse. I could feel my stomach get queasy and the hairs on the back of my neck stand up. I felt totally assaulted on an emotional level. I heard stuff like this in church growing up, and it just made it all come flooding back.

At this moment, in this public place, during an otherwise happy week, Susan felt like she had just been ambushed. She felt angry, depressed, anxious, and a little nauseated. She couldn't wait to get home to tell Liz about it.

When Liz arrived at home that evening, she could immediately tell something was wrong. Susan poured out her anger and hurt about the billboard. Liz responded, "Yeah, I saw that billboard yesterday and thought it was the work of haters. It's amazing to me how people use religion as a cover for their bigotry."

Susan couldn't believe Liz had seen the sign and not warned her about it. In fact, Liz's reaction was unemotional compared with her own. Susan wondered whether Liz could even understand how awful this felt. The couple had very different experiences and reactions. For Susan, her religious identity was being used to attack her sexual identity. Because Liz did not identify with a religion, she did not take it as personally as Susan did. Liz was, however, deeply affected by Susan's distress. Neither of them got much sleep that night.

When negative messages using religious language push Susan's buttons, Liz and their relationship are also affected. Despite all of the rational deconstruction, critical analysis, and theological reframing that Susan has done to move beyond her dogmatic fundamentalist religious roots, she still has moments where she is vulnerable to "having my buttons pushed." She still occasionally experiences self-doubt and wonders whether she really is accepted and loved by God. Susan has internalized these negative messages and experiences them as a personal attack on her identity. Liz has not internalized them, so she understands that they are not about her but about the "haters."

Clearly, the ultimate solution is to end toxic messages of hate and prejudice that use religious language as the delivery vehicle. Prejudice and bigotry that cite religious beliefs as justification are still, in the end, prejudice and bigotry. Susan understands this intellectually, and yet her emotions don't always obey her intellect. Liz seems to have a protective immunity to these kinds of negative religious messages that is protective. Like getting a flu shot each year, Susan wants to find ways to strengthen her own immunity to the destructive messages that occasionally blindside her.

Pause and Reflect

What messages about your lesbian, gay, bisexual, transgender, and/or queer identity or same-sex attractions did you receive from your religious or faith community? How did these messages make you feel? Do they still influence you on occasion?

Share a story with your partner about how religion has impacted you.

Liz listened carefully and nonjudgmentally to Susan as she shared the negative messages that she had internalized from her conservative religious upbringing. She validated the pain that Susan felt when she saw the billboard. Susan, on the other hand, expressed admiration and some envy for Liz's skill at deflecting these kinds of attacks. Liz shared how she learned to "look at the pointing finger" and keep the blame on the attacker rather than believing that the attack had any validity.

Once we have identified the negative, stigmatizing messages that we have internalized, we can start to do something about them. We can start to critically examine them. We can dispute these negative messages. Like Liz, we can look at the pointing finger and keep the responsibility where it belongs rather than accepting it.

With Liz, Susan practices verbalizing positive responses to negative messages. She works to avoid taking these messages so personally and to see that they are not really about her or her relationship. Instead, these messages are about the fear and ignorance of others.

Sometimes it is helpful to use humor to highlight the irrationality of negative messages. For instance, Susan shared that "I wrote an over-the-top, fire-and-brimstone sermon about the 'Abomination of Heterosexuality.' I delivered it in an academy-award worthy performance that totally cracked Liz up."

You might consider starting a collection of humorous plays, books, songs, comedy routines, quotes, and essays that talk back to religion-based prejudice. You may have other creative ideas for expressing your feelings, experiences, and perceptions through poetry, music, art, or photography. Many great works of art are expressions of artists' experience of the negative, as well as the positive, influence of religion on their lives and on society. Writing your own spiritual autobiography and sharing it with your partner can also be a way to critically reflect on the helpful and hurtful messages you have learned. The Guided Activity in this chapter can help you get started, or you might look for one of the many online resources that are available.

Ultimately, however, we need to claim a new story about ourselves that is free of internalized stigma and grounded in the affirmation of our authentic selves. Being whole (holy) or complete means being authentic and then sharing ourselves with our loved ones, our communities, our world. Well-being requires being our true self and not a false self that has been prescribed by a religious dogma.

Developing our spiritual strength, for most of us, starts with rejecting any message that devalues us. Instead of listening to negative messages, we can pay attention to our own inner wisdom and use it to guide us in expressing our authentic selves and in living with integrity. We can also find a community, religious or spiritual, that supports the expression of our authentic selves.

Guided Activity: Cultivating a New (Spiritual) Story About Your Identity

You and your partner may benefit from writing and sharing your spiritual autobiographies. Here are some questions to get you started. Part of the goal is to identify and talk back to beliefs that diminish you and focus instead on beliefs that support and nurture you as individuals and as a couple.

1. What role did religion or spirituality play in my family of origin?
2. Who were the significant people that influenced my spiritual development? What significant experiences with religion or spirituality (positive and negative) do I remember from my childhood, adolescence, and adulthood? (You might want to make a timeline of these.) How have these experiences influenced my self-concept?
3. How has my religious or spiritual background influenced my beliefs about myself and my relationships?
4. How have I incorporated, discarded, or changed these beliefs in adulthood?
5. How has my sexual identity shaped my understanding and experience of spirituality? My participation in organized religion?
6. How do my religious and spiritual background and my sense of self as a spiritual being impact (positively and negatively) my relationship with my partner?

Note. Astramovich, R. L. (2003). Facilitating spiritual wellness with gays, lesbians, and bisexuals: Composing a spiritual autobiography. In J. S. Whitman & C. J. Boyd (Eds.), *The therapist's notebook for lesbian, gay, and bisexual clients: Homework, handouts, and activities for use in psychotherapy* (pp. 210–214). New York, NY: Haworth Clinical Practice Press.

Susan and Liz decided that the central focus of their spiritual practice was to find ways to "let our light shine." They started by writing and sharing their spiritual autobiographies with each other. This activity gave them time to talk about their backgrounds and the messages they had been taught about their identities. They critically evaluated how these messages had shaped their own feelings and beliefs about their identities. They made a commitment to reject any belief that devalues them and instead focus on spiritual values that support their identities and their relationship.

Susan and Liz made a list of things they could do together that expressed their spiritual values. Their list included expressing their compassion, cultivating a sense of awe and wonder, and conveying gratitude and joy in their everyday life. Susan found that these qualities of spirit, or spirituality, strengthened her self-acceptance to the point that she could respond calmly to negative religious messages rather than react to them out of fear and self-doubt.

CONCLUSION

Some of you may have grown up in religious communities that taught you stories about yourselves that were destructive rather than constructive. Religion has often been misused to maintain the status quo and current power relations. Some religious institutions have served to maintain privileges for some while oppressing others. However, authentic, spiritual people have been at the center of compassionate social reforms to help others.

Embracing, cultivating, and expressing your spirituality is an antidote to the stigma that you may have internalized. Religious institutions and beliefs can be a source of support for your spirituality. You should not feel bad about learning negative religious messages, but as an adult, you can also learn to talk back to those messages. You can reject messages and beliefs that tear you down rather than build you up. The important thing is to increase your awareness of your own religious heritage and how it may have helped and hurt you. With this insight and awareness, you can extend compassion to yourself and then replace negative messages with feelings of appreciation for the many positive strengths, including spiritual strengths, that are part of your identities as lesbian, gay, bisexual, transgender, and/or queer individuals and same-sex couples.

CHAPTER 18

FINDING HIGHER GROUND

Some same-sex couple members grow up in families that participate in progressive religious or spiritual communities that support lesbian, gay, bisexual, transgender, and/or queer (LGBTQ) identities. These early influences may powerfully shape, in positive ways, couple members' feelings about themselves and their relationship. People who identify as LGBTQ and same-sex couples may search for this type of supportive community as adults. Organized religion can be an important positive support and resource for same-sex couples and their families.

Rhonda, 65, and Bonnie, 60, have been a couple for 30 years. They regularly take their youngest grandchild with them to church.

> Bonnie: I think that one of the hardest things about being a same-sex couple is that you don't get enough support in everyday interactions. We find that support in our church. We're really excited about taking our grandson with us because it is important to us that he have positive faith experiences.
>
> Rhonda: We have people come up to us and tell us they are glad we're there and they really appreciate our help with the children's activities each week. The whole church talks

regularly about being allies to the LGBTQ community, and they are really supportive of all kinds of social justice issues. That's a big reason why we wanted to go to church there.

Our sense of well-being can be enhanced simply by taking the time to recognize the positive messages and support that we have in our lives. Sometimes it's far too easy to focus only on negative experiences. Bonnie and Rhonda have gained this wisdom over the years. As Bonnie explained,

> Even after 30 years, my 85-year-old father still refuses to acknowledge my relationship with Rhonda. I probably spent 20 years fretting about it and trying to change him, but I finally realized that I needed to focus on all the people who love us and support us. A lot of those people are part of our church family. Our minister also makes sure that her sermons are inclusive. She has a way of delivering a sermon that is positive and encouraging, as well as challenging. We usually take notes and discuss her sermon while we eat our Sunday dinner. That's one of the highlights of my week.

Many same-sex couples do find religious communities that are affirming of their identities and their relationship. These communities can be an important source of meaningful connections to others and to their most deeply held values. Participating in an affirming faith community supports their health and well-being as individuals and as a couple.

If an affirming faith community is not available, couples can express their spiritual values through many pathways. For some couples, volunteering in the community or working for the preservation and renewal of the planet expresses their connection to their spiritual ideals. These and many other positive activities can be imbued with spiritual meaning and can contribute to our well-being.

How do your spiritual values and/or your practice of spirituality contribute to your well-being as individuals and as a couple?

Some couples create and foster a positive spirituality that is not connected to any organized religion. For example, Jerry, age 24, and Neil, age 28, have been together 2 years. They listed spirituality as one of the attractive qualities that first drew them to each other. Neil defined his spiritual practice as "being aware of the goodness of the universe, the goodness within people, and practicing compassion and loving kindness." Jerry believes that meeting Neil was not a coincidence because, as he said,

> Nothing happens by accident . . . Neil was literally an answer to my request for goodness in my life, so I think there's a force other than just ourselves that brings goodness into our lives if we are just open to it.

Jerry and Neil had a commitment ceremony to confirm what they call their "spiritual union." They wrote poems that expressed their love and devotion to each other and articulated their shared commitment to "leaving the world a better place than the way we found it." To witness their ceremony, which they held in their small apartment, they included another same-sex couple whom they consider their role models for a spiritually based relationship. This couple also pledged to provide support, encouragement, and accountability for Jerry and Neil's commitment to enacting their spiritual principles and values in their life together.

Jerry and Neil believe that it is very important that couples establish their own routines and rituals that support their spirituality.

Together they enjoy reading inspirational books and have "developed our own eclectic little brand of spirituality." They look forward to their evening reading ritual.

> Neil: We read something aloud, and then we discuss what we think about it. We both get greater clarity in terms of what we think, understand, and believe. That's really uplifting and enriching. Couples miss out by not sharing these kinds of insights with each other that help us grow intellectually and spiritually.
>
> Jerry: Spirituality is something that a couple needs to be able to share between themselves. I think our shared spiritual values give us grounding and help when we get stressed out about work or bills or whatever. It's the glue that holds us together and keeps us strong.

Jerry and Neil do not attend a church or formal religious meeting on a regular basis, but they have a vibrant spiritual life that fulfills both of them. They are not anti-church; they occasionally go to events at different churches with their family and friends. They attach no power to other people's religion-based condemnations of their relationship, so even when they occasionally encounter these toxic messages, they are able to talk about them and feel compassion for the unhealthy behaviors of people who are prejudiced.

They have attended talks by clergy or theologians. These talks spark interesting discussions between the two of them and deepen their understanding of each other and, as Neil said, "our place in the universe." Neil and Jerry find that keeping an open mind and learning about a variety of religious and spiritual experiences feeds their intellectual curiosity and spirituality in a healthy way.

Guided Activity: Cultivate a Positive Spirituality

Positive spirituality includes connection, compassion, and contribution. There are many ways to express each of these aspects of spirituality. Here are a few ideas for you to consider. Read this list and then make a list of your own. What activities support your connection, compassion, and contribution as a couple? Is there an activity in one of these areas that you would like to try?

1. *Couple's Sangha (connection).* Some of the couples we talked to enjoyed reading aloud to each other from inspirational books and materials. Couples may read a short, inspirational passage and then stop to reflect and discuss its meaning or relevance to their lives.

2. *Taking time to appreciate the positive (connection).* It's easy to forget to take time to express appreciation for the positive support that we receive. Expressing gratitude for the people, places, and experiences that bring us joy is an important part of cultivating positive spirituality. Take time to talk together about the things you are grateful for and that bring you joy.

3. *Creative activities (connection).* Couples can gain a shared sense of meaning and purpose from activities such as meditation practice, gardening, playing or listening to music, or enjoying other artistic expressions. What creative activities can you do together to inspire you and to foster a shared, positive spirituality?

4. *Consider service activities (compassion and contribution).* A positive spirituality is expressed in acts of compassion for ourselves and all sentient beings, including the plant and animal world. Compassion can be expressed in many ways. Couples can choose among a wide variety of charitable organizations and service activities that express compassion for others. Examples include local organizations that provide meals for people with AIDS, cancer, or housebound elderly people; groups that provide housing for the working poor; and child and adult literacy programs. Some couples use vacation time to work with refugee communities or to help rebuild communities destroyed by natural disasters. In what ways do you (or could you), as a couple, express your compassion and contribute to the world?

Note. O'Hanlon, B. (2006). *Pathways to spirituality: Connection, wholeness, and possibility for therapist and client.* New York, NY: Norton.

CONCLUSION

You and your partner/spouse may benefit from assessing how you incorporate positive spirituality into your life together. A positive spirituality and a sense of belonging to a community that supports your spiritual values is a resource that can enhance your sense of well-being. You can draw on your spirituality and spiritual resources when you encounter minority stress.

Many people who identify as LGBTQ have forged strong spiritual lives and values because their identities, and their faith, have been tested by their experiences of minority stress. By integrating the strength of their sexual identities and the strength of their spirituality, they enhance their well-being as individuals and as a couple.

Part IV

WORK

Most adults spend more time at work than in any other single activity. For this reason alone, our work environment has a significant impact on our relationships. We often "bring work home" with us. This means that we bring home emotions that the workplace has triggered. We bring home preoccupations about events that happen at work. We bring home our relationships with our coworkers, bosses, and people we meet in our work setting. We express our feelings about all of these interactions either directly or indirectly when we get home. The quality of our work life affects our couple relationship, for good or ill.

Likewise, we take our partners to work with us. Information about our home life may be shared in the workplace. Interacting with others in the workplace often involves disclosure of some of our personal life, including our relationship. Some workplaces make certain assumptions about our family life and what it looks like. For example, we may be expected to bring a spouse with us to a social event sponsored by our employer.

In this section, we examine minority stressors in the context of work and their possible impact on couples' relationships. If the workplace is a site of minority stress for one partner, then both partners are affected. For example, when one couple member is not protected by a nondiscrimination workplace policy that includes sexual orientation and gender identity, both partners may feel pressure to conceal their relationship in their respective workplaces.[1]

Thus, same-sex couples share the stress when one member experiences minority stressors in the workplace. As a result, work stress can easily become relationship stress. So, it is very important for couples to recognize the minority stress that either of them experiences in the workplace and effectively deal with the stress as a couple.

Research on individuals who identify as lesbian, gay, bisexual, transgender, and/or queer (LGBTQ) has found that many have experienced discrimination in the workplace and that most have experienced microaggressions and prejudice. These experiences range from heterosexist comments in a lunchroom conversation to being openly harassed or fired. Sometimes employees with same-sex partners find themselves passed over when they otherwise qualify and expect a promotion. Events like this may stress their career advancement and their family finances and leave them wondering whether prejudice against their relationship underlies the decision.

Other supervisor or coworker behaviors, such as unreasonable deadlines and expectations, persistent criticism, or excessive supervision, may leave members of same-sex couples wondering whether it is their identity that is being targeted. It is often difficult to prove that this kind of prejudicial treatment is because someone is in a same-sex relationship. That uncertainty makes the negative impact difficult to leave at the office. Rather, prejudice often follows us home, and we may rely heavily on our partners for support.

Any of these prejudicial events in the workplace, whether blatant or subtle, can create fear and anticipation of negative events in both couple members. Many couples depend on both partners' income to provide for their family. Same-sex couples may live in places where employment options are limited. These contextual factors exacerbate the effects of minority stress on the couple. Some workplaces have policies that explicitly protect employees who identify as LGBTQ. These policies are good for business, and it is becoming the norm for businesses and companies to have inclusive policies—they help increase employee recruitment, retention, loyalty, and job satisfaction.[2] Other workplaces do not have inclusive workplace protections, and still others explicitly discriminate against individuals who identify as LGBTQ.

Employees of the federal government and federal government contractors (by executive order) are protected against discrimination based on sexual orientation and gender identity. However, as of 2014, there is no federal civil rights legislation that more generally protects workers who identify as LGBTQ from discrimination. Some states and cities do have inclusive nondiscrimination protections. The protection linked to these laws may be broad or limited. Members of same-sex couples may be able to use these public policies to redress discrimination in the absence of inclusive workplace policies. Activities in the chapters that follow guide you to find what protections are in place in your state, locality, and workplace.

As important as workplace nondiscrimination policies are, it is even more important that these policies are reinforced by the behaviors of supervisors and coworkers. Some workplaces sponsor affinity groups for LGBTQ employees and their straight allies. The presence of these groups sets a tone and expectation of affirmation of same-sex couples and their families. In other job settings, the workplace culture for an employee with a same-sex partner is unclear or unsafe.

Couple members may also consider other factors, such as race and gender, when making decisions about disclosure. The more minority statuses that you have, the more hesitant you may be to try to integrate all of these identities into your workplace. The sad fact is that discrimination on the basis of sex, race, sexual orientation, gender identity, and other characteristics still exists in some workplaces. We need to continue working for equality in access to jobs and treatment on the job.

Couples often feel the tension between (a) being honest and open and yet (b) fearing negative consequences that could compromise their ability to support themselves and their families. As a result, most couples are out to different degrees in their work and personal lives, depending on how they assess all facets of their unique circumstances. Negotiating how to balance their lives together as a couple and their individual work lives can be a challenge.

Couple members tend to use three primary identity-management strategies at work: counterfeiting, avoiding, and integrating.[3] People who identify as LGBTQ may pretend to be straight while in the workplace, counterfeiting an identity as a way to avoid discrimination. Some people may change the subject as a way of avoiding disclosure when questions about weekend plans come up in conversations with coworkers. Employees who identify as LGBTQ may integrate their identities in their workplace, disclosing their identity and relationship in a variety of ways. They may also use a combination of these strategies.

People who use counterfeiting or avoidance as a way to manage disclosure experience less job satisfaction and more distress than people who integrate their identities, especially when their workplace is not discriminatory. However, in highly discriminatory workplace environments, being open about one's identity may expose the employee who identifies as LGBTQ to even more minority stress.[4] Workplace disclosure is a complex matter that both couple members must assess and manage.

Negative experiences at work and the lack of supportive workplace policies can trigger our internalized stigma. When self-doubt and negative messages make us self-conscious and preoccupied with how others are perceiving us, it can impact our job performance. We may try to cope with our self-doubt in ways that negatively affect our couple relationship. Workaholism and perfectionism (what we sometimes call the Type-A personality) can take a toll on the quality of our couple relationship. Or, we can shortchange ourselves by being so focused on our fears of roadblocks that we don't pursue our career goals and aspirations.

Research has shown that negative feelings about ourselves, our coworkers, and our jobs and experiences of prejudice at work can negatively impact our job performance, as well as our general well-being. In a work environment that promotes anxiety, fear, or anger, everyone suffers. However, when we feel that we are actively engaged in making a valuable contribution to our workplace and that we are valued for our authentic selves, our unique talents, and our personhood, we thrive and our workplace thrives.

Getting to know others at work is important to our individual well-being and also to our productivity and success. We need to be able to have authentic connections with the people in our workplace so that productive channels of communication and creative problem solving can flow. We and our coworkers should experience positive emotions (e.g., joy, interest, caring) at work on a daily basis. It's good for us, good for our families, and good for our employer!

In this section, we illustrate different ways that minority stress can originate at work and how it can affect couples' relationships. In Chapter 19, we focus on blatant discrimination in the workplace, as well as more subtle instances of prejudice that leave people feeling unsure or unsafe. Microaggressions sometimes seem to come out of nowhere and catch people off guard. We illustrate positive actions that couple members can take to recognize and address these minority stressors. In Chapter 20, we illustrate a range of work situations that require couples to spend energy deciding whether they should disclose their relationship. We offer a structured activity for assessing the impact of disclosure at work. In Chapter 21, we show how couple members may try to anticipate possible rejection and minimize the risk to their employment opportunities. We suggest positive ways to move through fears of rejection. In Chapter 22, we discuss how couples can become more authentic at work and thereby reduce internalized stigma and its influence on work behaviors and career decisions. Finally, in Chapter 23, we describe additional positive strategies that couples use to cope with minority stress in the workplace.

Workplace anxiety and stress drain the energy that we could be devoting to a productive work life and a happy home life. We need to reach out to others for support and affirmation. We need to nurture our relationship at home and take that positive energy into the workplace with us. Whether you experience minority stress in the context of work rarely or every single day, we hope that you find ideas in this chapter that you, as a couple, can use to successfully thrive at home and in your workplaces. Our work can be an important source of life satisfaction. When we bring our best talents and competencies, including all part of our authentic selves, to our workplaces, everybody wins!

NOTES

1. Rostosky, S. S., & Riggle, E. D. B. (2002). "Out" at work: The relation of actor and partner workplace policy and internalized homophobia to disclosure status. *Journal of Counseling Psychology*, *49*, 411–419. doi:10.1037/0022-0167.49.4.411
2. Badgett, M. V. L., Durso, L. E., Kastanis, A., & Mallory, C. (2013, May). *The business impact of LGBT-supportive workplace poli-*

cies. Los Angeles, CA: The Williams Institute, UCLA School of Law. Retrieved from http://williamsinstitute.law.ucla.edu/research/workplace/business-impact-of-lgbt-policies-may-2013/

3. Button, S. B. (2004). Identity management strategies utilized by lesbian and gay employees: A quantitative investigation. *Group & Organization Management, 29,* 470–494. doi:10.1177/1059601103257417

4. Velez, B. L., Moradi, B., & Brewster, M. E. (2013). Testing the tenets of minority stress theory in workplace contexts. *Journal of Counseling Psychology, 60,* 532–542. doi:10.1037/a0033346

CHAPTER 19

THE UNFRIENDLY WORKPLACE

Many workplaces have protections in place for employees who identify as lesbian, gay, bisexual, or transgender. However, many still do not. We have heard numerous stories from couples about experiences at work that felt unfair and discriminatory. For instance, many couple members have at some time in their work history failed to get a job, a promotion, or a raise that they felt they deserved. They still wonder whether their sexual or gender identity was part of the reason. Other couple members have told us stories about more subtle, but equally stressful, interactions that they had with coworkers that left them feeling confused, uncertain, and sometimes unsafe.

Workplace nondiscrimination policies that include sexual orientation (and, ideally, gender identity or expression) are intended to send a message to employees about values and expectations. Couple members that work in places that do not have these policies may be more likely to experience prejudice and discrimination. However, even in workplaces that do have inclusive nondiscrimination policies, members of same-sex couples may still encounter prejudice.

Candace, 52, and Carla, 48, have been a couple for seven and a half years. They are public high school teachers in different school districts. When Candace had to have emergency surgery to remove a tumor, Carla was denied a request for a 7-day leave to take care of her: "I was told that Central Office would have to dock my pay because my request was to take care of my partner instead of my husband or parent or child. I told them to dock it and walked out!" After threatening legal action and pointing out that she had accumulated more than 100 sick days, she was finally granted time off with pay. Carla said, "After everything that I have done for that school system for the past 15 years, I was furious that we were treated like that when we were already in the middle of a crisis."

To add to this blatant discrimination against her relationship, Carla was also hurt that none of the other teachers at her school acknowledged the strain and stress of Candace's illness. As she described,

> No one called. No one sent a card. No one asked about Candace. And I've been around long enough to know that this is not the usual response that teachers get from each other when they have illness in their families. I really don't know what to make of it. I'm not saying it was because we're gay, because no one actually said anything. That was the problem. No one said anything at all! Why am I treated differently than anyone else in the same situation would be? I can't think of any reasons other than the fact that my partner is a woman.

Carla is experiencing institutionalized discrimination because she is not protected by a family leave policy that includes same-sex couples. In addition, her coworkers' lack of support when she most needed it was upsetting. As is typical of people's feelings when they experience microaggressions, Carla was not sure how to interpret her colleagues' failure to express concern when she and Candace were going through a health crisis. The nagging thought in the back of her mind was that their silence was an expression of prejudice toward their relationship.

Pause and Reflect

Think of a time when you experienced overt prejudice in the workplace, or a more subtle form of prejudice. Share the story with your partner. Can you remember how you felt as an employee and how it made you feel about your employer? How did you handle the incident?

Depending on the specifics of the situation, we may decide to ignore a microaggression or we may decide to initiate a conversation about the incident. Either decision may entail a risk, depending on our employer and our situation in the workplace. Our partner can help us by listening carefully, by validating our feelings and experiences, and by helping us figure out how we want to respond.

On the one hand, if we repeatedly ignore experiences of prejudice, whether blatant or more subtle microaggressions, or fail to even acknowledge these incidents to ourselves and our partners, we may risk negative effects on our well-being. On the other hand, if we deal directly with prejudice, we may risk possible discrimination in the workplace. In dealing effectively with prejudice, we have to determine whether it is worth the risk, the effort, and the energy to address it directly.

If we decide to deal directly with prejudice, it is important to use our positive assertive communication skills. If our coworkers become defensive and angry when we try to communicate with them about their prejudice, our workplace climate will remain chilly. Responding effectively is important, and it takes effort and skill.

Jeff, age 27, has experienced prejudice at work. Last week, a coworker posted an e-mail that contained an offensive joke about gay people. Jeff got no indications that anyone else found the joke to be inappropriate. Nevertheless, he decided that he had to say something, so he told his coworker, in private, that he found the joke to be in poor taste. The coworker immediately got defensive and told Jeff that he shouldn't be so overly sensitive, it was just a joke, after all, and he'd heard gay people make even coarser jokes, so "what's the big deal?" This incident contributed to Jeff's negative feelings about his coworkers and his work environment. According to Jeff,

> Especially since I was the only one who seemed to think that the joke was inappropriate and offensive. It's hard to be in an environment where you hear antigay remarks and then try to be happy about your work or anything else.

To add to his minority stress, Jeff perceives that he is excluded from normal conversations about spouses and significant others:

> I've worked there for 5 years and people know me and Walker. Yet, they never ask about Walker or what our plans are for the weekend. I'm not a part of the normal social interaction that goes on. On the other hand, I can count on some implied sexual remark from this one guy if I say I can't go with the group to lunch because I'm meeting Walker. All of these "small" things add up and put me on edge.

Perhaps the worst incident, according to Jeff, happened several months ago. Jeff was in the break room chatting with a female coworker that he knew. The woman handed Jeff a religious tract and told him that her church offered "special therapy" for people like him. Jeff felt blindsided. After handing back the tract and telling the woman that he was offended, he reported this incident to the human resources manager. Jeff recalled the manager's reply:

> She said that it was a private interaction and there was nothing she could do about it. She said since the woman wasn't my

supervisor that it wasn't harassment or anything. She wouldn't do anything about it. She didn't seem to care about how it made me feel.

Jeff described the effect of these cumulative unpleasant interactions: "I'm more guarded and more self-protective. I figure that there are a number of coworkers who do not accept me and my relationship with Walker." Walker noted that Jeff was tense and depressed when he got home from work:

> Of course it has an effect on us. If Jeff has a work event to attend, either he doesn't want to go at all or he wants to go by himself because people are so hostile. So if he doesn't go at all, he is maybe hurting his career, and if he goes without me, then he is hurting us. It feels like a no-win situation!

Walker went on to say that he felt a sense of relief when he took a job with a large retail company that had a written policy in their employee handbook that included sexual orientation, in contrast to Jeff's company:

> It made me feel a lot more comfortable at work, so I don't worry about someone firing me because I'm gay. That makes it a lot easier, especially since we feel a lot less secure about Jeff's situation at work. Still, it's hard to see Jeff come home so frustrated and unhappy.

Jeff decided he needed to do something positive about his workplace. He made an appointment to talk with his employer about forming an employee resource group to address lesbian, gay, bisexual, transgender, and/or queer (LGBTQ) workplace issues. He used online resources available from the Human Rights Campaign and Out & Equal Workplace Advocates (see Additional Resources).

Following the helpful suggestions he found online, he looked around for two other interested and motivated people to help him. They started meeting for lunch once a week. So far, they have checked their workplace policies about employee groups to make sure that they are abiding by all the rules. They have also drafted a mission statement for the group, set some goals, and made a plan.

Jeff is feeling good about his positive efforts to make a difference in his workplace. He enjoys updating Walker about the progress that he and his two coworkers are making. Walker is happy that Jeff comes home energized rather than depleted, and he likes their two new friends. This weekend, he plans to help the fledgling group design an attractive website.

Like the couples in this chapter, you may have experienced blatant discrimination, prejudice, or microaggressions in your workplace. It is important for couples to identify, label, and validate each other's workplace experiences. Giving each other this kind of support is invaluable. It is also important to find positive responses to help alleviate stress. The Guided Activity may help organize your thoughts and responses as a couple.

CONCLUSION

Improving assertiveness skills is an important and positive coping strategy that can help you as a couple deal with minority stress at work so that your negative feelings do not encroach on the quality of your home life. These skills can help you with the day-to-day interactions that you have with coworkers and supervisors.

Inclusive nondiscrimination policies do help to create a climate that makes it less acceptable to express prejudice against LGBTQ-identified people or same-sex couples. When nondiscrimination policies are in place, couple members feel more empowered

Guided Activity: Assessing Each Partner's Workplace

1. Label the blank columns with each of your names. Look at each item on the list and put a check in the column beside the items that describe your workplace. In the final row, give your workplace climate an overall rating.
2. When you and your partner have completed the chart, notice the differences between your workplaces. How do these differences impact your life together? How do they impact your relationship with each other?

Workplace Climate	(Your Name)	(Partner's Name)
Inclusive nondiscrimination policy		
Benefits for same-sex spouse/partner		
Workplace group for LGBTQ-identified employees and their straight allies		
Inclusive language in official documents		
Inclusive conversations with coworkers		
Coworkers support relationship		
Overall, on a scale from 0 (*not at all*) to 10 (*extremely*), how welcome and affirmed do you feel in your workplace?		

3. What is one positive action that you can take to improve your workplace for LGBTQ employees? What is one thing that your partner can do to help support you in taking this action?

Note. LGBTQ = lesbian, gay, bisexual, transgender, and/or queer.

to assert themselves when they experience either blatant prejudice or microaggressions at work. Workplace nondiscrimination policies that include sexual orientation are important to same-sex couples. When one partner works in a safe setting that is free of prejudice and discrimination, the other partner in the relationship also benefits.

CHAPTER 20

CLEANING OUT THE WORK CLOSET

Decisions to conceal or disclose one's sexual identity or same-sex couple relationship are as diverse as the couples that we interviewed. Every couple has to weigh the costs and benefits and come to decisions that make sense for each partner's particular circumstances. Some people are totally out at work, whereas others may be totally closeted. However, for most people, coming out in the workplace is an ongoing series of decisions. Couple members tend to disclose their relationship to people they trust and tend to not disclose to people that they anticipate will be prejudiced.

The decision to disclose is as much a couple decision as an individual one. Having to make decisions about disclosure or concealment at work is one of the minority stress factors that can have huge implications for same-sex couples. Jobs, careers, and future promotions and recommendations are at stake. There is certainly no one-size-fits-all answer for couples.

Couples must take many factors into consideration when discussing disclosure at work. Economic and educational privilege plays a role, as do race, ethnicity, age, sex, locale, and many other circumstances. Couples make a range of decisions about disclosure at work. Within this range are as many possible variations as there are jobs, couples, and contexts.

Kate and Jill have been together for 11 years. They still wrestle with how out to be in their jobs. Kate, a 35-year-old police officer, had this to say about disclosure:

> It's an ongoing challenge for us, especially how to handle introducing Jill to the people that I work with. I think it's the polite thing to do, but she really doesn't want me to. We happen to be in a city that has a fairness ordinance. I feel like it's very important to be out in my profession to the extent that I can and when it's relevant. On a day-to-day basis, I'm just doing my job and my home life is not relevant. But, I don't make a secret of the fact that I have a female partner. Most of the other officers that I work with have met Jill, at least briefly, and they can surely put two and two together. So far it has not been a problem.

Jill sells office equipment primarily to small business owners. Unlike Kate, she is not out to many people at work. As she said,

> If I'm meeting with customers, I am very careful to monitor myself and what I say. It's not that I outright lie to people. I just try to avoid personal topics because I need to get along with everyone. I don't want to lose a sale! I have to appeal to my customers in a certain way. It sucks. I really hate that about my job.

Kate and Jill typify couples in which one person is more out at work than the other. This difference in itself can increase the stress that a couple experiences. Like many couples, Kate and Jill have to make decisions on a regular basis about concealing or disclosing their identities. They both think that it is preferable to be out. Kate doesn't want to conceal her identity or their relationship. Jill, on the other hand, sometimes feels that she has to. Weighing the benefits and risks and making decisions about when to come out is a chronic stressor.

Kate and Jill are similar to other couples we have talked with; They feel dishonest and uncomfortable when they hide their relationship.

> Kate: I fully understand and support Jill's need to conceal our relationship when she is trying to target certain business customers. We have bills to pay, after all! But that doesn't mean it feels right.
>
> Jill: I appreciate that we don't pressure each other to be out to everybody or get upset if one of us doesn't introduce the other one as her partner. We're flexible and understanding about those decisions. I admire Kate for being as courageous as she is in her line of work and with the guys she works with. I'm not sure I would be that courageous if I were in her shoes.
>
> Kate: [Nodding] Yeah, but it does feel terrible to have your partner introduce you to someone from work as "a friend." I wish it wasn't that way. It's hard to have a partner who doesn't claim you at times, even though you understand why! And, honestly, Jill sometimes comes home a little testy just from all the strain. We have stopped going out in public as much. It's too stressful. I'm nervous about how I should react if we run into one of her big clients. How should I act? This stress definitely affects how we live our life together.

Couples frequently told us that it was much easier to "pass" or "fly under the radar" before they met and became a couple. Talking about our spouses, partners, and families is part of typical social interaction at work. Hiding that we are in a committed same-sex relationship feels dishonest and disrespectful. Hiding and concealing, as we have previously noted, can also feed our internalized stigma by increasing our negative feelings about ourselves. In this way, minority stress compounds.

Some couples find it challenging to deal with their coworkers' and clients' heterosexist assumptions about them. Making decisions on the spot about how to respond to questions or assumptions about one's relationship status can be very stressful for couple members who are unsure about how they will be treated. Their anxiety and fear about the consequences of disclosure is part of minority stress.

Clint, age 35, has been with Ed, age 36, for 11 years. They have a young daughter. Clint is out in some work settings and not in others. As he related,

> In my job I travel to different plants. I'm not out when I go to the plants that are in more conservative parts of the country. When I go to those plants, I'm as straight as I can be. Sometimes someone will ask me about my wife. I say, "No, I like to play the field." They assume I'm divorced since they know I have a daughter. Even so, it's okay for me to be "a player" but it is not okay to be gay.

At one plant where he has worked for several years, Clint found that it was becoming harder and harder to conceal his relationship with Ed. He thinks that the general manager is aware that Ed is more than Clint's housemate, even though Clint has not directly acknowledged the partnership. As Clint said,

> I'm sure he's figured it out, and if he asks me, I will tell the truth. On the other hand, I seriously doubt that he will ever ask. But

then it feels even weirder when someone else asks me in front of him if I have a girlfriend. I just try to avoid personal conversation.

Ed has also had uncomfortable experiences with disclosure at work. Unlike Clint, Ed considers himself completely out at work. He displays family pictures of himself, Clint, and their daughter on his desk. He shares stories about their family trips with all of his coworkers.

Recently, however, a new employee came into his office to chat for a few minutes and after looking at the picture on his desk asked Ed if the other guy in the picture was his brother: "I just blurted out, 'That's my husband.' I think I may have made him uncomfortable and maybe I wasn't very sensitive to him. It felt terribly awkward for both of us, I think."

Ed's and Clint's stories typify the stress at work that follows others' erroneous assumptions. Awkward interactions with coworkers, bosses, or customers can increase stress. Assumptions of heterosexual identity feel disconcerting. In these interactions, couple members are forced to instantly decide how much they are going to disclose to the person who is assuming that they have a different-sex husband/boyfriend or wife/girlfriend. They may internally debate whether to correct them, change the subject, or let them keep assuming. Bearing this extra cognitive load can be mentally exhausting.

Ed's sense of responsibility for his coworker's feelings is also common. It can be frustrating to be in situations in which we are correcting other people's erroneous assumptions. Taking on too much of the responsibility for how others feel when we correct their faulty assumptions is yet another piece of the minority stress pie.

Couples have many different ways of handling the disclosure or concealment of their relationship in their work environment. Whether you are out to everyone at work, out to some trusted others, or not out to anyone, these decisions affect the couple, not

Guided Activity: Weighing the Costs and Benefits of Disclosing at Work

The following questions and statements can help you and your partner examine and evaluate your disclosure decisions at work.

What are the benefits of being out at work?

1. I can be honest with my coworkers about our relationship.
2. I can invite coworkers over to our house or entertain business associates in our home.
3. I can take my partner to functions at work and other social events.
4. I can take advantage of employee benefits for our family.
5. I can be a role model at work.
6. Other benefits of being out are _____ .

What do you feel are the benefits of not being out at work?

1. I am safer physically and/or emotionally.
2. My job will not be in jeopardy if I am not out.
3. I am more likely to be promoted if I am not out.
4. I can be more effective in my job if I am not out.
5. Other benefits of concealing my relationship at work _____ .

What are the costs of not disclosing your identity or relationship at work?

1. I have to worry about someone finding out about my identity and/or relationship.
2. I am isolated at work.
3. I can't be authentic and honest at work.
4. I have to monitor my pronouns.
5. I can't have coworkers or business associates over for dinner.
6. I can't bring my partner to social functions.
7. I have to worry about running in to customers or coworkers outside of the office when I'm with my partner.
8. I am seen as single even though I am in a committed relationship.

(continues)

Guided Activity: Weighing the Costs and Benefits of Disclosing at Work (*Continued*)

9. I feel like I'm disrespecting my relationship by hiding it from others.
10. Other costs of concealing my relationship at work are _____.

When you have each shared your answers to the preceding questions, discuss the following questions with your partner:

- Which of the benefits of disclosing vs. concealing your relationship in the workplace do you experience?
- How do these costs and benefits affect your disclosure decisions?
- How do your disclosure decisions affect your relationship?

Note. Hollingsworth, L. A., & Didelot, M. J. (2003). Out in the workplace: A cost–benefit view. In J. S. Whitman & C. J. Boyd (Eds.), *The therapist's notebook for lesbian, gay, and bisexual clients: Homework, handouts, and activities for use in psychotherapy* (pp. 268–274). New York, NY: Haworth Clinical Practice Press.

just the individual. You and your partner may find the Guided Activity helpful in weighing the costs and benefits of disclosing your relationship at work. (Keep in mind that the costs and benefits may be financial, psychological, social, emotional, or even physical.)

CONCLUSION

It is certainly worthwhile to weigh the costs and benefits of either concealing or disclosing your same-sex relationship at work. Disclosure decisions can have both positive and negative consequences. You as a couple need to assess the costs and benefits of your disclosure decisions and find positive ways to cope with the stress of these decisions so that your relationship stays strong and flourishes.

If you are a couple that is not out in the workplace, you can protect your well-being by making sure that you have some strong social connections outside of work that support your couple relationship. Work may consume a large portion of your daily life, and social isolation is not healthy. If you are not out as a couple in your respective workplaces, find other positive relationships outside of the workplace that affirm your couple relationship. Also, periodically take time to reevaluate your disclosure decisions and how they affect your couple relationship.

CHAPTER 21

TESTING THE WATERS AT WORK

Past experiences of discrimination and prejudice can easily make us guarded with our coworkers, supervisors, clients, customers, and others in our workplace. We can easily become preoccupied with how people at work are responding to us or how they might respond to us if we came out to them. We don't even need to have personally experienced prejudice and discrimination at work; just knowing about others' experiences is often enough to make us anxious and watchful. It is important to remember that all types of prejudice in the workplace have a negative impact on productivity for all workers.

Many of us have trained ourselves to watch for the smallest nonverbal signs that we are about to be rejected. We look for the tell-tale frown or the uncomfortable silence. We listen for clues to whether we are being accepted or judged. We monitor our own behaviors to make sure that we are fitting in at work.

Our watchfulness and guardedness, when accompanied by anxiety, is sometimes called *hypervigilance*. Trying to anticipate rejection by being hypervigilant is a common way of coping with minority stress. Hypervigilance can give us a comforting sense that we are more in control of our environment, although the reality is that we are not in control of others' behaviors and beliefs. We are only in control of our own.

If we have experienced prejudice, we don't want to be caught off guard and risk being hurt or humiliated, especially in a work setting. We do what we can to try to control and avoid these kinds of experiences. Extreme hypervigilance can exhaust us mentally and physically and affect workplace satisfaction and productivity.

Anticipating rejection at work can be a major source of stress for a couple. In interviews, couples frequently share a common coping strategy that they use to try to anticipate and protect themselves from rejection. They look for information or clues in their work environment about the climate for people who identify as lesbian, gay, bisexual, transgender, and/or queer as well as people with other minority identities. Couples use these clues to determine how they might be treated at work if they disclose their same-sex relationship. Then they test the waters in ways that feel least risky to them.

Each couple must assess whether their fears of rejection are realistic and whether their coping strategies are effective. Overusing certain coping strategies can have unintended effects on the couple. In this chapter, we illustrate these coping strategies and suggest ways to evaluate their usefulness.

Paul, age 34, is a middle-school science teacher. Even though he is a well-liked and award-winning teacher in his district, he still worries that if people knew about his relationship with Chris, he might be treated unfairly or even fired:

> Once a week, at least, I will hear one of the other teachers talking about "the tragedy of kids being gay" or the "downfall of traditional families" and how that accounts for our students' academic problems. So, I'd be crazy to mention my relationship with Chris at work, even though we've been together for almost nine years. You have to almost put up a wall and filter your conversation with the other teachers and especially the parents because you just never know what the reaction is going to be, unfortunately. I'm in the habit of being very careful about everything I say.

Paul also worries that if people knew he was gay, they would misinterpret his natural friendliness and concern for his students:

> I'm afraid that if the other teachers and the parents knew I was gay, one of them, and all it would take is one, would accuse me of trying "recruit" their kid. Some people really still think like that. I'm sure it would only take one parent to raise a question or plant a doubt in the other parents' minds. I don't know what Chris and I would do if that happened. We need this job until he gets his business established. So I do everything I can to make sure that I don't say something that would jeopardize that. That means I don't mention Chris. Ever. I don't use the *we* pronoun. And I make sure that I never so much as pat the shoulder of one of my students.

Like Paul, many couple members may want to try to control what others in their workplace know about them and their relationship. They may closely monitor what they say. They may try to control others' perceptions of them because they assume people around them will be prejudiced.

Couple members may worry that even an ordinary conversation about going with their partner to see a new movie could be perceived as "flaunting a gay lifestyle." The stress of spending the workday anticipating rejection can easily follow them home and affect their relationship. It can impact their overall life satisfaction and well-being. As Paul shared,

> I get worn out at work worrying about everything I say and everything I do. My energy is zapped by the time I see Chris in the evening. On really stressful days I just want to eat and watch TV until bedtime.

One couple member's anxiety and fear can easily affect the other couple member's behaviors, as well. As Chris described,

Because Paul is so worried about someone finding out about us, it makes it hard for me to be out. I would like to be more out, and sometimes we argue about it. I think he could be more out if he would just relax about it, but he doesn't feel safe at all, so I have to respect that and support him. Teachers have it rougher than anybody, if you ask me. Administrators and parents get paranoid about gay teachers. Paul certainly knows the school system better than I do, and I certainly wouldn't want him to lose his job. But it stresses me out when we are out and I feel like I have to hide our relationship in order to protect him. Staying home and watching TV gets boring, but at least at home I'm not having to deal with Paul's anxiety about who sees us together.

Paul's minority stress is negatively affecting his health and his relationship with Chris. His fear is keeping him stuck. The choices

---

Pause and Reflect

Write down your answers to the following questions. You will use them later in the Guided Activity.

a. At work, under what circumstances do you tend to be hypervigilant about the prejudices of others? Make a list of times this week where you find yourself trying read how people at work perceive you. How often do you wonder about whether others' reactions to you are different because you identify as lesbian, gay, bisexual, transgender, and/ or queer or are in a same-sex relationship?

b. How much self-monitoring or self-censoring do you engage in at work? Watch yourself for a week to see. (Keep a log on your phone or write a note to yourself.) How many times can you catch yourself editing your partner's name out of conversations? Are there other ways that you censor your conversation at work because you are in a same-sex relationship?

that he makes in reaction to his fear are making his life more, not less, difficult.

It is important for Paul and Chris, and all couples, to acknowledge the realities of discrimination and prejudice. However, once this fact is acknowledged, it is up to Paul and Chris to make new, more empowering choices about how they will respond.

One empowering response might be to refuse to focus on fear and negativity. Ruminating about negative experiences or fears of negative experiences makes things worse, not better. Once we recognize a situation for what it is, we can make choices that will support our well-being.

Paul might choose, for instance, to focus his attention on his life outside of work to make sure that he and Chris are filling their lives with purpose, meaning, and positive emotion to balance out the stressful work environment. Once Paul is reenergized with positive emotions about his life instead of weighed down with worry, he might find that there are many other choices that he can make at work. Some of these choices might be risky, and therefore scary. They might push Paul out of his comfort zone. Staying stuck, however, is more painful than facing our fears and taking risks that are ultimately empowering. Chris can remind Paul that he has the resources to handle rejection and need not spend his life fearing it.

Couples may test the waters to determine whether the benefits of disclosure outweigh the risks and stress of constant self-monitoring and concealing their identities and relationship. Couples that we have talked to are endlessly creative in how they test the waters at work. For instance, some couple members seek information from colleagues about their boss's attitudes and beliefs and the overall climate for diversity in their workplace. They devise all kinds of ways to get information to help them determine how others might perceive them and how safe it is to be honest and authentic.

By far the most common strategy we hear about is "letting people get to know me first" before disclosing one's same-sex relationship. Joan, age 25, explained,

> When I started my new job, I hated feeling like I was hiding my relationship with Mai, but I purposely didn't put it out there in the beginning. I think it works out a whole lot better if people get to know you as a person and then find out you're in a same-sex relationship. Then it's just one aspect of who you are. You're not hitting them with it all at once. It's good to break in the homosexually challenged people gradually.

A related strategy that couple members describe is watching for the smallest signs of rejection: a tone of voice, a phrase, a look. Joan's partner, Mai, age 27, scrutinized her manager's reaction very carefully when she first introduced Joan: "I saw a flicker of surprise in his eyes." By that Monday, word had quickly gotten around the store. That evening, Mai told Joan, "I noticed some coldness and discomfort from a couple of my coworkers. I wasn't sure what to make of it." As she described,

> I can pick up on people's vibe. Also, I listen carefully for any kind of prejudice toward not just gay people but toward other groups of people as well. If a coworker expresses racism, for instance, I know that there is a high likelihood that they will reject me for being in a relationship with Joan. Prejudice is difficult for most people to hide. You just have to tune in carefully to what they say and watch what they do. Of course, by the time I get home, I'm emotionally drained from all the fantasies I have in my head about why someone said this or did that. For instance, a few weeks ago one of my colleagues brought in sandwiches from [a fast-food chain that had very publicly provided financial backing for anti–gay marriage policies] for everyone for lunch. I couldn't believe how insensitive that was. Actions speak louder than words, that's for sure! A few words

197

of support from even one of my coworkers sure would have been nice to hear at that moment! Instead, I felt my wall get a little bit higher and thicker that day.

Carefully observing the verbal and nonverbal actions of coworkers and supervisors (and clients or customers) and then trying to interpret these actions is a skill that many same-sex couple members have practiced for many years. These skills are used to make decisions about how much self-monitoring and censoring is necessary and how much disclosure is safe.

Observation skills are highly useful in many situations! On the other hand, sometimes we overuse our skills, even to the point that they become more harmful than helpful. Discerning when to be wary and guarded and when to be relaxed and open are also skills that require practice.

Keen observation skills can be turned into a positive coping strategy. Finding even one ally at work makes a world of difference to job satisfaction and overall well-being. This work ally serves as an important source of validation, perspective, or advocacy.

How does a couple decide whether one or both of them are being too guarded at work? Sometimes your partner can help you decide to what extent you are only doing what is necessary to protect yourself and to what extent you may be creating unnecessary stress. Your partner can help you perform a reality check to see how much of your anxiety and hypervigilance at work is following you home and into your relationship. The Guided Activity may help you to structure this discussion.

CONCLUSION

Coping with stress can, itself, be stressful! Hypervigilance, self-monitoring, and testing the waters are all survival tactics that may help you cope with the prejudices of others and the threat of dis-

---

Guided Activity: Reality Checks for Hypervigilance

Sometimes we are not aware of the extent to which we self-monitor or engage in hypervigilance in our work environment. The first step is to become aware of our own behaviors so that we can decide which ones are working for us and which might need to be modified. The Pause and Reflect activity earlier in this chapter asked you to make a list of times this past week that you self-monitored and censored, or felt hypervigilant about prejudice at work. Use that list to share the following with your partner:

1. For each circumstance you listed in the Pause and Reflect exercise, make a note beside it indicating how you felt. Did you feel stressed or relieved? happy or sad? energized or depleted? anxious or relaxed? What other feelings did you have?
2. What were your coping strategies? What are the pros and cons of the coping strategies you used?
3. How do these incidents of hypervigilance and self-censoring at work affect your relationship with your partner? Do they increase or diminish your well-being as a couple?
4. Brainstorm with your partner about how you might turn your hypervigilance into an asset at work. How might you use this skill (and other strengths) to find an ally at work?
5. What can you and your partner do to protect and nourish your relationship in the face of this minority stressor?
6. What small action can you and your partner take in the next week to support each other in your work environments?

crimination in the workplace. These are highly useful skills that you may have developed in response to the very real discrimination and prejudice that you have faced. They are adaptive in many instances. These coping strategies can also increase your stress.

It is important to assess how these skills function in your life and how they affect your relationship. You as a couple can recognize when you are using these skills and reaffirm that the problem is not your relationship or your identities. The problem is stigma and discrimination and their real consequences in your lives. After recognizing that hypervigilance and self-monitoring are understandable responses to stigma, you can then decide how to best protect your relationship from minority stress at work and your attempts to manage it.

CHAPTER 22

ARE YOU FOR REAL?

Internalized stigma includes the collection of erroneous beliefs about lesbian, gay, bisexual, transgender, and/or queer identities and same-sex relationships that we have been taught by our families, our religion, our communities, and the media. Many same-sex couple members have been exposed to messages that their identities and their relationships are inferior to heterosexual identities and different-sex relationships. These negative messages are false and damaging. They can also interfere with our ability to have a satisfying and productive work life by keeping us isolated, disconnected, and perhaps anxious or depressed.

Negative messages about our identity and our relationships need to be corrected and replaced with positive beliefs about who we are. We start this process by paying attention to when and how we experience internalized stigma. At one time or another we may all feel stress from internalized stigma, including while we are at work. Catching ourselves reacting to the negative messages in our heads is an important step in unlearning the stigma and relieving the stress.

Juan, age 32, is fairly reserved about his personal life while he is working. On the other hand, he does not hide his 6-year relationship with Al, age 33. Nevertheless, from childhood he was taught negative stereotypes about gay and bisexual men. He has lingering self-doubts that run through his head at work:

> I'm a fitness trainer. I sometimes question, "Can a gay man do this job?" Because I'm the only gay man and the only Hispanic person at my gym, I often think I have to work doubly hard and be extremely professional at all times in order to prove myself. It's like I have to constantly show everyone that I'm worthy, competent, responsible, smart, and hardworking.

Juan is painfully aware of the negative stereotypes about his ethnic identity, as well as his sexual identity. Although he knows that these stereotypes are not true, he feels like he has to work hard to disprove the stereotypes that he assumes his clients, boss, and coworkers believe. As a result of his negative assumption, which may or may not be accurate, Juan is self-conscious when he interacts at work. At home, Al notices that Juan is often tense and is driven to take too many clients and work very long hours. Although Al is supportive of Juan's goal to succeed at work, he sometimes perceives that Juan overworks to the detriment of their time together.

Al, on the other hand, works in a restaurant, where he has cultivated his persona as "The Gay Guy." When asked how he feels about this role, Al says that playing up the stereotypes is strangely protective at work but takes a lot of energy: "I can pretty much say any outlandish thing I want to. I can be bitchy. I can be flaming. People just accept it because I'm 'The Gay Guy.' I just beat 'em to the punch!"

Although some of his persona is adaptive, Al plays on negative stereotypes as a defense mechanism. In doing so, however, he expends a lot of energy and to some extent is incorporating these negative stereotypes into his own self-concept. Recently, the manager expressed concern about these behaviors and how they were impacting his job performance.

Juan often reminds Al that "The Gay Guy" is largely an act. He knows that Al hides many tender, compassionate, and caring qualities behind his work persona. Although Juan understands that Al's behaviors at work are protective, sometimes he fears that Al will actually become his "Gay Guy" persona and lose the qualities that Juan most loves and appreciates.

Dealing with the minority stress that results from internalized negative stereotypes is difficult and requires self-awareness. Juan and Al are both reacting to negative societal messages. In some sense, these negative stereotypes are controlling their behaviors and preventing them from expressing their authentic selves.

Juan and Al assume that their coworkers, clients, and customers harbor negative attitudes toward them because they are gay. This triggers their own internalized beliefs that they may not be good enough because they are gay and exacerbates the stress they feel at work. Reflecting on the negative stereotypes they have been taught and observing how these messages influence their behaviors at work is a first step. Then, adopting more positive beliefs and actions will help them to protect their relationship from the stress of their working environments.

Pause and Reflect

Think about your work persona. In what (even small) ways does this persona incorporate, hide, or obscure your authentic identity? How might your work persona impact your relationship with each other?

Our partner or another ally can often help us figure out the extent to which our behaviors at work are adaptive versus limiting. Our partner and allies can also help us critically evaluate how

203

much our own internalized stigma, rather than current realities in our workplace, are influencing our behaviors. The key is to start by identifying when, where, and how we are responding at work to negative beliefs and stereotypes we harbor about our identities.

Al and Juan spent some time talking about their work personas and how these personas served to protect and at the same time limit them. Al wondered whether being "The Gay Guy" at work kept him from being taken seriously by his manager. Was he contributing to his own lack of advancement by limiting his expression of his authentic self? Likewise, Juan wondered whether his workaholism might be preventing him from forming the kinds of genuine and authentic relationships with his clients and coworkers that would actually improve the quality of his work as well as help him feel more support and less stress.

Juan and Al both recognize that reducing their work stress could improve their home life. These discussions about their work

---

Guided Activity: Becoming More Authentic at Work

Embracing and expressing our authenticity is the antidote to internalized stigma. Discuss the following questions with your partner. Be open to each other's perspectives, insights, and suggestions for being less reactive to internalized stigma and more authentic in your work life.

1. What are your strengths in the workplace? What strengths do you have that you are not currently using at work?
2. What keeps you from being more authentic at work?
3. What is one small positive thing that you could do to be more authentic at work?
4. Make a career plan that takes into account your strengths, your goals, and your authentic self.
5. How can you support each other in moving toward a more authentic work life?

situations also led them to larger questions about meaningful work and its role in their lives. They started to reimagine their careers and their goals for aligning their work with their authentic selves and their life as a couple.

CONCLUSION

Believing the negative messages that you may have been taught may keep you from being your authentic self at work. When you react to your internalized stigma, you may find yourself engaging in behaviors like perfectionism, people pleasing, procrastination, or passivity. You may focus too much on comparing yourself with others, criticizing, or being overly apologetic. These and similar behaviors may help you cope with or manage your negative feelings. Ultimately, however, they may limit your success and satisfaction.

As your awareness increases, you can contemplate changing your beliefs and attitudes. Changing these beliefs about yourself can help you cope more effectively with the other minority stressors and the general stressors you face at work. It is important that you treat yourself and your partner with compassion and acceptance during this process of awareness and change. With new awareness of how internalized stigma increases the work stress that affects your life and your relationship, you can refocus your energies on contributing your unique strengths, skills, and talents at work.

Your partner and your relationship can be sources of great support and encouragement in changing your internalized stigma into positive self-acceptance. When you respond to others at work from a place of authenticity and wholeness, instead of reacting from a place of self-criticism and self-doubt, your work life will benefit. Then you will bring home less stress and your relationship will benefit also.

CHAPTER 23

TAKING PRIDE TO WORK

Discrimination and prejudice in the workplace are common sources of minority stress for same-sex couples. However, it is important to recognize that there are also many examples of positive and supportive workplace environments. In previous chapters, we have urged couples to expand their support networks in the workplace and to work for inclusive policies and laws. It is important to create a positive work environment for all employees.

We can start by being open to finding support at work. Sometimes we close ourselves off from others because we have already decided that positive support is not going to be available. If we want others to be open, then we must be open, as well. People who identify as lesbian, gay, bisexual, transgender, and/or queer (LGBTQ) are not the only group that has to deal with prejudice and discrimination in the workplace. Others need our support at work too!

Sometimes we are guilty of acting on our own negative stereotypes about our coworkers on the basis of their age, background, ethnicity, religion, or other factors. It is not surprising that when we are busy looking for the subtlest signs of possible rejection, we tend to overlook many neutral or positive reactions that don't align with our automatic assumptions about people. Instead, we need to remember to look for evidence that disproves the negative stereotypes and assumptions in our heads instead of only looking for evidence that confirms our negative beliefs about others. A good practice is to start out by assuming the best about our coworkers. Instead of constantly worrying about whether someone will act with respect toward us, assume that they will. This doesn't necessarily mean throwing all caution to the wind. As Felicia, age 26, told us,

> I got a tip once from another lesbian, who told me that she just assumed support and that allowed her to talk very naturally at work about her partner and their life together. When I started assuming the best instead of the worst, I found out that she was right! People tend to live up to or down to our expectations of them!

We do not want to minimize the real impact of minority stress at work. But we are suggesting that when you come home from work and start to talk about your day with your partner or spouse, try to include positive events. This ritual will keep you attuned to positive interactions that happen, lessen the stress you bring home, and increase the positive emotions that you and your partner can share together.

Remember Jeff and Walker from Chapter 19, in this section? After Jeff's encounter with a coworker who was promoting prejudice against gay men and lesbians in the workplace through a religion-based pamphlet, Jeff and Walker both started avoiding people at work that they knew to be religious. They started assuming the worst.

It was important for Jeff and Walker to confront their assumptions. Walker met someone at work who was very religious and who also supported his and Jeff's relationship. That surprising interaction prompted Jeff and Walker to sit down and have an honest discussion about their perceptions of others and how often they anticipated rejection. They realized that they had biases based on age, as well as religion. As Walker stated,

> I realized that I would either not talk about anything personal around older people or I would censor and just say that *I* did something over the weekend instead of *we*. I just assumed that the woman in the office that I take the mail to everyday would be a bigot because she's older. Then I realized I had no basis for that assumption. She had never been anything but nice to me. I even remembered that when I complimented her on her hair, she said how much she loved her stylist and how he and his partner were "great boys." Of course she thinks all men under 40 are "boys," so that was a good thing.

Jeff and Walker both realized that they did not have to be constantly on guard at work. They came home with positive stories about their interactions. It lightened the mood at dinner and made evenings more relaxed and happy. This strategy also helped when something not so positive did happen at work. Jeff said,

> If someone tells an antigay joke, I don't automatically imagine everyone is laughing anymore. I actually notice people who are *not* laughing. I notice other people giving stern looks to indicate their disapproval. It's a start, and it makes things feel not quite as bad. Although not having any of those remarks at work would be best.

Pause and Reflect

For the next 7 workdays, bring home positive news about your day. Highlight every positive interaction or event, no matter how small! Little shifts in our own behaviors can make a big difference in our mood and our well-being.

LGBTQ-identified employees tend to know more people from different parts of the workplace. They have wider networks because they look outside their immediate work area for other people who identify as LGBTQ and their straight allies. This kind of networking benefits the worker and the workplace. For example, Laura, age 56, has been a manager for more than 10 years at one of the largest employers in her city. She recognized the positive benefits of networking:

> I know people from every department in the company. I know people from the custodial staff, the assistant to the division leader in IT, a vice president, a senior HR person, and a security officer. I know people all over the place. So when there is a problem, I usually know someone to call, personally, who can help resolve the issue. My colleagues are always amazed that I know all these people, but really, it's just because we are all gay. It's this great resource that helps me to be effective in my job. And they can call on me for support. It's a big win for the company when it supports LGBTQ employees being out and knowing each other.

Networking with other people who identify as LGBTQ and their straight allies, and with their partners and families, is important to employee effectiveness and productivity. Creating opportunities for employees to talk with each other should be a part of every employer's strategy. These relationships provide a boost to the bottom line for the employer and help employees who identify as LGBTQ build their professional and personal support networks.

When couple members have this kind of support available, they experience less minority stress at work, which means they have less stress to bring home. Less stress at home and work is associated with higher levels of worker productivity and more relationship satisfaction. It's a win–win for everyone.

Candace and Carla (Chapter 19) and Paul (Chapter 21) are all teachers. Finding support at work is important for them. They may look within their districts or states, or they may turn to national organizations to network with other teachers who identify as LGBTQ. Paul, for example, contacted the GLBT caucus of the National Education Association (www.nea.org) for information. Candace and Carla actively reached out to other gay teachers in their area. They recently befriended a couple from a nearby town. This friendship offers a chance to get social support and to swap stories and share teaching strategies. As Carla said,

> We have benefited in many ways from meeting John and Howard. They actually know some other gay people at our schools that we invited to join us. We aren't nearly as stressed about our jobs now that we know there are other people out there we can talk to about them.

When people find positive social support at work, they are more likely to have the energy for addressing systemic issues. Personnel policies in the workplace, for instance, often suffer from inertia that is only interrupted by a change in law or demands from employees. This situation is especially true in smaller workplaces. Changing workplace policy, and culture, to be supportive of same-sex couples often requires that employees ask for the change.

Many couple members told us that the only way that their workplaces would change would be for more and more people to come out at work. These couple members expressed a strong sense of responsibility for being out at work. Laura felt she had an important role to play:

> As a person who is gay but also economically and educationally privileged, it is important for me to stand up and say I'm gay and be a good representative of the community. I think a lot of times people have stereotypes, and I don't fit a lot of

those stereotypes. I think it's important for me to say, "There are gay people in this industry, and you guys need to change the way you treat people." That's the only way it will happen.

Laura asked her employer to provide equal access to health insurance for same-sex partners. Even though she and her partner, Medha, did not need the benefits, she wanted her company to be more inclusive. She made the argument that most of the other companies in her industry offered the benefits. She also requested that the company's nondiscrimination policy be updated to include sexual orientation and gender identity. As she related,

> No one had thought about it. They assumed that it was already covered somehow or that it was unnecessary. I told them it was important to send a message by being explicit. How can we compete for the best talent if we don't have an inclusive policy? Even many straight people have started looking for that as an important indicator of workplace climate.

Making these requests and working for positive change helped Laura deal with her minority stress at work. Championing this cause also made her a better partner at home because she focused on sharing the positive progress she was making at work. That inspired her partner, Medha, to ask for changes at her workplace. Workplace equality became a goal they could work toward together.

Couples who have privilege based on, for example, their race, socioeconomic advantage, education, or position in their company can use their privilege to bring about positive change in their workplaces. Sometimes people who identify as LGBTQ underestimate how much positive influence they can have on those around them. They fail to consider their privileged status because they are so focused on their oppressed status. The Guided Activity will help you create a plan to bring about a more positive workplace for everyone.

> ## Guided Activity: Finding Positive and Supportive Resources
>
> Small actions can make a big difference. With your partner, complete the following two activities to increase your professional network and support for workplace equality.
>
> 1. Organizations such as Out & Equal (www.outandequal.org) are available to help those who are dedicated to bringing equality to the workplace. Explore the website and then share three things that you learn from your exploration. How might the things that you learn be applied to your workplace? What would be your first step toward improving workplace equality?
> 2. Complete an online search of professional organizations in your field. Make a list of employee groups or organizations for people who identify as lesbian, gay, bisexual, transgender, and/or queer that you might check out. Think locally and nationally. How can these resources be used to help you create and support workplace equality in your profession, area of work, or workplace?

CONCLUSION

You as a couple can take positive actions, supporting each other as you each confront minority stressors in the workplace. It is important to recognize that there may already be more support available than you realize. Relaxing your defenses and being your authentic selves at work will help you develop the support you need and want. These positive actions can also create opportunities for changes that will improve the workplace for everyone.

Noticing and reporting on the positive things that happen at work is one way to start. Finding support and building a network can help end isolation at work and provide other sources of support for your relationship. Working to create a more positive workplace benefits you, your relationship, your coworkers, and your employers.

Part V

NEIGHBORHOODS AND LOCAL COMMUNITIES

In their daily lives, same-sex couples run errands, go out to eat, take their kids to school, interact with their neighbors, mow their lawns, walk their dogs, frequent local businesses, and otherwise participate in community life. Their neighborhoods and local communities provide a sense of belonging and connection to a place. These local communities may also be a source of minority stress. In Part V, we focus on same-sex couples as they live and interact within their local communities.

We all want to feel safe where we live. When we think about safety, we may typically think about crime in our neighborhood. For same-sex couples, safety also includes feeling comfortable and secure as we interact with others in our community. We may experience acceptance or rejection in our communities. Most likely, we experience some of both.

In the mundane everyday tasks of life, we may experience typical stressors like having too many bills to pay or running late for an appointment because of heavy traffic. Minority stress adds to those everyday stresses and affects our sense of security and sense of well-being in our community. Minority stressors in our communities can range from a "weird look" from a store clerk to physically threatening incidents including vandalism or harassment. Stigmatizing interactions within a community context take many different forms. In 2006, our research team conducted a national survey on the impact of referendum votes on state constitutional amendments restricting the definition of marriage to "one man and one woman." In the survey, we asked about local interactions. We found that overhearing or participating in conversations that included negative messages about people who identified as lesbian, gay, bisexual, transgender, and/or queer (LGBTQ) and about same-sex couples had a negative impact on well-being, as did exposure to stigmatizing messages on yard signs, bumper stickers, or billboards. We found that these local interactions increased the stress of same-sex couple members[1] and members of their family of origin.[2] On the other hand, prejudicial events can inspire communities to act in positive ways. Acts of violence, threats, or discrimination against individuals who identify as LGBTQ or same-sex couples can prompt communities to work together to create a safer environment. Individuals often show resilience and grow stronger in the face of these kinds of prejudicial events.[3] Even so, prejudicial events are harmful. The ultimate goal is to eradicate stigma.

Communities can be small or large. They can be centralized or more dispersed. They are brought together by some commonality. Communities are often constructed around a physical location. They also form around shared religious, racial, and ethnic identities. These communities are often very important to people and connect them to their families and their histories. Belonging to these communities is important to well-being.

Same-sex couples must often negotiate their place within these communities, as well as their larger community. Couples who also have additional identities that are stigmatized on the basis of age, race, ethnicity, social class, or physical or intellectual challenges may face complex issues in finding a supportive and inclusive community. Even within LGBTQ communities and organizations, couples in which one or both members identify as bisexual or transgender may find it difficult to find a sense of belonging. When couple members encounter stigma in their communities, negative feelings about their identity and their couple relationship (internalized stigma) may be triggered. Couple members who struggle with internalized stigma may be particularly vulnerable to encounters with prejudice. They may spend considerable energy trying to anticipate and avoid other people's prejudice. The anxiety and isolation that accompany this coping strategy can negatively affect their well-being and their relationships.

As a result of their experiences with prejudice and anticipation of prejudice in their communities, couples negotiate how out to be. This, of course, is not a one-time decision. Rather, couples are continually faced with deciding whether to disclose their relationship in the many interactions that they have in the course of a day. For example, some couples may try to blend in within their neighborhood and simultaneously be more visible by joining an LGBTQ social group or political organization.

Same-sex couples live in all kinds of neighborhoods, from the most rural to the most urban. Few live in what might be called "gay neighborhoods." Same-sex couples who live in rural areas may not have access to a local organized LGBTQ community. They may not know even one other same-sex couple in their area!

Regardless of where a couple lives, it is important to establish some type of supportive community. Social isolation is not good for anyone. Positive social connections and a sense of belonging are fundamental human needs. Research shows that same-sex couples benefit from the social support that comes with access to an LGBTQ community. Creating this access is an important goal for couples and for the community as a whole.

Our research with same-sex couples reinforces the importance of creating positive experiences for ourselves and others in our communities. Our experiences of social exclusion can propel us to be more compassionate and inclusive of others. Our research has found that forging positive social connections and working to enhance the LGBTQ community and the general community are strengths of people who identify as LGBTQ. These strengths may contribute to couple well-being.

Communities can communicate positive messages of acceptance and support through, for example, nondiscrimination ordinances and workplace policies, marriage equality, affirming religious congregations, schools with Gay–Straight Alliances, and LGBTQ-specific resources. Ideally, same-sex couples see themselves represented in wedding announcements and stories in the local paper. They can name local religious organizations, congregations, and clergy that are affirming and supportive of same-sex couples and their families. They have friends who identify as LGBTQ and straight allies and access to at least one visible LGBT community organization. Their children know other children with same-sex parents and see their families represented positively in school. They participate in community organizations that are inclusive of all families. They know of LGBTQ-identified clergy, politicians, and artists who are visible and respected members of their local community.

Vibrant communities are populated by flourishing residents. When we enjoy a sense of security and belonging in our community, we can relax, feel connected, and contribute to our community. Studies show that this kind of relationship to our local community is associated with positive well-being.[4] In Part V, we illustrate the minority stressors that same-sex couples may encounter in their daily lives in their neighborhoods and local communities. As illustrated in previous chapters, minority stress factors form a reciprocal process. One factor can trigger others. For example, in Chapter 24, we illustrate the all-too-common ways that couples experience prejudice in their local communities. Their fear or anticipation of being a target of harassment or prejudice, the subject of Chapter 25, may lead them to be, understandably, hypervigilant about their surroundings in order to protect themselves. Couples may respond to their fear of being stigmatized by concealing their relationship when they interact in their communities, the topic of Chapter 26. Our negative feelings about ourselves or our relationship can be triggered when we are busy concealing our individual and couple identity. In Chapter 27, we show how internalized stigma may be triggered by experiences in our neighborhoods and local communities. Together, the stories in this section demonstrate how anticipating rejection, hypervigilance, and concealment function as coping strategies, and how they can also contribute to stress. We suggest several strategies that can help interrupt this process. In Chapter 28, we make further suggestions for building support networks and positive community relationships that can enhance couple well-being.

What is the climate in your community? The climate of a local community is shaped by the economy; educational and employment opportunities; racial, ethnic, and religious diversity; and many other cultural and sociopolitical factors. The climate is also shaped by how inclusive and supportive the environment is for diverse families. Recognizing incidents that trigger minority stress and marshalling available support in communities are important for same-sex couples.

Same-sex couples have many reasons for living in their communities. Couples everywhere can take steps to create strong social networks that support their relationship. They can actively cultivate positive identities. They can engage with their communities in ways that provide a sense of meaning, purpose, and belonging that will enhance their life satisfaction.

NOTES

1. Riggle, E. D. B., Rostosky, S. S., & Horne, S. G. (2009). Marriage amendments and lesbian, gay, and bisexual individuals in the 2006 election. *Sexuality Research and Social Policy*, *6*, 80–89. doi:10.1525/srsp.2009.6.1.80

    Rostosky, S. S., Riggle, E. D. B., Horne, S. G., & Miller, A. D. (2009). Marriage amendments and psychological distress in lesbian, gay, and bisexual (LGB) adults. *Journal of Counseling Psychology*, *56*, 56–66. doi:10.1037/a0013609
2. Horne, S. G., Rostosky, S. S., & Riggle, E. D. B. (2011). Impact of marriage restriction amendments on family members of lesbian, gay, and bisexual individuals: A mixed-method approach. *Journal of Social Issues*, *67*, 358–375. doi:10.1111/j.1540-4560.2011.01702.x
3. Russell, G. M., Bohan, J. S., McCarroll, M. C., & Smith, N. G. (2011). Trauma, recovery, and community: Perspectives on the long-term impact of anti-LGBT politics. *Traumatology*, *17*, 14–23. doi:10.1177/1534765610362799
4. McLaren, S. (2009). Sense of belonging to the general and lesbian communities as predictors of depression among lesbians. *Journal of Homosexuality*, *56*, 1–13. doi:10.1080/00918360802551365

    McLaren, S., Jude, B., & McLachlan, A. J. (2008). Sense of belonging to the general and gay communities as predictors of depression among gay men. *International Journal of Men's Health*, *7*, 90–99. doi:10.3149/jmh.0701.90

CHAPTER 24

GETTING A BAD DEAL

Same-sex couples may encounter prejudice in many forms in their neighborhoods and local communities. The threat of physical attack, a hate crime, is very real for some couples. Couples may be disparaged in hostile verbal attacks. Or couples may encounter more subtle forms of prejudice called *microaggressions*. These incidents commonly involve verbal comments or nonverbal responses to a couple as they interact in their community.

Whether overt or subtle, these experiences of prejudice have a cumulative effect on couples' stress. It is important to recognize and acknowledge this stress. Experiences with prejudice lead to the expectation of more experiences of prejudice. This heightened anticipation of prejudice can negatively affect couples' quality of life and well-being.

Corey, age 27, and Brett, age 26, illustrate the stress of being verbally harassed, often by strangers, as they go about their daily lives:

> Corey: Sometimes people see a couple like Brett and me and they either say something or look a certain way at us. Most people look and then they snicker, but most don't even have to say anything. I remember this one guy walked by us, and

when he got far away from us he yelled, "I hate fags." I turned and said something back to him. He kept walking and I kept walking. Brett doesn't like it when I talk back like that because he thinks they just want to make me mad, so they are "winning." I say something back because I don't want people to think they can treat us like that.

Brett: You know that boy that you said was staring at you in the store yesterday? I'm pretty positive that when he and his dad were walking out they were making fun of us being gay. That's more typical of what happens to us. People disrespect us or give us an odd look.

Corey: Well, they don't look at you as much as they look at me. I present myself as more stereotypically "gay" than you do.

Brett: That's true.

Corey: I get the odd looks because I look the part. I like to strut my stuff, honey!

Brett: It frustrates me, though, whenever people give us "the evil eye." But it's not as bad here as it is in some places. People think we're flaunting the fact that we're gay, but we're just being ourselves.

Corey: Yeah. We can just be minding our own business, out shopping together, and we have to put up with comments from some jerk. It's annoying, to say the least.

Verbal harassment or certain looks and whispers trigger fears in couples that they could be physically attacked. As a result, couples have to negotiate how to handle these incidents. Like many couple members, Corey feels that it is important to directly confront strangers who verbally harass them: "If I don't stand up for me; if I don't love me enough to stand up for me, how in the hell can I expect anybody else to stand up for me?" Brett, however, prefers to cope by ignoring the negative comment or verbal attack: "Having someone yell 'faggot' at you just comes with the territory," he maintains. "I just tell myself this is a reflection on them, not on us."

Corey's preferred coping strategy makes Brett anxious when they are out together. He perceives Corey's coping strategy as aggressive and dangerous. On the other hand, Corey thinks Brett is too passive and believes they must have enough self-respect to challenge any disrespectful treatment they encounter.

Pause and Reflect

Think of a time that you experienced an incident of harassment or other expression of prejudice in your community. How did you feel? How did you respond? To what extent do the two of you agree on how to handle these incidents? If you have different ways of dealing with other peoples' threatening behaviors, what are the pros and cons of each approach?

It is important that couple members discuss these issues and the best way to handle them when they arise. Remember that the source of the problem is the perpetrator of the harassment. Clearly, the problem is not you or your partner. Beyond verbal comments, the concern about potential violence is also extremely stressful. We return to the stress that comes with this fear and anticipation in the next chapter.

Some couples have negative experiences with vendors, salespersons, and people that they hire to provide services to them. Some couples experience overt prejudice. Other couples may suspect that any rude treatment or poor service they receive is because they are a same-sex couple. These kinds of microaggressions can cause a couple to deliberate very carefully about where to do business. Couples may be especially cautious when hiring people to do work in their home.

Darla, 31, and Yvonda, 29, have been a couple for 3 years. Recently, they purchased a new bookcase at a local store. They ran into problems when they went to the warehouse to pick it up.

> Darla: The guy who was loading the bookcase got angry when we suggested how we wanted it wrapped up and loaded onto our truck. He screamed at us: "Get your fucking dyke asses out of here." We immediately went back into the store and told the managers, who apologized to us and gave us the refund that we demanded. The next day, however, the manager called and said that he had talked to the employee and thought there was fault on both sides. No way are we going there again! And we are telling everyone else we know not to go there!
>
> Yvonda: It was an awful experience, and nothing ever happened to that man. It was a good reminder that some people are looking at us and judging us in a negative way. That was the first time that we experienced anything like that. It has kind of set us up to be more nervous when we have to deal with businesses we don't know.

Heterosexist incidents or microaggressions, which are a type of prejudice, may not be as overtly hostile as the incidents described so far in this chapter. Microaggressions usually occur when people make false assumptions, often based on stereotypes. These microaggressions may leave the couple feeling stressed about how to respond. For example, Darla and Yvonda planned their wedding a couple of years ago, which involved going to a local department store to register. Yvonda discussed the incident:

> The salesperson asked me, "Is one of you the groom and one of you the bride?" I laughed and said, "We're both the groom."

She told us that one of us had to register as the groom and one as the bride. Then she told Darla that she looked more like a bride, because she is more "girly" than I am. The whole time I'm stunned that this conversation is actually happening. It was very offensive, but I honestly and truly think this salesperson thought she was just being friendly and funny!

Both of these couples, Brett and Corey, and Darla and Yvonda, also recalled the stress they experienced during the anti–gay marriage restriction debates in their states. Darla and Yvonda remembered the yard signs with negative messages urging voters to deny them the right to marry. They had to pass by these signs when they walked together in the evenings and anytime they left their house to drive to work or to the store. As Darla said,

Frankly, it was impossible to not take it personally. Most of our neighbors know that Yvonda and I are a couple. We're good neighbors! We're quiet. We're friendly. We participate in our neighborhood clean-up. Why would they want to discriminate against us? Why would they vote to make us second class citizens? It hurt like hell and made me just want to pack up and move! But when I asked our next-door neighbor why they had a sign like that and why they were supporting this amendment that hurt our family, they just said they didn't mean anything personal by it. They didn't have anything against us; they just believe marriage is between a man and a woman. No offense intended! I told them it is very personal to me!

Brett and Corey spent many Saturdays canvassing their community before a November ballot initiative. After the marriage restriction amendment passed with more than 70% of the vote, they were depressed and discouraged. As Brett said,

The people of our state sent us a strong message that day that we are not welcome and that despite our contributions to our community, they don't want our family to be recognized. It felt like a big slap in the face. I thought about all the people we had talked to over many weeks and wondered who I could trust to be supportive of us. I just felt alienated from everyone.

Recognizing and labeling prejudice and discrimination in our interactions with people in our communities helps us to externalize, rather than internalize, the problem. In other words, our relationship is not the problem. Prejudice and discrimination are the problems. By placing the blame for creating these stressors where it belongs, our focus can shift to generating positive strategies for dealing with the stressors in our lives.

Taking positive action in your local community is one strategy for dealing with prejudice. Be sure to patronize the gay-friendly and socially conscious businesses in your area. Some communities have compiled listings. Like Darla and Yvonda, you may have to compile your own list through trial and error and then share that information with friends and supportive neighbors. Don't underestimate your power as a consumer. This form of activism can be very effective.

Also, consider volunteering some of your time to an organization that promotes peace and justice or that serves people who have suffered because of injustice. Volunteering is very effective in increasing feelings of well-being. Investing in our communities gives us a sense of meaning and purpose in our lives. These types of shared experiences and activities can also increase couple well-being.

After the passage of the anti–gay marriage restriction amendment in their state, Brett and Corey adopted a "movement perspective."[1] Like other important civil rights and social justice movements, the goal of ending stigma and discrimination and achieving full equality requires us to take a long view of social change. Keeping this perspective has helped Brett and Corey continue to move forward rather than stay stuck in their feelings of anger, sadness, and loss. As Corey said,

> After a big pity party, we decided to take a stand and become even more politically active in our community. We want to be part of some badly needed changes. We worked for marriage equality and also for an inclusive nondiscrimination law locally and in the state. There are also changes that need to be made for older people who identify as LGBT and who might not have family to take care of them. We need to help everyone.

Guided Activity: Working for Positive Changes in Our Local Community and Beyond

Create a plan as a couple for making positive contributions to social justice in your local community. Consider the following steps.

1. Make a list of positive actions (big or small) that would contribute to the long-term goal of social justice for same-sex couples and individuals who identify as lesbian, gay, bisexual, transgender, and/or queer.
2. Do some research to find out what local community organization or organizations you might be interested in joining. If you live in a rural community, there may informal networks of leaders and helpers, such as schoolteachers, clergy, or social workers who would welcome your assistance.
3. Look on social media sites for ways to volunteer in your local community. What kind of volunteer work would feel empowering and satisfying to you as a couple?
4. Use your answers above to make a list of activities that you would enjoy doing as a couple and that would benefit some need in your local community or neighborhood. Pick one activity to do together in the next 30 days. Make it a date!

Brett and Corey's activism and movement perspective help them cultivate hope, optimism, and other positive emotions that enhance well-being. A movement perspective helps couples keep in mind that social change does not happen overnight. While working toward social justice, couples can also engage in other meaningful activities that benefit their local community.

Darla and Yvonda, for example, contribute to their community in many ways. They enjoy regularly volunteering with the local animal shelter. Once a year, they use a week of their vacation to work on a women's build with Habitat for Humanity. They are energized by working together in their community. Through their volunteerism, they have met several straight couples with similar values and commitments. These new friends are quickly becoming Darla and Yvonda's straight allies on LGBTQ-related issues in their community.

CONCLUSION

Dealing with prejudice from others in your local communities can be stressful. It is important to remember that you do have choices. You can choose to take positive action that connects you to each other and your community. By taking the long view, persevering, and cultivating hope and optimism, you will increase your relational well-being. By engaging with your communities, you will increase your communities' well-being.

NOTE

1. Russell, G. M. (2000). *Voted out: The psychological consequences of anti-gay politics.* New York, NY: New York University.

CHAPTER 25

I WANNA HOLD YOUR HAND

The all-too-common expressions of prejudice described in the previous chapter naturally cause same-sex couples to try to avoid these experiences. They may try to anticipate when and where these types of incidents might occur. This strategy may give couples some sense of control over their environment. While this strategy is understandable and often adaptive, hypervigilance takes more energy than people often realize.

Hypervigilance takes effort. More important, it takes energy away from enjoying our lives in our communities. The fear of being targeted or the anticipation that we are going to be rejected by neighbors and others in our local community is the focus of this chapter.

Recall from Chapter 24 that Darla and Yvonda had a wedding ceremony a couple of years ago. As they made their wedding plans and hired vendors in their local community, they anticipated that the local businesses they contracted might have biases against same-sex couples. They were careful to explain to each vendor that this was a contract for service (catering, photography, flowers, etc.) at a wedding between two women.

> Darla: One of the most nerve-wracking things was hiring vendors. We felt obligated to be really clear that this was

a gay wedding with two brides. Then I would ask if that was going to be a problem and steel myself for the answer.
Yvonda: That's certainly something straight couples don't have to worry about!
Darla: Yeah, I was very anxious about other people being negative. The first few calls we made I worried, "Oh, am I going to get an ugly response?"

Weddings are stressful, and planning takes a lot of work and effort. Darla and Yvonda had the added minority stress of anticipating that the vendors they approached might discriminate against them. Indeed, one photographer was "a little weird about it," and one dress fitter turned down their business because they were a same-sex couple. However, they did not have as many problems as they had anticipated.

Yvonda: We got a lot of, "Well, honey, I don't care. I've got friends who are gay." Or, "My sister has a friend who is gay." It was kind of funny.
Darla: And one of the photographers e-mailed me back, "Aren't you paying?" It was like, "Why would that be an issue?" So it turned out to be a better experience than I expected it would be. I expected that we would have more problems than we actually did.

Even when our positive experiences outnumber our negative experiences, it is more likely to be the negative experiences that we replay in our minds. This is true for everyone. Our tendency to focus on negative interactions or on "the worst case scenario" may be an ancient survival mechanism that has outlived its usefulness in modern times. Regardless of the reason, our emotional brains continue to anticipate threats to our emotional and physical well-being.

> **Pause and Reflect**
>
> Susan Jeffers, in her book *Feel the Fear and Do It Anyway,* reminds us that at the root of all of our fears is a lack of trust in our ability to handle whatever experience we have. When we are anticipating negativity from others, we can remind ourselves (and each other) that whatever happens: We Can Handle It. Can you think of an instance in your community where you and your partner could have put this advice to good use?
>
> Note. Jeffers, S. (1987). *Feel the fear and do it anyway.* New York, NY: MJF Books.

Darla and Yvonda made "We Can Handle It" their mantra during their wedding planning. And they did! They were pleasantly surprised that most of the problems they anticipated didn't happen. A few incidents that they didn't anticipate did happen. For instance, the reception hall cancelled their reservation 2 months before the ceremony, saying they had double-booked the space. Darla and Yvonda didn't think this cancellation had anything to do with their same-sex relationship, but, still, the mantra came in handy! They just looked at each other and said, "We can handle it," and got busy locating another venue for their reception.

Our fears of rejection are well-founded. It is a fact that people who identify as lesbian, gay, bisexual, transgender, and/or queer (LGBTQ) experience stigma, discrimination, and prejudice. Being cautious, guarded, and anxious in some situations is adaptive and entirely rational. A few couples we interviewed fear that they will be targets of violence because they are a same-sex couple. Aaron, age 26, described his fear for his physical safety when he walks around his community:

> The problem with being gay is that I feel that everyone knows I'm gay. Todd and I could be walking down the street, and while I don't think that it's obvious that I'm gay, it's still a scary thing. We are constantly on edge wondering who knows we're a couple and who doesn't. Hopefully one day we will get to the point that nobody cares and we don't have to hide it from anyone. Right now, though, we just wait for someone to spray paint something hateful on our front door. It's the fear that kills me. You just never know what might happen.

This fear of potential violence can naturally lead to hypervigilance. Couples talked to us about how they go into "protective mode" when they are in public places, especially if they are going someplace unfamiliar. They scan the environment to determine whether there is any danger and carefully monitor their own interactions. As Aaron stated,

> Our rule is no affection in public. I'm so afraid that sometimes I don't even stand too close to Todd. The problem is that if we go out to a straight bar and we've had a couple of drinks, he gets affectionate and wants to hold my hand or put his arm around me. And I'm like, "We're gonna die, kid." He tends to have a more positive attitude about other people, and I'm always looking around. I don't feel comfortable. I wish I could feel more relaxed about it, but I don't.

Aaron's fear is understandable. Still, he is trying to relax a little for the sake of his outgoing and extroverted partner and their relationship. As he explained,

Todd is a very expressive person and doesn't give a damn what people think. I'm probably overly concerned, and sometimes that's a detriment. I'm trying to get to the point that I can tolerate having his hand on my arm without flinching and pulling away. It really hurts his feelings when I do that, even though he understands it's just an automatic reflex.

This situation can take a toll on relationship satisfaction, so it's important that couples come up with a plan that will meet their needs. Aaron and Todd start by talking about and acknowledging their dilemma. They externalize the problem (as Marcus and Nathan did in Chapter 16) by reminding themselves that their environment is the source of this problem, not each other.

Todd expresses appreciation for Aaron's desire to keep them safe when they are out in public. Aaron expresses appreciation for Todd's affectionate nature and his pride in their couple relationship. They decide that Aaron will give Todd a signal if he feels it isn't safe. They laugh about how to avoid looking like he is a baseball coach giving the signal for stealing second base. This signal will cue Todd to hold off on the affection. Aaron, on the other hand, says he will make conscious efforts to be more physically affectionate and responsive to Todd's affection whenever they are with friends, in a place they feel safe and at home.

In our interviews, both female and male couples described how they "watch their back" out of fear that they would be targets if they were perceived to be a same-sex couple. They described how they carefully observe the people around them and take note of what they look like. They are conscious of any stares or whispers. They try to figure out how open others seem to be and how strangers might respond to them as a couple.

"All of these things are things that I consider when I'm in public with Todd. I'm not paranoid, but I am very cautious," said

Aaron. "The fear of being beaten up is a little seed that I have in the back of my mind. You have to learn how to read other people and the environment."

Sometimes our anticipation of rejection is so strong that we project it onto other people and situations regardless of what is actually happening. Aaron realizes that there are times when he projects his worst fears onto others:

> Aaron: Sometimes I feel like people are looking or saying something under their breath whether they are or not.
> Todd: Sometimes they are. I'm pretty observant. But a lot of times they aren't even paying any attention to us at all.
> Aaron: I know that's probably true, but even after being out for seven years, I still feel very self-conscious, like everyone is looking at us and judging us for being a couple.

Todd and Aaron talk about these incidents as a way to discern how much hypervigilance is helpful and how much may be harmful to their well-being. Some couples may restrict their activities because of their fear of rejection. Over time this strategy can lead to too much isolation and can compromise couples' well-being. Our partners (and our friends) can help us put our fears and assumptions to a reality test to evaluate the level of psychological or physical danger that is really present.

Our hypervigilance can also be put to good use. We can choose to focus our attention on times that we are not being rejected or discriminated against. This technique is called *finding exceptions to the problem*.[1] Noticing all the times when the problem is not happening gives us a new vantage point that helps us gain insights into the problem and ourselves. Couples can make a conscious effort to recount the times that their expectations of rejection were wrong.

Aaron and Todd, for instance, were delighted to be included in an impromptu cookout with other couples in their apartment complex. "I almost fell over on the ground because I couldn't believe that the people across the hall made a point to invite us!" exclaimed Aaron. "I had been avoiding them, but they reached out to us!" They also recounted the respectful treatment that they received from the maintenance workers who repaired their air conditioner. "I have to say that the overall degree of acceptance is much more than I ever anticipated," said Aaron. "As important as these positive experiences are, it's easy to forget them and focus on all of the negative experiences that we've either had in the past or we're afraid we'll have in the future!"

Aaron recognizes that he may overestimate the percentage of time that people are responding negatively. When Todd and Aaron are out together, Todd estimates that they get "a look" about 15% of the time. "It doesn't happen that much. But I can tell when someone is watching us or wondering what our relationship to one another is. At least it seems that way . . . and at least sometimes it's probably true," Todd said, chuckling.

Aaron admits that it helps to do a reality check when he is feeling guarded:

> I know that Todd has not experienced racism and homophobia to the extent that I have. I've had more negative experiences, and it can make me overly cautious. I have to remind myself to take another look and ask myself, 'Am I reading this wrong?' Because sometimes I do. Between the two of us, we need to help each other find a balance!

CONCLUSION

We recognize the unfortunate reality that people who identify as LGBTQ and are members of same-sex couples do experience stigma, discrimination, prejudice, rejection, and victimization within their

Guided Activity: Using the ABC Technique to Analyze Your Fear and Anticipation Experiences

Before we can change or modify our behaviors, we have to first become aware of when the behavior occurs. Try to catch yourself anticipating rejection or prejudice as you go about your daily interactions in your community. (Take a look back at Part III, Chapter 16, to remind yourself of how Rae and Brooke used the ABC technique to identify Rae's fear of being rejected by her physician.) Keep a log or notes on your smartphone or other device that includes the what, where, when, and how you felt. Schedule a talk time with your partner and share your logs with each other. Below are some examples of one partner's log.

> *Tuesday.* I was on the way to meet my partner at the gym to work out when I suddenly remembered that I had on a very colorful rainbow shirt that had "Celebrate Queer Identities" written in big letters across the front. I turned the car around and went back home to get a different shirt because I anticipated that I would be outing myself and risking negative reactions. I felt anxious and then guilty for caring what strangers at the gym think. My partner and I have been going to the same gym for years and probably people know we are a couple, yet I still took time to go home and change my shirt.

> *Friday.* We were standing on a fishing pier enjoying the sunshine. My partner of 10 years suddenly threw his arm around me and planted a kiss on my cheek. I stiffened and told him there were fishermen watching us. When I thought about it later, I realized that particular display of public affection would have been considered completely normal for any straight couple. No one would have looked twice. That is what heterosexual privilege is, and it makes me angry. Most of all, I get annoyed with myself for being unwilling to assert my "gay privilege." That is, act like a normal couple instead of being anxious and hypervigilant.

Couples can help each other to analyze these experiences using the ABCs of cognitive behavior therapy that we introduced in Chapter 16.

> **Guided Activity: Using the ABC Technique to Analyze Your Fear and Anticipation Experiences** (*Continued*)
>
> Practice answering the following questions about the two events above. The first one is completed for you as a demonstration. Then apply the ABC technique to your own experiences in your log.
>
> A: *Activating* event: Had on a queer shirt on the way to the gym.
> B: *Beliefs* (thoughts about the event): People will stare at me (or worse).
> C: *Consequences* (emotional and behavior): Felt bad, anxious, mad at myself. Turned around and went home to change.
>
> The ABC technique is designed to help you become aware of how your anxiety and fear and behaviors in response to anxiety and fear (C) are caused by the thoughts that you think (B) and not by the actual event (A). To change the emotional and behavior consequences (C) requires changing the thoughts (B).
>
> Can you think of positive thoughts to replace the anxiety-producing thoughts in the two scenarios above? For example, in the first scenario, the partner might decide to replace his negative thought with a positive thought such as, "I look really good in this shirt!"

communities. Fear and hypervigilance can take a toll on a couple's well-being. Many of you may have trained yourselves to anticipate the worst reaction rather than the best reaction. This strategy helps you to maintain your sense of control over your environment. The bottom line, however, is that you are only in control of your own choices. You as a couple can become more aware of your hypervigilance and make choices about your responses to help yourself thrive and flourish in your community, rather than live in fear.

NOTE

1.   Miller, S., Hubble, M., & Duncan, B. (Eds.). (1996). *Handbook of solution-focused brief therapy.* San Francisco, CA: Jossey-Bass.

CHAPTER 26

OUT ON THE TOWN

Couples who are out in almost every sphere of their lives told us that they still conceal their relationship at times as they go about their daily lives in their local community. Most frequently, they conceal their relationship by monitoring how they introduce their partner. They may also carefully monitor any display of affection in public. Even seemingly small decisions—for example, "Do we put a rainbow sticker on our car?"—become a momentous decision about disclosure for some couples.

On the other side of the coin are the couples who constantly have to disclose their relationship because people assume they are siblings or roommates, rather than a couple. These couples may not even be fully aware of the fatigue that they experience from having to correct people's assumptions and misperceptions about them. Interracial couples, in particular, shared with us their frequent experiences of feeling invisible as a couple because they were of the same sex and different races.

Donna, 62, and Tamara, 65, are an interracial couple who have encountered racism and heterosexism in the 35 years that they have been together. On the one hand, they intentionally conceal their relationship when they do not feel safe. On the other hand, they feel invisible because people in their community often assume that they are not together. Donna shared how racism and heterosexism affect their daily life as a couple in their community:

> I constantly experience, as a White person, what it means to be with somebody who is an African American in a racist, as well as heterosexist, society. When we go to the grocery store people look at us, but then when we check out, nobody seems to think that we're together. Or when we rent a car, I have to do the renting because sometimes the price is higher or the type of car we want suddenly isn't available if Tamara walks up to the counter. It makes me incessantly aware of the prejudice in our society.

Donna and Tamara constantly have to make decisions about when to disclose their relationship. Tamara acknowledged, "Sometimes it just feels like it's not worth the hassle to correct people's assumptions about us. It just takes too much effort. We just let them assume whatever they want to. It's easier that way." Donna said,

> It gets tiresome to have to come out as a couple over and over again. What really bothers me is that some people act as though it would be an insult to ask us if we're together. Like, what century is this? It's like Black people and White people can't be friends? Can't be partners? Others just assume that I'm straight. Last weekend for instance, we had a salesperson at our house measuring for new carpet. Tamara and I are standing there talking to the guy, and then he asks me if my husband would be able to reconnect the electronics once the new carpet was installed. I think my jaw actually dropped for a minute. I just stared at the guy for a few seconds because the question was so offensive on so many levels! But then I just mumbled something about there being no need to worry, I'd

take care of it. It just wasn't worth the trouble of correcting all his assumptions.

Donna and Tamara continually make disclosure decisions. In the course of one weekend, they may make several decisions. After the carpet salesperson left their house on a Saturday morning, they walked to their favorite bakery. They ordered their usual, coffee and blueberry scones. According to Tamara,

> Every couple with a man and a woman was treated like they were together. But we were asked if our bill was "together or separate?" It's assumed that we are separate unless we say otherwise. Really, it's a small thing, but still it's annoying, especially since we go to that bakery together a lot. It would be nice to feel at home there without having to make a big deal about coming out to the servers.

Tamara and Donna are a quiet and reserved couple. They work tirelessly behind the scenes in their local community. They joke about their invisibility and things they can do to make themselves visible. They fantasize about wearing bright T-shirts with arrows that say, "She's my husbian." "It's not like we're closeted," said Tamara. "But we do tend to avoid the limelight. That's just our personalities."

Tamara and Donna had a similar experience of invisibility at the gym on Friday night where they take line dancing classes and water aerobics. Donna said,

> People in our class are friendly. They have great energy, although we are probably the youngest people in the class. I think they all assume that we're just friends rather than a couple. Friday night a woman in the class asked Tamara if she had children, and Tamara gestured to me and said, "*We* have two daughters and a 3-year-old grandchild." I watched the look of surprise spread across the woman's face, so I jumped in and tried to make a joke about subjecting her to the 600 pictures of our grandson that I carry on my phone. I'm always on standby to relieve any awkwardness when we out ourselves. It seems to be my job to ease any tension. Tamara tolerates other people's reactions better than I do. When the woman quickly excused herself and dashed out the door to her car I assumed it was because we had just made her uncomfortable. It makes me sad when things like that happen.

Avoiding public affection is another common strategy that couples use in their efforts to conceal their relationship in environments where they feel unsafe. Couples do not always agree about when and where they should avoid showing affection toward each other. For example, Donna is more willing than Tamara to hold hands in public:

> I'll grab her hand when we're out walking sometimes. Tamara usually gives my hand a squeeze and then immediately drops it. To me, walking and holding hands with your partner should be as common as seeing a heterosexual couple hold hands. When Tamara holds my hand, it signifies to me that she is proud of our relationship. Holding hands when we walk around our own neighborhood makes me feel close to Tamara, but makes her more anxious and nervous. I certainly don't want her to feel that way! So we generally don't hold hands, even in our supposedly safe neighborhood.

239

Tamara and Donna also talked about how they let their neighbors gradually get to know them before they disclose their relationship. Tamara said,

> We don't immediately introduce ourselves as "the lesbian couple next door." When we moved into our house 10 years ago, we certainly didn't introduce ourselves as a couple right away. We got to know our neighbors and let them get to know us. When one of our neighbors figured it out and started interacting with us as a couple, we relaxed and started referring to each other as partners in front of him and his wife. We figured he'd pass the word! Now we just assume that everyone on our street knows that we're a couple.

Donna and Tamara have learned that it is important to talk about these types of interactions. They need to recognize the cumulative stress that these incidents can produce. Concealing one's couple relationship can take a toll over time. Concealment, if overused to cope with prejudice and fear of discrimination, can lead to feelings of distance, disconnection, and isolation, which negatively affect couple satisfaction.

Although there are times that Donna and Tamara choose to not disclose their relationship, they do consider themselves out in their community. "We just don't feel obligated to correct people all the time when they make assumptions. We just don't want to spend our energy that way," says Tamara. "We pick our battles," adds Donna. "If we see someone *else* is being discriminated against, we tend to be quicker to say something."

Most couples are surprised by the number of disclosure decisions that they regularly make. Most of these are made without much thought. You may want to try the Guided Activity below to gauge the amount of energy and effort you expend making decisions

Guided Activity: Disclosure Log

Use a chart like the one below to log your disclosure decisions during one typical week. Also note how you felt about each interaction and each decision. At the end of the week, share your log with your partner. Are there interactions that you would handle differently in hindsight? How do you feel about your disclosure decisions? How much stress did you feel? What can the two of you do to lessen the effects of this kind of minority stress?

Sample disclosure log

Interaction or incident	How I felt	How I handled it	Total stress level (0 = *no stress at all*; 10 = *extremely stressed*)
Server in cafe	Annoyed	Rolled my eyes and didn't say anything	5
Neighbor at the cookout	Anxious and preoccupied about whether to come out to her	Disclosed our relationship	9
Grandchild outed us at the park playground	Anxious in that moment about what all the parents would think	Smiled and laughed at our grandchild's innocence	7

about disclosing or concealing your relationship. Then compare your actual log with your answer to the Pause and Reflect activity you completed earlier.

CONCLUSION

As a couple you may frequently have to make disclosure decisions as you go about your daily lives in your communities. Coming out is not a one-time event! Because you may have acclimated to having to conceal or disclose your relationship, you may not realize how much stress you have accumulated over time. You may have found many helpful ways to manage this stress. It can help to use humor and get social support from other same-sex couples; friends who identify as lesbian, gay, bisexual, transgender, and/or queer; and straight allies. Finding positive ways to manage the stress of frequent disclosure decisions as you go about your daily lives in your communities is important to your well-being.

CHAPTER 27

WHAT WILL THE NEIGHBORS THINK?

Internalized stigma is absorbed from our culture and may cause us to experience negative emotions, such as unease, anxiety, depression, or self-doubt. In this chapter, we focus on the everyday interactions in our neighborhoods and local communities that can trigger these negative thoughts and feelings about our identities and our relationship. Dealing with internalized stigma is a two-step process. The first step is to recognize when interactions or incidents provoke these negative feelings. The second step is to respond in ways that help us (instead of further distress us).

Danielle, 42, and Cirleen, 45, have been a couple for 15 years. While Cirleen was out of town, Danielle went to the local coffee shop for breakfast. A server who had waited on them several times over the past year came over to take her order. Seeing that Danielle was alone, the server remarked, "I'm sorry to see you in here alone. Breakups are hard." The comment left Danielle feeling uneasy and wondering if she and Cirleen looked like they were not happy together.

As she and Cirleen discussed this incident later, Danielle was able to name the implicit negative message that seemed to underlie the server's statement. The negative (and false) stereotype about same-sex couples is that their relationships are inherently unstable.

Danielle and Cirleen have built a strong, committed relationship for 15 years, and the interaction with the server triggered this negative message about lesbian relationships. Danielle realized that she has internalized this message because of the negative cultural stereotypes about same-sex relationships. This negative implicit message provoked negative feelings.

The subtle or implicit nature of the message can make it more challenging to catch during the moment that it is happening. In hindsight, and with Cirleen's help, Danielle was able to recognize that the statement was stigmatizing and prejudicial, although this was probably not the server's intent. Danielle and Cirleen speculated that if Danielle had been married to a man for 15 years, the server would have probably asked, "Where's your husband?" instead of assuming that they had broken up.

As Danielle recounted this interaction and shared her feelings with Cirleen, she could recognize that social stigma was operating, which helped her to shift her own feelings of unease. Now she was able to access understandable feelings of anger. Instead of blaming the server or feeling bad about herself or her relationship, Danielle focused her anger on the real problem—stigma in society.

Danielle and Cirleen brainstormed how they might handle these kinds of interactions in the future. With the focus on the inappropriateness of the statement, Danielle practiced saying with appropriate assertiveness, "Why would you make that assumption? It's sad that people assume the worst." Notice that this response holds the server accountable while challenging her with a question. It is not the goal to blame someone for internalizing these insidious and pervasive cultural messages. The goal is to challenge ourselves and others to critically examine them and their impact.

We need to practice responding authentically, honestly, and with mutual respect and compassion. Assertive responses maintain our own integrity while still being respectful and relational. In this way, everyone has an opportunity to learn and grow more mindful and thus participate in changing these messages.

Danielle's encounter at the coffee shop is just one example of the many similar interactions that couples may experience in their neighborhoods and communities. It is almost inevitable that our internalized negative beliefs and feelings will get triggered on occasion. After all, we have been socialized in a society where these negative messages are pervasive.

It is important to recognize when our own internalized stigma gets triggered. It is also important to avoid being critical or judgmental toward ourselves when we get triggered. Even if it is after the fact, a part of our learning to respond assertively to these messages requires that we first be able to simply notice when they are happening. Danielle's first clue, for instance, was that she felt uneasy and sensed that something was "off" in her interaction with the server. Making a safe space to process these events with our accepting and nonjudgmental partner gives us needed validation and help in generating effective ways to respond.

Danielle and Cirleen were able to generate and practice empowering responses for future interactions that might take place. Although they don't want to become hypervigilant in their interactions with

---

Pause and Reflect

1. When was the last time your internalized stigma was triggered in the course of your daily life in your community?
2. How did you feel? What did you do?
3. What was the implicit (or blatant) negative message about your relationship or your identity that you were reacting to?
4. In the future, what assertive response could you use during this kind of interaction? (Help each other distinguish between possible assertive, aggressive, or passive responses.)

---

others, they do want to have empowering responses ready to use. They want to be able to respond in a way that keeps the focus on the problematic beliefs and messages in the culture rather than allowing their energies to be sapped by negative thoughts and feelings about themselves and others in their community.

Stigma is a story that we have learned. Who benefits from this story? This story serves the purpose of maintaining the social hierarchy that privileges different-sex relationships and devalues same-sex relationships. Challenging and disrupting this story threatens this status quo.

It takes courage to live a different story, a story of pride and self-acceptance. When we live positive stories of thriving and flourishing as same-sex couples, we are creating a new reality. We are part of creating a better world for everyone. Sean and Jake, who we introduced in the very beginning of this book, are living a new story of pride rather than the old story of stigma. To do this, they had to first notice when and how their interactions with their neighbors reflected The Old Stigma Story (TOSS). As they reflected on their experience of buying their house and moving into their charming subdivision, they pinpointed several interactions that triggered TOSS and their negative feelings about themselves as a couple. For instance, the day they moved into their house a neighbor in their cul-de-sac came over to greet them. As they talked in the yard, the neighbor seemed confused about who the homeowner was and puzzled over the relationship status of the two men. "Did you boys buy the house together?" asked the neighbor. At face value, this question seemed innocent, but in that moment Sean and Jake were both aware of suddenly feeling uncertain and uncomfortable about disclosing their relationship. This interaction triggered an anxious feeling and negative thought that perhaps they would not fit in with their new neighbors. Suddenly they felt fearful that they might be mistreated because of their relationship. TOSS was clearly operating.

Sean and Jake also recognized their tendency to overcompensate for being the only gay male couple in their neighborhood by making sure that they have the perfect house and yard. They had no rainbows, nothing that stood out, and nothing that "looked gay." Whether they were working in the yard, barbequing with friends, or walking the dog, they self-consciously asked themselves, "What will the neighbors think?" Sean said,

> We live in a small town, and while I think everybody on our street knows we're gay, we try not to force our lifestyle on our neighbors. Straight people have this idea of what they think gay people are like; a lot of them may not like the idea of living next door to a gay couple. We don't have a gay pride flag hanging on the porch, and there's no physical contact in the yard. That might make our neighbors uncomfortable. We try to be sensitive to that.

Like many couples, Sean's internalized stigma is driving some of his thoughts, feelings, and behaviors. He is preoccupied with how his straight neighbors view him and Jake. He tries to control how their neighbors respond to them by working hard to follow the implicit and unspoken rules so that the neighbors are comfortable and not threatened by the "gay lifestyle." Sean and Jake assume that others have negative views and will not be accepting. This assumption that others will judge us is common and is a stressful manifestation of internalized stigma.

When we project our own internalized negative beliefs onto those around us and then try to control those negative beliefs, we do ourselves, and others, a disservice. In effect, we reinforce negative beliefs by shaping our behaviors around them as if there is something wrong or shameful about us. Although we think we are controlling others' perceptions of us, we are actually being controlled by our own negative beliefs and assumptions and our projections of these negative beliefs and assumptions onto our neighbors. We are hooked by TOSS.

To change this story internally, Sean and Jake first remind themselves that they are not the problem. Their relationship is not the problem. The problem is the negative beliefs and messages about their relationship that we have all been taught. The problem is stigma, and it needs to be "Tossed"! This story is only a story, and an unhelpful one, at that. This unhelpful story is not them. It is not their identity as a couple.

Sean and Jake work hard to catch themselves projecting their own negative beliefs onto their neighbors and then reacting to those negative beliefs. By recognizing how they get triggered into colluding with and reacting to the negative stereotypes about gay male couples, they have taken the first step toward their goal of living more authentically and joyfully in celebration of who they are as individuals and as a same-sex couple.

To get a visual of what living more authentically would look like, they practiced the Guided Activity. The goal is to live a new story about themselves and their relationship. Their new story is characterized by pride and self-acceptance rather than stigma. Part of their vision of themselves living more authentically (regardless of what the neighbors might think) involves volunteering as a couple with their neighborhood association. See where your new story might take you.

CONCLUSION

The negative thoughts and feelings that you may have about yourself and your relationship are the results of negative messages you have been taught. These stigmatizing messages are not true. They are the result of prejudice that you are taught in your culture. By

Guided Activity: Creating a New Story About Our Relationship

Find a quiet and comfortable spot where you can relax. Spend a few minutes observing your breathing and quieting your mind. When you are ready, imagine that everyone in your neighborhood or community is an ally for those who identify as lesbian, gay, bisexual, transgender, and/or queer (LGBTQ). Take your time and picture your neighbors. Imagine that each person celebrates and supports your relationship in the same way that she or he supports different-sex relationships in your community. In other words, imagine that stigma does not exist. Imagine the quizzical looks that your neighbors give when someone asks about prejudice against same-sex couples. It has completely vanished from your community. Same-sex relationships are no more or less remarkable than different-sex relationships. Take time to imagine. The problem of stigma is gone. There is nothing to internalize because stigma against LGBTQ identities and relationships is nonexistent.

With stigma gone, how do you interact in your neighborhood or community? How do you behave? How do you feel? What do you do that you might have avoided in the past? How do your behaviors change now that stigma is nonexistent? Imagine, as if you are watching a movie, what your day would be like and how you would think, feel, and behave with your neighbors and others in your community.

When you have completed the visualization, take a few minutes to reflect on what you learned. How has internalized stigma interfered with your authentic living? Are there small actions that you could take (regardless of what the neighbors think or what you imagine that the neighbors will think) that are congruent with an authentic expression of your identity and relationship?

recognizing that the problem originates in societal prejudice, you can begin to isolate and deal with the problem constructively.

Your authenticity is a key contribution you can make to your neighborhood and community. Allowing yourself to buy into and participate in a story that stigmatizes your identity and relationship robs you and your relationship of your authenticity. A new story can free you from internalized stigma so that you can live confidently in who you are as an individual and as a couple.

CHAPTER 28

IT'S A BEAUTIFUL DAY
IN THE GAYBORHOOD

What does it mean to belong to a community? Communities can include temporary communities that gather periodically, such as once a year at an annual party or festival. Communities may be smaller groups that meet more regularly for a specific purpose, such as a reading group that meets at a local bookstore. A community can also be large and virtual, such as online communities that communicate regularly but are not in the same location.

There are many ways to build and connect to positive community support. We encourage same-sex couples to look around at their local communities—their town, their neighborhood, and their immediate surroundings. Couples may also look online for other couples with similar interests or issues.

Same-sex couples, like all people, benefit from being a part of a strong and positive community. Strong and positive communities are social networks characterized by people who have a sense of responsibility for each other's well-being. Strong communities may form for the explicit purpose of bringing about positive social change.

Communities provide information, support, and resources that are made available as needs arise. Being a part of a positive community helps same-sex couples to manage minority stress and enhance their health and well-being. Many couples want to be a part of a community, but sometimes they don't know where to start looking.

Montel, 24, and Clark, 25, have been a couple for 2 years. A year ago they moved together to a new city to start new jobs. Montel noted that it is challenging to establish a sense of community in a new place: "We aren't into the bar scene, so we have had to look for other ways to connect to the LGBTQ [lesbian, gay, bisexual, transgender, queer] community and to the larger community."

Montel noticed that their new city, despite its relatively large population, did not have a gay and gay-friendly men's chorus. Because he and Clark first met each other in a men's chorus, they loved the idea of starting a chorus in their new community. As Clark described it,

> This gave us a chance to meet and really get to know a lot of people. A chorus is usually very diverse; it includes people from a lot of different places and different backgrounds who work in a lot of different types of jobs. And when you plan things and work together for a goal, like practicing for a concert, it brings you together in a really nice way. It's also a way to work with other organizations in town, partnering to raise money for a local service organization that helps people in the community.

Initially Montel and Clark spent several months doing an informal needs assessment. With some other community leaders, they decided that there was enough interest and excitement about starting a chorus that they put together a small planning committee. Within a few short months they had made many new friends as a result of their work on this project. Before they knew it, they were holding the first rehearsal and planning a holiday concert to raise funds for the LGBTQ community center in town.

Clark and Montel have found a way to contribute their unique talents and interests to helping create positive community support for themselves and others. They are thrilled with the new friend-

Pause and Reflect

With your partner, go on a "scavenger hunt" for needs in your community. Identify at least three community needs that would benefit from your unique strengths, talents, and interests. Pick one that you both would enjoy and plan a date that involves this volunteer activity.

ships that they are making and are feeling at home in their new community. They also like the idea of giving back to the community through a charitable organization.

Sometimes the best way to plug in to your community is to examine your own needs for support. For instance, Carrie and Elizabeth are retired health care professionals who have been a couple for about 25 years. They live in a midsized city in a state that does not have an inclusive nondiscrimination law. They have both worked in a local organization to persuade legislators, but so far to no avail. Elizabeth and Carrie felt very discouraged after the last legislative session when a "fairness" law died in committee. Elizabeth says about the experience,

> Oh, we knew we wouldn't really do it, but we talked about selling our house and packing up and moving someplace that is friendlier to gay people. We are very disturbed by the message that antigay legislators send in our state. And one of them represents our district! It makes our state feel like a very unfriendly place to live.

Carrie and Elizabeth started looking around their neighborhood for support. They noticed that several other same-sex couples had moved into their charming, 1960s era, working-class neighborhood. Carrie contacted these neighbors to see whether they would like to help her form a "gayborhood association." At first, the idea was somewhat whimsical and fun. But before she knew it, Carrie had a membership list that included more than 50 same-sex and straight-ally households. The list is still growing.

Last spring, the Gayborhood had a well-attended and highly successful potluck picnic in a city park that adjoins the neighborhood. At the family-friendly gathering, approximately 75 people played croquet and bean bag toss, ate lots of good food, and shared conversation and laughter. The district representative even attended to meet and greet her constituents.

The Gayborhood has also sponsored yard sales, environmental clean-up days, and garden tours. Carrie occasionally writes emails to the listserv that shares local needs, neighborhood improvement projects, issues of concern, and celebrations. Neighbors post questions seeking everything from garden advice to the names of good contractors. Carrie muses about her feelings about the neighborhood now: "Even though not everyone in the neighborhood has joined, having the group makes this place feel friendlier. More people smile and wave at us when we walk around the neighborhood. Just that change alone is encouraging!"

The Gayborhood association has generated a strong sense of community and positive belonging in this diverse neighborhood. Members are joining all the time and from all over town. There are no membership fees! The group likes to joke about creating new membership categories, like "honorary" or "alumni," for people who have moved out of the neighborhood or who have never actually lived in the neighborhood but want to. The positive energy of this LGBTQ and ally community is contagious and powerful!

Our own sense of purpose and fulfillment increases when we invest ourselves in our communities. When we contribute to our community, we experience a sense of belonging that increases our well-being. Having a positive sense of belonging to one's community is important for individuals and couples.

Guided Activity: Assessing Your Community

What do you think of when you think of your community or communities? Is it your neighborhood? The lesbian, gay, bisexual, transgender, queer community? A small group? A virtual online community of people with similar interests? What communities are you and your partner a part of?

Draw a picture of your communities. Your picture might look like a map, or it may be more abstract. Does it look like a big set of overlapping circles? Or a flower with petals that each form one part of your community? Share your picture with your partner. Then discuss the following questions.

1. How do you feel about your neighborhood/community?
2. What community resources contribute to the well-being of your relationship?
3. Are there resources available that you are not taking advantage of?
4. What would have to happen for the two of you to feel a greater sense of community belonging? What might you do to help initiate this change?

CONCLUSION

Although virtual communities have helped to end the isolation of many people who identify as LGBTQ, it is important that you also connect to, and participate in, local communities. Some may need to unplug and step outside your own homes and offices in an effort to engage with your community. Sometimes the opportunities to engage already exist; other times we must be active in creating new opportunities for ourselves and others.

A positive connection to others is important to couple well-being. Social support, positive connections, and a sense of belonging are basic human needs. Contributing your time and energy to building positive community will help to reduce the effects of minority stress for everyone.

Part VI

LAWS AND POLICIES

Same-sex couples live in a constantly changing legal and policy environment. This environment has the potential to create tensions related to minority stress for the couple. Laws and policies affecting the recognition of their relationship status are important for all same-sex couples, but these are not the only laws and policies that affect them. Laws governing immigration, inheritance, parental rights, and nondiscrimination are just a few of the other laws that couples potentially need to know about. For example, in the workplace, nondiscrimination and relationship recognition policies affect couples and their decisions. Also, policies in schools impact same-sex couples and their children.

Relationship recognition and marriage equality immediately come to mind when discussing legal issues that impact same-sex couples. However, marriage equality does not solve the problem of minority stress for same-sex couples. Couples may still face challenges and stress related to encounters with prejudice and disclosure decisions about their relationship. It is also important to remember that even after marriage equality is fully implemented in the United States, marriage equality is not recognized in every country around the world. Additionally, many same-sex couples will choose to not get married; the recognition of those relationships is no less essential.

Many laws besides marriage equality and marriage recognition affect the lives of couples. Some states have statewide nondiscrimination laws that include sexual orientation. Unfortunately, fewer states have laws that also include gender identity. Other states simply have executive orders that are more limited in scope and lack many of the qualities of a law. A majority of states and the federal government lack these inclusive protective laws (as of 2014).

These policies have real effects on couples. For example, we have found in our research that couples who live in states that have inclusive nondiscrimination laws experience less minority stress and are more likely to disclose their relationship. However, couples who live in states without inclusive protections may experience increased minority stress about disclosure and risks of discrimination.[1] Also laws governing inheritance are very important to same-sex couples. Each state has a set of laws governing who has the right to property if a person dies without a properly executed will or trust. Regardless of laws governing relationship recognition or marital status, same-sex couples must proactively establish their inheritance rights. If these rights are not established, the law grants rights to property to the "next-of-kin," often parents, siblings, or other legal relatives, leaving a surviving partner with no rights.

In the past, few laws have protected the relationship of same-sex couples during a medical crisis. We have probably all heard a heart-wrenching story about a partner in a same-sex couple being kept from the side of their seriously ill, injured, or dying partner. Recent changes in federal rules regarding the treatment of patients in medical facilities have prompted hospitals to recognize the important relationships of all patients. However, these policies are far from perfect and may fail to be enforced at a crucial moment when a couple is in a medical crisis. Same-sex couples are at risk for discrimination in health care settings when they travel to places that do not recognize their relationship or are being treated in medical settings where personnel act in a discriminatory or prejudicial way toward them.

Advance planning is a proactive step toward establishing rights for a relationship. These rights need to be clearly established regardless of legal relationship or marital status. Advance planning is a positive activity that affirms our commitment to our relationship. However, engaging in advance planning may also cause minority stress. For example, trying to find an affirmative, competent provider (e.g., a lawyer or a doctor) may elicit fears of discrimination. Couples need to directly deal with these minority stressors so that they can take steps to protect their relationship.

Immigration policy has had a profound impact on the lives of binational same-sex couples. Although immigration law also affects heterosexual couples, same-sex couples face additional challenges. Recent modifications in federal policy have made it possible for a U.S. citizen to sponsor residency in the United States for a same-sex partner or spouse, but there are still challenges in this process. Binational couples must cope with their fears that disclosing their relationship may put them at risk for prejudice and discrimination, both in the United States and in another country.

Policies in the workplace may or may not recognize same-sex couples' relationships and protect these employees from discrimination. Even when one couple member is covered by an inclusive policy at work, the other partner may not be. To access an inclusive workplace policy such as family leave, an employee has to document the same-sex relationship, which may put the employee at risk for discrimination. This common situation presents a disclosure dilemma for couples as the threat of discrimination and even job loss may be very real.

Educational opportunities and the school environment are extremely important to parents. Individual districts and schools vary greatly in how they implement laws and policies. For same-sex couples, it is important to understand the laws and policies that are available to support children in their learning environment. Dealing with disclosure decisions, prejudice, and discrimination in schools can be stressful for couples and their children. Couples may find themselves having to force schools to enforce the law and provide equal educational opportunities and a nonthreatening learning environment for all students.

Laws and policies cover groups of people in society. To change laws or policies, a couple must work within a larger system such as a workplace, a city, or a legislature. Working on behalf of social justice typically means organizing groups of people to negotiate changes to institutional policies that are discriminatory. In some situations, this kind of activism exposes a couple to discrimination and increased risk of experiencing minority stress. Couples need to monitor the effects of their social justice activism on their relationship to make sure that they are protecting their health and well-being.

For example, if we want our partner to be recognized in our workplace, we must go through the appropriate channels to appeal to the management to implement an inclusive policy. This type of activism requires a lot of time, effort, and persistence. Although some types of activism may increase the minority stress that we feel, our research suggests that this kind of activism is also empowering and enables us to develop and use our strengths on behalf of social justice.

In this section, we present several scenarios in which laws and policies can contribute minority stress for same-sex couples. In Chapter 29, we discuss different ways that marriage equality may impact couples. To show that marriage equality will not magically eradicate minority stress for same-sex couples, one couple in this chapter illustrates how civil marriage can increase the risk of discrimination. In Chapter 30, we offer a scenario in which debates over the law, which often include negative stereotypes and messages, can trigger internalized stigma for couple members. The couples in this chapter illustrate some of the ways to counter these negative messages. In Chapter 31, we discuss advance planning as one way that couples can positively deal with the lack of relationship recognition. We illustrate how couples can face their fear of rejection, which can be a barrier to advance planning. In Chapter 32, we tackle some issues that parents may face. State laws governing adoption may cause significant minority stress when both parents are not legally recognized. Finally, in Chapter 33, we illustrate how law can be used in positive ways to confront discrimination and to create a more positive environment for same-sex couples and their families.

Social stigma is often codified in discriminatory laws and policies. Even neutral laws can be interpreted in prejudicial ways. Institutionalized stigma increases the minority stress of same-sex couples. They must respond to the immediate situation even as they work for long-term change. Working to repeal discriminatory laws helps to reduce social stigma and promote equality. Inclusive laws and policies will further help to reduce social stigma. While progress toward social equality continues, same-sex couples need to stay informed about the impact of the current laws on their relationship and mindful of the work that still needs to be done.

NOTE

1.   Riggle, E. D. B., Rostosky, S. S., & Horne, S. (2010). Does it matter where you live? Nondiscrimination laws and the experiences of LGB residents. *Sexuality Research and Social Policy, 7,* 168–175. doi:10.1007/s13178-010-0016-z

CHAPTER 29

GOING TO THE CHAPEL

You've probably heard the old adage "Louise and Hank sittin' in a tree, K-I-S-S-I-N-G. First comes love. Then comes marriage. . . ." This children's rhyme has traditionally paired different-sex partners. Now, the rhyme has been updated, and we can start with a same-sex couple! "Luis and Hank sittin' in a tree, K-I-S-S-I-N-G. First comes love. Then comes marriage. . . ."

Marriage is a public institution. Through civil marriage, couples publicly declare their commitment, and the state recognizes that commitment for legal purposes. Civil marriage is now available to same-sex couples in the United States (although those marriages are not yet recognized in all states as this book goes to press). However, marriage rights for same-sex couples are not universally recognized throughout the world.

Civil marriage is accompanied by language for referring to our partner and our relationship to our partner: "We're married and this is my spouse/husband/wife." These labels have a shared cultural meaning that conveys our relationship status. Marriage symbolizes the acceptance and celebration of a relationship. Marriage creates an important mechanism for same-sex couples to have equal access to all of the rights and responsibilities of marriage if they so choose.

Luis, 60, and Hank, 65, have been a couple for 33 years. They are preparing to retire. Luis is originally from another country, where his family of origin still lives. Luis and Hank have been planning to move back to Luis's home country after retirement to be near to Luis's family.

Luis and Hank entered a civil marriage in their current home state in the United States when marriage for same-sex couples became legally recognized there. They are happy to be able to enjoy the rights and security that their civil marriage has provided.

> Luis: I have some chronic health problems, so being married has made us feel more secure in knowing that Hank always has the right to be with me if I have to go to the emergency room.
>
> Hank: This has become a big issue for us when we talk about moving somewhere that won't recognize our marriage. I feel like we will lose that security. But we also want Luis to be near his family. It would be easy to just stay here, but that would force us to give up something important just because of some stupid law. It feels so unfair.

Marriage inequality or the lack of legal recognition of the relationships of same-sex couples, whether in the United States or in other countries, has the potential to impact the opportunities and choices of same-sex couples. This inequality also triggers minority stress. Luis and Hank realize that even though they enjoy the rights of marriage where they currently live, legal discrimination elsewhere places burdens on them as a same-sex couple.

> Hank: We argue about this plan sometimes, because Luis feels so strongly about moving near his family but I don't want to lose our rights. We really don't know what to do.

Luis: I would like to believe that there will be marriage equality everywhere in the next decade, but realistically we can't count on that. That makes us feel like our plans for the future are in limbo, which is hard to deal with. We need to come up with some kind of plan.

Luis and Hank recognize the stress that marriage inequality creates for them. They also recognize that they need a positive plan for their future. They realize that they need to find specific information about relationship recognition for same-sex couples for all of the places that they regularly travel to as well as the country to which they plan to move to Luis and Hank decide to find some outside counsel through organizations that advocate for LGBT rights worldwide.

Pause and Reflect

What types of legal relationship recognitions are available to you as a same-sex couple? Civil marriage? Civil unions? Domestic partnerships? Some other type of relationship recognition (e.g., reciprocal beneficiaries)? What are the rights that are provided by these legal relationships? What rights are not provided that you need to secure in other ways (such as writing a will or powers of attorney)? When you travel to different places, do you know whether your relationship will be recognized? Are there ways to find out and to secure your rights in those locations?

Access to civil marriage is socially and legally important for same-sex couples. However, marriage equality can raise a different set of issues related to stigma and discrimination. Some of these issues may seem counterintuitive at first glance. After all, sometimes we buy into the good-time feeling that marriage equality will eliminate all stigma and discrimination.

Maria, 41, and Rachel, 44, have been a couple for 15 years. They live in a state with marriage equality. They want to get married. However, they realize that getting married will make their relationship public because marriage records are public and are published in the local newspaper. For Maria, this is not a problem. For Rachel, however, disclosure has always been an issue.

Rachel works as a teacher in a religiously affiliated school. She believes that she could lose her job if the school finds out she is in a same-sex relationship. Although many people at the school know about her relationship, Rachel thinks that getting married would be "too public, too much in-your-face" and would cause parents to complain to the school administration.

Maria understands and wants to support Rachel, but she also wants to get married. Rachel wants to get married but not at the cost of her job. She wants to wait until she can find a new job in a school where she is protected by a nondiscrimination policy, but she is uncertain how long that will take.

Maria: I want to get married. It's legal now. We should celebrate us. We've been together longer than most of the couples in my family. I don't want you to lose your job. I understand that part. I want to do whatever you are comfortable with, but I also want to do what is right for us. Haven't things changed? Do we really have to still worry about all this? Surely you wouldn't get fired for getting married, would you?

Rachel: The problem is that they don't have to fire me outright or say why they are doing it—they can just not renew my contract. It's a private school. They get away with a lot of things. I want to marry you more than anything, but I don't want to jeopardize my job and our financial future. I saw a report on the news about a guy who got married in California and lost his job. Our wedding should be a glorious thing, not a risky thing!

Both couples in this chapter face difficult discussions and decisions because of discrimination in the law and in the workplace. Discrimination causes minority stress for these couples. For Luis and Hank, marriage equality has had immediate benefits, but marriage inequality elsewhere could cost them the opportunity to move to where they wish to retire. Maria and Rachel would also receive immediate benefits, but the potential cost is Rachel's job and half the couple's income.

Because Luis and Hank have a few years before retirement, they set a deadline for deciding about moving. They decide to wait 3 years, when Luis turns 63. Then they will reassess the legal climate in Luis's home country and weigh their options. They take positive action and begin to research local LGBT groups in Luis's home country to make social connections there and to find out how they can join in the fight for LGBT and marriage equality. They also join a group that works for LGBT rights internationally. They want to turn the stress of discrimination into positive action by working towards marriage equality for everyone, everywhere.

Maria and Rachel also set a deadline. Rachel will actively look for another job in a school that provides inclusive protections, thus increasing her job security.

Maria: It's important to us to celebrate our relationship and not let other people dictate whether we get married or not. So, I took Rachel to her favorite restaurant on the beach for a weekend getaway and asked her to marry me. She said yes, and we are engaged! We're both excited about getting married! Our families and friends are having an engagement party for us! We're getting married next summer! Hopefully Rachel will have a new job by then, but if not we'll deal with whatever happens as a happily married couple!

Rachel: I know that not all couples can risk losing a job, but I think we have figured out a way to make it work. We want to adopt a child and start our family as soon as possible. The state will recognize our family. Hopefully my new workplace will, too.

Legal rights are important for couples to understand and discuss. Unfortunately, discrimination and the minority stress that accompanies it are real. Couples need to understand the impact of laws on their relationship and their options for positively dealing with discrimination.

Guided Activity: Assessing Your Legal Rights and Options

Collecting this information may take some effort and some research. Having this information, however, provides a base of knowledge for making important decisions for your relationship.

1. Make a list of benefits you would receive as a couple from legal relationship recognition. For example, are there federal benefits that you would receive? State-level or local benefits? Benefits at work?
2. Is there any risk of discrimination from exercising your right to legal relationship recognition? (Be realistic but not alarmist.) If there is a risk, what positive actions can you take to minimize this risk?
3. What can you do to work for equality for everyone? Full equality also includes working for equitable treatment and protecting the relationship rights of couples who choose not to get married.

CONCLUSION

Marriage, domestic partnership, or commitment ceremony—how you as a couple wish to celebrate your relationship is a very personal decision. There are many different forms of relationship recognition that are also legal contracts that come with responsibilities, rights, and visibility. You need to assess and decide for yourself what form of relationship recognition is right for you and what rights you need to secure to protect your relationship.

CHAPTER 30

STEPPING OUT AND LOOKING IN

Public debates over existing or proposed laws often include negative stereotypes and negative messages about people who identify as gay, lesbian, bisexual, transgender, and/or queer (LGBTQ) and about same-sex couples that are propagated by those who oppose equality. For instance, recent marriage equality campaigns, and the court cases that have followed, have provided a platform to some groups to convey negative messages about same-sex couples. Television, radio, newspapers and magazines, billboards, bumper stickers, yard signs, social websites, and tweets deliver negative messages that are hard to ignore. Avoiding exposure to these negative messages may be impossible at times.

For some partners in same-sex couples, these negative messages may, as they are intended to do, trigger our internalized stigma. We know that these negative messages about our identities and relationships have triggered our internalized stigma when we find ourselves feeling bad about ourselves or insecure about our relationship in reaction to things we hear. These negative feelings are a minority stressor and can be harmful to a couple's well-being. Couples may need to recognize and deal with the fallout from these toxic messages in their environment.

Andy, 53, and Stuart, 49, have been a couple for 19 years. They survived the very contentious and public debate over a marriage restriction amendment to the constitution in their state that unfortunately passed. Andy and Stuart were very active in campaigning against the amendment. They even agreed to be interviewed by the local newspaper. Their activism exposed them to a barrage of hate speech on one occasion, and they routinely encountered many negative messages. Although participating in the fight for marriage equality was energizing, the exposure to these negative messages also took a toll on their relationship. As Andy describes,

> It's not that I really believe these hateful messages in my e-mail and on TV telling me that my relationship isn't worthy and won't last. But, day after day after day of being verbally assaulted every time I turned on my computer or went to a rally . . . it all took a toll on me and I know it was hard on our relationship. It was a constant struggle, just against all the religious stuff I thought I had dealt with—being told I was going to hell for who I loved. I think at some point in the campaign I started to think about whether Stuart and I would really be together for the rest of our lives. Even though we've been committed and settled down for years, I found myself feeling insecure, like maybe they're right, somehow.

Stuart had a hard time dealing with Andy's sudden doubts about the relationship. He tried to pull back from the campaign so they would not be exposed to so much negativity, but Andy insisted the fight was too important. Stuart told us,

> I could see that Andy was fighting himself as much as them. He was fighting discrimination, but he was also fighting his own doubts about himself and us. Every time someone told us we were going to hell, a part of him seemed to be deflated, and it took a lot of energy to fight that.

Whether the law in question is about marriage equality or restrictions, nondiscrimination, bullying, partner benefits, or any other issue of importance to same-sex couples, negative stereotypes used by opponents of equality are toxic. These negative stereotypes are intended to invoke stigma and bad feelings for the purpose of maintaining the status quo of inequality. Even when we are winning political battles, we are still exposed to these toxic messages and the stress that they create.

For Andy and Stuart, it was important to step back and identify these negative messages. They had heard them so often that they seemed to fade into the background, but they still had an impact. Even after bracing himself for the hate messages he found in his e-mail, Andy would be exhausted after reading them. Stuart would try to comfort him, but sometimes Andy seemed to pull away instead of accepting the comfort. Stuart would get frustrated and say, "It's a self-fulfilling prophecy. If they stress us out enough, of course relationships like ours will suffer and of course some of them might break up as a result!"

Stuart and Andy needed to take care of themselves and their relationship. Activism on behalf of equality can be empowering and

---

Pause and Reflect

Sometimes we forget how important it is to take care of ourselves so that we can live, love, and work with joy and effectiveness.

1. Make a list of self-care activities that the two of you engage in when your internalized stigma is triggered in the context of working for social justice. Self-care activities can include any positive activity that renews and rejuvenates your spirit.
2. Examine your list to see if there are other positive, spirit-renewing activities that you might add.
3. Discuss with your partner how to balance activism and self-care in your lives together.

can give us a sense of purpose and meaning in our lives as we work toward a better future for everyone. Activists like Stuart and Andy must also take good care of their emotional and physical health.

One way that Andy and Stuart dealt with the stress of their activism was to attend a workshop for activists that focused on self-care. They learned about the importance of balancing the intensity of community activism with self-care activities that restore and replenish. To begin their self-care, they took some time out to reflect on and discuss their experiences and feelings with each other. Andy gained some insight into his feelings: "I think part of it is just feeling ineffective and like I can't control things. So, to try to get some control, it's really tempting to just give up."

They also learned a technique in the workshop called the *counterargue* that they use to combat the assault of negative messages that trigger their own internalized stigma. Stuart summarized the method:

> Counterarguing means *talking back*. We learned to say out loud the bad things being said about gays and lesbians and then to counter with what is really true about us. A couple of years before the [marriage restriction] campaign, we were active in fighting for the nondiscrimination policy for the city we live in. Looking back, even though we won, it was still a stressful time. We certainly could have used that counterargue technique during those days, too. Whether we win or lose, we never get to stop fighting against all the misinformation and ignorance about us that is out there. Even counterarguing takes energy! But we try to keep our eye on the end goal: just being treated like everyone else.

Counterarguing is a useful technique for dealing with stresses that come from negative messages that trigger internalized stigma. Whether one or both partners are being triggered, the couple suffers. Couple members can help each other in the face of negative messages. Once they have identified the negative messages that drive discriminatory policies, they can respond with a counterargument and restatement based on the truth about their lives and identities.

For Stuart and Andy, the fight for marriage equality is just a beginning. There are also battles to fully implement marriage equality and relationship recognition and to pass nondiscrimination laws at the federal level and in all states. The sense of social justice extends beyond the U.S. to working towards equality in other nations as well. Stuart and Andy remain active, but they also realize that this kind of long-term activism is stressful for them. Andy explained:

> Part of me just wants to be an "old married couple" who sits at home and watches TV. Then I feel guilty, like I'm not doing enough. That makes me feel like maybe the [opponents of equality] are right—I just don't care about anyone but myself. Then I remember how committed we are. How much we do. We will keep fighting in any way we can, but we do have to be careful to recognize our limits and take care of our relationship. That's not selfish. That's being healthy.

For same-sex couples, activism is an important affirmation of our relationship and connection to our community. We want to make the world a better place! Being active means putting ourselves out there and being exposed to negative messages. This exposure may trigger our self-doubt or internalized stigma. It is also an opportunity to learn about ourselves and change these negative messages into positive ones. Finding ways to counter negative messages with positive messages about our identities and our relationship helps us and helps our community.

Through their activism, Stuart and Andy have learned a lot about the policies in their state and other states (and countries). They have also learned a lot about interacting positively with their community. Together, they are learning about the self-care and limit setting needed to sustain themselves in these activities.

Guided Activity: Generating Counterarguments and Restatements

1. What are the civil marriage laws in your state? Do these laws support marriage equality or marriage inequality? What message do these laws send to you and your partner about your relationship?
2. What are the nondiscrimination laws in your state? Are these laws inclusive or noninclusive? What message do these laws send to you and your partner about equality in your state?
3. What are the other issues that have been debated in your state that impact same-sex couples or individuals who identify as lesbian, gay, bisexual, transgender, and/or queer? What are the messages you and your partner have heard or seen in the course of these debates?
4. Look at the negative messages you identified above. Try restating each in a truthful way. For example, if your state had (or still has) a marriage restriction amendment, one message you may have received is that your relationship is not equal to those of your different-sex neighbors. A positive restatement might be

> Our relationship is equal to our neighbors. We love each other and are committed to each other. We pay our taxes and work hard. We have made a good life together that we are proud of.

Try this counterargument and restatement technique with the negative messages you listed above. For each negative message, write a statement that affirms your right to be treated equally. Also, don't forget to focus on the positive messages that you have encountered in your environment. For example, Stuart and Andy frequently remind themselves that their city passed an inclusive nondiscrimination policy. They focus on feeling affirmed by that policy and being happy that they have that kind of support in their local community.

CONCLUSION

Encountering negative messages may trigger internalized stigma. These messages may be difficult to avoid, especially during public debates. Laws that are designed to denigrate same-sex couples or individuals who identify as LGBTQ are ever-present forms of institutionalized prejudice. You as a couple need to recognize the messages, negative and positive, that laws and public debates about laws convey. You can learn to recognize the effects that these laws have on your well-being and then actively counterargue, promote positive messages, and support each other in balancing activism and self-care.

CHAPTER 31

GOOD HELP IS HARD TO FIND!

Laws may be helpful or they may be stigmatizing. Because laws are technical and are backed by the force of the state (government), we often need assistance when dealing with the law (and the government). We also sometimes need to use the law in times of crisis. All of these factors can make us feel vulnerable to rejection when we are dealing with legal issues and the people who should be helping us with legal matters.

The historical nonrecognition of same-sex relationships, and sometimes the persecution (and prosecution) of same-sex relationships, has left a legacy of distrust among many people who identify as lesbian, gay, bisexual, transgender, and/or queer and same-sex couples. Even in states with full legal marriage equality, prejudice and stigma remain an issue. Yet, at some point in their relationship, most same-sex couples need the services of legal, financial, or other professionals. Accessing these services requires disclosing their same-sex relationship, which may be a barrier for couples who fear that they will be treated poorly by these professionals. Couples hesitate to get the help that they need when they are not sure how they will be treated.

Couples want competent service from a professional with whom they feel comfortable. Although there are many wonderful professionals who are knowledgeable and supportive, same-sex couples don't always know how to find them. Even in larger urban areas, it may not be obvious which lawyers or financial planners are "gay friendly" or "LBGT-competent." In smaller or rural locales, it can be even tougher to find service providers that meet these criteria because there simply are fewer choices.

Rejection by a service provider is not the only fear that same-sex couples may have. The legal documents themselves can trigger fears and anxiety. For some couples, the fear that these documents will disclose their same-sex relationship and lead to discrimination in the future is a significant obstacle. Sometimes it seems easier to avoid the whole issue rather than deal with all of these fears.

Shirley, 45, and Taylor, 44, want to write their wills and find out what else they can do to protect their relationship and their rights in the event of an emergency. They have had many discussions, but have reached an impasse.

> Taylor: We have no clue how to find a lawyer that we will feel comfortable talking to and who will know what to do. We live in [a medium-sized city] and there seem to be plenty of lawyers around, but we don't know any of them or anyone who has used them for this kind of thing. What if we go in and the lawyer doesn't like gay people? Then he won't do a good job. We could drive to [a larger city], but it seems like a lot of effort to find someone there and then make the trip. So, we just keep putting if off.
>
> Shirley: We know that we really need to write a will because we've seen people lose their homes and everything else because they weren't married and one of them died. The family can just swoop in and take things. It's easy to use the excuse of not knowing a lawyer who will treat us right, but the other part

is that having a will would probably cause problems with our families, and we just don't want the drama. They treat us okay, but if I tell my mom that I'm leaving everything to Taylor, she'll start asking about Grandma's china cabinet or other things that have been in our family for years. I don't want to have to justify mine and Taylor's relationship yet again and point out that she wouldn't treat my brother's wife like she treats Taylor.

Taylor: So it's easier to avoid all of this and not deal with lawyers who may not like us because we're lesbians, or with family who barely tolerate us. It's like, if we just don't talk about it, we won't upset anyone else. But that doesn't do us any good, so we just get upset when we think about it.

Shirley and Taylor thought that marriage recognition in their state would solve all of their problems. But inheritance laws in states do not automatically leave all property to a surviving spouse when there is no will or advance planning documents. Shirley and Taylor still need to write a will and other documents to make sure that their property goes to the other in case of death or that the surviving spouse would have full access to their shared finances. They also need a financial planner who understands the financial implications of being a same-sex couple. That adds one more "friendly" professional they worry about trying to find.

Beyond getting the documents, Shirley and Taylor have worried about what would happen if one of them got into an accident and their relationship was revealed through those same medical advance planning documents that are supposed to help them. As Shirley said,

You just don't know who you'll be dealing with around here. If we write up these powers of attorney for each other, we're

---

Pause and Reflect

What legal protections do you have in place for your relationship in the event of a crisis? Make a list. At minimum, do you have

a. a will or living trust (stating who should get your property when you die)?
b. a power of attorney for health care (designating the person who will make decisions about your medical care in case of a crisis)?
c. a power of attorney for finances (designating the person who will make decisions about your money and assets in case of a crisis)?
d. a funeral plan (including who will make decisions)?
e. a living will (stating your wishes about life-prolonging treatment options in case of a crisis)?
f. designated beneficiaries on transferable accounts (e.g., retirement savings) and on life insurance policies?

---

putting in writing that we're a couple. And while we of course want to be there for each other in case of emergency, we've heard the horror stories about what happens when some mean nurse or doctor finds out a patient is gay. So having the documents takes away one stress and adds another. We just talk ourselves in circles trying to figure it out.

Fears of rejection from those we count on to help us create advance planning documents and from those we count on to enforce them can be huge obstacles to this necessary process. We can overcome these obstacles by keeping our focus on the reason we need to engage in this process. Protecting our relationship, reinforcing our commitment to each other, and expressing our love are the top reasons why couples overcome their fears and actively engage in advance planning.

Shirley and Taylor decided to make an action plan. The first thing they did was write a "mission statement." This statement outlined their commitment to each other and included their commitment in the event of a crisis such as a medical emergency.

This type of mission statement will help a couple to focus on protecting their relationship. After all, this is the most important issue. Taylor and Shirley explained how creating a mission statement and literally putting their relationship at the top of the list helped them to focus.

> Taylor: I thought it was a little corny, but it really did help to write out a mission statement. We tell each other that we love each other all the time. This statement just made it concrete and literal. Then we could look at our relationship and say to each other, "How are we going to protect this thing that we value so much?"
>
> Shirley: Yeah, Taylor thought it was a little weird when I said we had to write this down, but then we got into it. It really drove home the point that we need to put our relationship first. Then everything else could fall into line after that.
>
> Taylor: Then we could talk without getting stuck on what to do about our families in terms of our wills. It's still tricky, but we can see what we're doing this for. We can see that even if we're afraid of a negative reaction or rejection, we still need to think about us first.

The next step for Shirley and Taylor was finding friendly professionals. They asked their friends about attorneys they knew or that they had used for any reason. They drew up a list of questions, created a script for a telephone conversation, and then made the phone calls. In those calls they simply asked whether the attorney did estate and personal planning. Then they asked if the attorney had worked with same-sex couples before. If they got affirmative answers to both of those questions, then they would ask more questions about their specific needs.

Shirley explained that making the first couple of calls was a little nerve-wracking because she didn't know what she would do if the person who answered said something rude.

> Shirley: I was just nervous. I don't know anything about dealing with lawyers really. But I looked at our mission statement and said to myself, "What's the worst thing that could happen? Someone will tell me I'm going to hell? I've heard that before!" But I was pretty sure that wasn't going to happen. It was just my anxiety talking. So I made a few calls. Yeah, a couple of people who answered the phone for these attorneys seemed a little surprised about what I was asking and said they weren't sure. One person was a little curt. But I don't know if that was my anxiety or maybe that person just always sounds like that. I said something to Taylor about it, but we decided to just move on. One office actually referred me to a lawyer that they knew worked with same-sex couples. That was cool! So in the end it was not the bad experience that I expected.
>
> Taylor: It's amazing how much stuff we make up in our heads. We create these disaster stories that keep us from doing things. We realized that, yes, we could get some rejection. But we knew we needed to get past that or we might really face a disaster someday.

It's okay to acknowledge that it is scary and anxiety provoking to think about something bad happening to your beloved partner. Now it's time to face your fears rather than avoid them. Use the Guided Activity to help acknowledge your fears, reaffirm your values and commitment to each other, and complete the process of advance planning.

Guided Activity: Advance Planning

Use the following steps to guide you in making a list so that you and your partner can recommit to your values and move forward with the important process of advance planning.

1. Write a mission statement for your advance planning. Why is it important to you as a couple to engage in these activities?

2. Look online or buy a book to help you map out the basic documents that you need to create. These documents include a will or trust, powers of attorney, and insurance beneficiaries. If there are sample forms online, print them out. Fill out as much as you can. If you get stuck on something, move on! If you don't know if you need a particular document, add it to the list anyway so that you can remember to ask an attorney.

3. If a will is at the top of your list, find an attorney that you are comfortable with who can help you. Start by asking five friends the name of the attorney they used to create their wills. Contact a local organization for people who identify as lesbian, gay, bisexual, transgender, and/or queer and ask for recommendations or look online. Call the attorney's office and ask whether that attorney has created wills and documents for same-sex couples. Don't be afraid to ask for an estimated cost if that is part of your concern.

4. Make an appointment and keep it! If you have to arrange to travel to a larger city, then make plans to do so. Turn the event into a celebration of your relationship.

5. Repeat the process for other services you may need. For instance, make a financial inventory. Find a list to help you inventory your real, tangible property. Make a list of your assets and where all of your money and investments are located. Use the strategy in Point 3 above to find a financial advisor with whom you feel comfortable. Make an appointment for a financial checkup and consultation.

CONCLUSION

Various laws have historically put same-sex couples at a disadvantage, and some policies continue to do so. Taking proactive steps to protect your relationship is vitally important and necessary. Fears of rejection can prevent you from taking the necessary actions to protect your relationship. We can talk ourselves in circles and end up where we started, or we can follow a step-by-step process and get moving! Just moving through the process takes the focus off our fears and our projections and keeps us focused on the important task of protecting our relationship. We feel better when we do not let our fears interfere with achieving our important goals.

CHAPTER 32

YOURS, MINE, AND OURS

Laws can be a significant source of minority stress for same-sex couples who are parents. These parents can easily find themselves at a legal disadvantage in relation to their own children. As stressful as it is to think about being kept from the bedside of a partner in a medical emergency, it is equally unthinkable to be kept from the side of one's own child.

In most states, nonbiological or nonadoptive parents have no legal parental rights. Laws and policies defining parental rights may discriminate against and disadvantage same-sex couples. For example, many states have birth certificates that provide spaces for the name of a mother and a father, but not two mothers or two fathers, or two "parents." Even when the child is conceived within the same-sex relationship and both partners are in all respects the child's two parents, many states only recognize the biological parent as having rights.

Adoption is not a right provided to same-sex couples in every state or, in the case of international adoptions, in all countries. Same-sex couples may have to pretend that only one partner is adopting a child as a single parent. In some states, a second-parent adoption may be available at a later time. In other states, this may not be an option.

Legal disadvantages in the recognition of parental rights for both partners in a same-sex couple causes stress for parents and children. When parental ties are not recognized, that parent is at constant legal risk of losing contact with or custody of their child. The emotional toll must be managed as constructively as possible.

Harold, 35, and Ray, 32, have a 4-year-old daughter, Ashley. Ashley was adopted by Harold as an infant. Because Harold has more job security as a medical technician and his family is close by, the couple reasoned that he would be seen as a better candidate to adopt a child than Ray, who was still finishing his nursing degree at the time of the adoption. Ashley is a happy, growing child. However, she has special needs that require frequent visits to health care professionals and physical therapists.

Both Harold and Ray care for Ashley equally at home, but when it comes to doctor visits, it is Harold who must take her. Because Harold is listed as her "father, single" on the adoption papers, the medical facility has explained that they must treat their situation accordingly. Ray and Harold have talked about second-parent adoption, but their state is not friendly to second-parent adoptions by same-sex parents. They are talking to an attorney, but at this time Ray's parental rights are still nonexistent in the eyes of the law. For Ray and Harold, this situation is very stressful.

> Ray: I don't count at all in the eyes of the law. It's horrible that I can't even take Ashley to the doctor for a routine visit, let alone in case of an emergency, which we haven't had, thank God. Hopefully we never will. Harold has signed a paper that gives me as many rights as possible to make medical decisions in an emergency if he is not around, but even that document is limited. It's terrible the way the law treats us.

Harold: We're both her daddies. Ashley is certainly clear about that! And her doctors and nurses know that we're both her parents, and they have tried to help us, but in the end they tell us that they have to follow the law or they can get in trouble. Trouble for what? Helping two dads take care of the child they both love more than anything?

Ray: We know it's going to be the same when she goes to school. Harold will be treated as her "real" father. It will always come down to Harold being the only dad that counts, legally.

Harold: Our attorney advised us to establish a record showing Ray is Ashley's dad. You know, like a paper trail that documents that he pays for things. Showing that he spends time with her. Showing that we both care for her; that we have both always been her dads. We're doing that even though it's degrading and stressful. I know Ray feels really insecure, and I do, too. But if something happened to him, I would still have Ashley. If something happened to me, who knows what some crazy judge might decide?

Harold and Ray need to find positive ways to deal with this stress caused by legal discrimination. They are working with a lawyer and taking steps toward second-parent adoption. They regularly check on changes in the law and court cases that may be useful to them.

Pause and Reflect

What laws in your state affect you as parents? Try doing some research on websites to find out, or ask other same-sex couples who have kids what their experiences with legal issues have been.

When we interview couples who are raising children without the benefit of both being legally recognized parents, we always recommend that they find a local attorney who can help them come up with the best strategy for establishing legally recognized parental rights. We know that locating an attorney involves time and expense. This solution may not always be feasible for a couple raising a child. Other strategies may be necessary, so getting accurate and helpful information is crucial.

Allison, 28, and Pat, 29, just had twins. The children were conceived via artificial insemination and Pat is the birth mother. Unfortunately, in the state where they live, Allison is not able to be listed as a parent on the birth certificate.

Allison and Pat have limited monetary resources, most of which goes toward buying diapers for the children, paying rent, and putting food on the table. They knew money would be tight, but some complications have made finances even tighter than usual. Although they know that they should contact an attorney about Allison's rights as a parent, they cannot afford it at this time.

> Pat: We feel bad. We know we need to talk to a lawyer, but we just can't pay one right now. Even an extra hundred bucks is just not in our budget right now. We planned and saved up money for all the medical expenses, but all it took was a few extra expenses to wipe us out.
>
> Allison: We have jobs. We're working and making money. But honestly we're back to living paycheck to paycheck. We have been trying to get information online and we've been talking to people that we meet. We both feel vulnerable at this point. I'm the twins' mama, but not in the eyes of the law.

Other same-sex couples in your state can be a great resource for finding out how to establish legal rights. Also, every state has a lesbian, gay, bisexual, transgender, queer (LGBTQ) group that works toward legal equality. Contacting that group and requesting that they do a workshop specifically for same-sex parents could help to organize and disseminate information effectively.

Allison and Pat did contact an LGBTQ rights group in the nearest large city. That group provided them with names of other parents to contact. They arranged to meet and talk about their options for creating, as soon as possible, legal parental rights for Allison.

> Allison: It was a big help. They knew a couple of shortcuts for creating a type of guardianship status for me. We can try to do that without a lawyer, although it doesn't solve our long-term problem of how to make me the twins' legal parent. We also talked about planning a workshop with some other parents. We're new parents and we don't have a lot of time and energy for this, but it's a relief just to be doing something positive. We also learned how to establish a record of us both being parents to the twins.
>
> Pat: I can't remember ever feeling this vulnerable. It's a horrible feeling that we can't both be automatically seen as the babies' parents. It makes me so mad sometimes, but then I figure I better put that energy to good use. For all the talk about "family values," this state sure isn't interested in supporting our family. Talking to the other parents helped. Hopefully we can get organized so we can help other parents, too.

For same-sex parents who are in a similar situation in their state, the Guided Activity may help to empower them. These steps will guide you in affirming your family and working for changes that will benefit all parents and their children.

Guided Activity: Confronting Legal Discrimination

Make a schedule for taking the following three steps to affirm your family and establish your legal rights as a parent. Set a deadline for completing each step.

1. Create a family portrait. With your children (if they are old enough), draw a picture of your family. Label yourselves with whatever names your child uses for you and whatever nicknames you may have for your child. Frame it or put it on the refrigerator to remind yourselves of the beauty of your family. Take a picture and post it online to share with friends and family. Remind yourself that this family is what you are protecting!

2. Communicate with other families about the types of legal issues they have encountered and how they have handled them. You can look for these families in your community, online, or by contacting local organizations. Ask them to share some of the ways they have handled the stress of legal discrimination. Share strategies for establishing legal rights.

3. Become involved in local organizations that work to elect public officials who affirm people who identify as lesbian, gay, bisexual, transgender, and/or queer (LGBTQ). Work to elect representatives to your state legislature who affirm people who identify as LGBTQ to your state legislature. Then lobby those legislators for laws that protect your family. A simple letter talking about your family and the need for equality is a good start. Equality in parental rights is in the best interest of the child!

CONCLUSION

When stress is caused by legal discrimination, parents must be proactive. It is important to take time to affirm and celebrate your family. You can also be creative in establishing legal connections between both parents and child or children. Remember that changing discriminatory laws and policies is a long-term process. Gaining the support of others in similar situations can help as we all work together to ensure that all parents and children have the support they need and deserve.

CHAPTER 33

UNTIL *ALL* ARE EQUAL

Know the law! Or at least know enough to know when you need help. That's the first step for same-sex couples who need strategies to deal with legal disadvantages in the current, ever-changing environment. Whereas in the previous chapters we discussed the minority stress created by discriminatory laws and policies, in this chapter we discuss how knowing the law can help to counter disadvantages or create advantages.

Use the law! Some laws are blatantly discriminatory. Other laws can help same-sex couples to create as many legal rights as possible to protect their relationship.

Laws change! Sometimes laws change rapidly. Keeping up with changes in the law and how those changes impact you as a same-sex couple is important.

Change the law! If a law is discriminatory or disadvantages your relationship, be active and tell your legislator. Legislators, no matter how negative they may be about rights for individuals who identify as lesbian, gay, bisexual, transgender, and/or queer and equality for same-sex couples, still need to hear from you. They need to hear your story. Join with others at the local or national level to work for change and equality for everyone.

Kai and AJ both turn 30 this year. They have been together for almost 5 years. They have been steadily working toward establishing their rights as a family. Two years ago, they decided to do an annual legal and financial inventory over the 4th of July holiday, which is also their anniversary. For some couples this may not seem like a very romantic anniversary activity. Kai and AJ like to use the occasion, which is easy to remember, as an opportunity to celebrate their commitment and their progress toward their goals for their family.

First, Kai and AJ made a list of documents they needed for advance planning. Then, they made a timeline. Kai shared with us,

> I don't want to think about anything bad happening to either of us, and we're young so it's not like we really think we're going to die or get sick, but I don't want that to keep us from protecting ourselves. So we made a plan and that made it easier because we could tackle things one at a time.

AJ was in charge of finding an attorney to help them create the documents. AJ identifies as transgender and is especially interested in finding legal and financial services that are affirming. AJ recounts the process,

> I talked to several people and did some research online. I came up with a list of possible attorneys and called each office and asked a series of questions like, "Have you worked with same-sex couples? Have you worked with any transgender individuals? Are you familiar with what our legal issues are?" It was hard to put myself out there. It ended up that everyone was very nice and honest. One lawyer told me he does family law but had never dealt with these issues and recommended someone else. At least he was honest. One lawyer

said that she had never worked with a transgender person but that she had worked with same-sex couples and was willing to do some research. We ended up going to her because she seemed honest and open.

Kai was in charge of the property and financial inventory. Kai found an outline online to use. Insurance company websites often have forms for creating a real property inventory. Kai made a written and video record for their insurance and for their use in advance planning. They put all of their financial information in one place so they could easily look at it. Kai explained,

> It really didn't take as long as I expected it to. It is one of those things that you put off for a long time because you think it will take forever, but when you start, you realize you'll be done in a few hours. Then I felt much better, like we were a little more protected now. That felt good.

AJ used the same procedure they used to find a lawyer to find a financial advisor. They wanted help figuring out all of the consequences of various decisions about beneficiaries and inheritance. They had a jointly titled house and car. They are talking about the option of getting a civil marriage, but they have serious ethical objections to participating in an institution that does not recognize all forms of families. They explored investments for retirement and for securing their financial well-being, taking into consideration their plans to add a child to their family. AJ told us,

> We definitely feel more prepared. We know there are still some laws that work against us, but we at least we know what they are. Knowing the details of our situation is better than not knowing. It makes it easier to cope. We can take positive action

and make a plan for us. We feel good about starting a family and dealing with some of these challenges. We are very happy with our lawyer and financial advisor.

Pause and Reflect

What are your legal, financial, and advance planning goals? What information do you need to gather to determine how to achieve them? Revisit the Guided Activity in Chapter 31. Assess where you are in terms of completing your tasks.

Advance planning is a cause for celebration. Advance planning is also an ongoing process. Checking in on your plan at least once a year is a good idea. Then celebrate that you have checked in and that you are making progress.

We have already pointed out in previous chapters how knowing about nondiscrimination workplace policies can be helpful. If your workplace does not have inclusive policies already, then working toward inclusive nondiscrimination and benefits policies is important. It is a great opportunity to find allies and work with other people for a common cause.

Local, state, and national laws or executive orders are also important to know. Having inclusive laws or policies in place can help to set the tone locally, in a state, or even nationally. We each have skills and talents that we can lend to the cause of equality.

Mario and Theo live in a state with an inclusive nondiscrimination law; marriage equality; and affordable, accessible health care. To some people it might seem like they have it made. But Mario and Theo recognize that they still have a responsibility to work for equality for everyone, everywhere.

For Mario and Theo, being active gives them a sense of purpose and adds meaning to their lives and their relationship. They recognize that they can use their privilege as men to speak out for accessible reproductive health care for all women. They recognize that they can use their privilege as citizens of the United States to work with groups who advocate for immigration policy reform.

Working for changes in laws and policy gives a focus to Mario and Theo's passion for social justice. They know that laws can be used by everyone once they are passed.

> Mario: We know that the laws privilege us. We benefit in many ways. Being gay has helped us realize that we do have to work for the rights of everyone. We get discriminated against, so we know what it's like. We know what it's like when people try to silence you.
>
> Theo: We have made some great allies in our work with different groups. When we show up to volunteer at an immigration rights rally, they know that we are gay men and that we care. It helps us bridge communities. We see these same people, who are straight, showing up at Pride day. That sends a powerful message that we are all working together. Politicians notice that. Companies notice that. It's like, if you mess with one of us, you mess with all of us. We want to keep working to build these bridges and expand these connections.

Same-sex couples recognize that they have been treated like second-class citizens under different laws and policies. They also recognize that even in areas where there is legal equality, there is a need to keep working for full equality. Using the law is one tool. Expanding the law to support the full equality of everyone is an important goal.

Guided Activity: Using the Law for Good

Previous activities have guided you to find out which laws affect you as a couple and how to use those laws to protect your relationship. This activity guides you through a values inventory. Then you can work to create or change laws that support your values.

1. What do you value? What policies are connected to those values? For example, let's say you list "health" under your values. Under policies, you may then list "health insurance."
2. Do the policies that impact you support your values? Do these policies treat everyone equally? For example, does your company offer health insurance to you but not to your partner? Does your company offer health insurance that excludes coverage of reproductive health needs for women?
3. What social privileges do you have? How can you use these to create or change policies that affect you? For example, are you privileged because you have a social status that is valued over others? Are you male? White/Caucasian? Highly educated? Have a high income? Able bodied? Identify as Christian? How can you use your privileges and your compassion for others to work for just policies for everyone?

CONCLUSION

Celebrate your relationship and commitment by figuring out how to use all available means to protect your family. Working together to complete advance planning tasks shows your commitment to peace of mind and security for your family. Make a plan and reward yourself when you have completed this important task.

Although some laws still discriminate against same-sex couples, using available laws and legal strategies will help alleviate some of the minority stress caused by legal discrimination. You can celebrate your relationship and commitment to each other by working for social justice for everyone. The meaning that you derive from this work adds to the quality of your life and your relationship. Working together to change discriminatory laws shows your commitment to the future. Working together for equitable policies enhances your connections to others and demonstrates your compassion.

CONCLUSION: A FUTURE WHERE WE THRIVE AND FLOURISH

What does the future hold for same-sex couples and their families? As we look around the country, and around the world, we see many positive changes happening. Marriage equality and relationship recognition are becoming realities for more and more people throughout the world. Same-sex–partnered politicians, athletes, and entertainers are in the spotlight. Out of the spotlight, same-sex couples are quietly and visibly contributing to their local communities as they coach their children's sports teams, shop in local businesses, take part in religious activities, and volunteer to make their communities better places to live for all. As a result of all of these positive changes, young people who identify as lesbian, gay, bisexual, transgender, and/or queer (LGBTQ) are imagining a future for themselves that many same-sex couples thought improbable only a dozen years ago.

As we contemplate the future of same-sex couples and their families, we like to imagine that our great-grandchildren will find a copy of this book, long forgotten, in a dusty old attic. We imagine that they will marvel that there was a time (not so long ago) when same-sex couples were discriminated against. For their generation, it has become a strange and disturbing historical fact. In their world, a same-sex couple is no more or less remarkable than any different-sex couple.

In this future world, same-sex couples will meet, fall in love, and begin the challenging work of building a life together. Like all couples, their relationship will benefit from financial and emotional stability, good communication skills, and social support. They will need to cope with the stresses of daily life. They will need positive experiences, positive emotions, and positive connections to strengthen and sustain them.

There will always be a need for books that can help couples build their relationship skills, but we look forward to the time when same-sex couples do not need additional support and resources for dealing with stigma and minority stress. Until that day, we hope that this book can provide a helpful resource and source of social support. We hope that this book serves as a reminder that we need to recognize the humanity and dignity of all by treating everyone, including same-sex couples, with respect and kindness.

In this book, we have focused on how minority stress shows up in the lives of same-sex couples and what they can do about it. However, we know that there are as many manifestations of minority stress as there are same-sex couples. We are not able to address all of the many factors that influence couples' lives. Minority stress is complicated and exacerbated by factors such as immigration issues; having multiple stigmatized identities; or living with HIV/AIDS, chronic health conditions, or disability. Couples must consider and address the specific circumstances that are connected to the minority stress in their own lives.

Of course, being happy together is about more than effectively coping with minority stress. As important as it is to deal with minority stress effectively, happiness is more than the absence of stress. Happiness is living a life of vitality, meaning, purpose, and fulfillment.

WHAT DOES IT MEAN TO *THRIVE?*

We want same-sex couples to *thrive!* We thrive when we enjoy psychological well-being. Same-sex couples thrive when partners work together to identify and mobilize strengths and resources to meet the challenges of minority stress. Through this process, we sharpen our skills and develop our strengths and use these to embrace life and live well. This is the essence of not just surviving our challenges but thriving and flourishing in our lives.

The ultimate solution to minority stress is to put an end to stigma and discrimination. All of us, LGBTQ people and allies, need to use our strengths and whatever privilege we enjoy on behalf of social justice for all. Using our strengths and resources on behalf of others is one way to thrive and flourish.

Drs. Huppert and So at the Well-being Institute at the University of Cambridge (UK) have discovered 10 features of flourishing. We flourish when we (a) have people in our lives who care about us, (b) are learning and growing through active involvement and engagement in life, (c) feel a sense of accomplishment, (d) are calm and peaceful, (e) are able to bounce back from life's setbacks or adversities, (f) are optimistic about the future, (g) have energy and vitality, (h) feel positive about ourselves, (i) feel satisfied and happy with our lives, and (j) have a sense of meaning and purpose and feel that we are doing things that are valuable and worthwhile. How many of these features characterize your life together? Which of these features would you like to enhance in your life together?

WHAT CAN WE DO TO THRIVE AND FLOURISH?

Couples thrive and flourish when they identify and use their strengths to cultivate positive identities, form a strong commitment to each other, assert appropriate boundaries, create supportive relationships with others, and contribute to their families and communities. The good news is that you can start with any one of these goals, because they are all connected. Improving skills and resources in one area will have positive effects on the others.

Cultivate a Positive Identity

When the stigmatizing beliefs that we were taught get triggered, we may have negative thoughts and feelings about ourselves and our relationship. Think of these negative messages as an annoying radio station with lots of static. We need to turn off the negative noise.

We need to proactively create our own playlist. We need to be listening instead to messages that enrich our lives. One place to start is to ask yourself and your partner the simple question, "What's positive about your LGBTQ identity? What's positive about being a same-sex couple?" These stories, along with stories of people you know and meet, can serve as sources of inspiration. Use these inspirations to identify your individual strengths and skills, and use them to cultivate your positive identity as individuals and as a couple.

Strengthen Your Commitment

What does it mean to be in a committed relationship? Our gender socialization, our socioeconomic class, our communities, and the dynamics of our families of origin all shape how we envision commitment in a relationship. One of the positive aspects of having an LGBTQ identity is that we have the space to critically examine gender rules and traditional relationship scripts and ask, why? Then, we are also free to ask, why not? We can write our own relationship script and create our own vision of commitment that works for us.

What are the rules that govern your relationship? What are the agreements that the two of you have made? What does it mean to you to be a couple? Clarifying what being a couple means to both of you and how you define being a couple to yourselves and others helps build emotional security and stability in your relationship. The actual agreements that you make are less important than the commitment you express in the process of making these agreements. Being explicit about your expectations for each other and your relationship will go far in helping you work together as a team to meet each other's needs and strengthen your commitment.

Assert Appropriate Boundaries

It is challenging to draw appropriate boundaries with family members or anyone who devalues or refuses to recognize one's same-sex partnership. In collectivist cultures, group identity and the greater good of the community is prioritized over individual identities and needs. For couples whose values are more collectivist, it can be particularly challenging to assert one's individual and couple identity.

The dignity and integrity of our couple relationship is integral to our well-being. We can call attention to and label disrespectful treatment from family members or others in our social environment. Learning to assert appropriate boundaries in these situations is an important skill that contributes to the well-being of our relationship.

When couples are caught up in the minority stress process, they may forget to work together as a team to address these challenges. They may forget that their relationship deserves top priority. Couples who thrive and flourish make their relationship a priority by devoting time to creating an empathic, intimate, egalitarian, and joyful life together.

Create a Support Network

Couples need strong social support. Ideally, we have a minimum of six to eight people whom we can count on for ongoing support for our couple relationship. This stable, cohesive group of family and friends does not magically appear. We need to be proactive and create mutually supportive relationships by investing our time and energy in creating and maintaining them.

Our supportive family and close friends provide physical, emotional and material support when we need it. These are the people who serve as our confidants, role models, mentors, and devil's advocates when we need them. It takes time, but creating a support network is one of the best investments that a couple can make on behalf of their relationship.

Generate Your Couple Well-being

An important task in our adult development is *generativity*, which means making a contribution to the lives of others. Adults frequently say that working with children or parenting is one of their most rewarding generative activities. Our interests, imagination, and unique strengths can lead us to engage in any of a variety of generative activities. For instance, any type of social justice activism or any compassionate act on behalf of others can form our generative legacy.

For couples, engaging in generative activities together helps to cultivate well-being. Remember, small actions matter! Contributing to a better community or to future generations helps foster our own well-being in the face of minority stress.

HAPPY TOGETHER

Remember that according to science (yes, science!), love is the master strength. As we age, the capacity to love and be loved is the strength most clearly associated with life satisfaction.[1] When we cherish, cultivate, and take pride in our love for each other, we create a lasting happiness that strengthens our relationship. Strong, happy same-sex couples who are living with pride and authenticity will make the world a better place for everyone to live, happy together.

NOTE

1. Isaacowitz, D. M., Vaillant, G. E., & Seligman, M. E. P. (2003). Strengths and satisfaction across the adult lifespan. *The International Journal of Aging & Human Development, 57,* 181–201. doi:10.2190/61EJ-LDYR-Q55N-UT6E

ADDITIONAL RESOURCES

BOOKS

Ameli, R. (2014). *25 lessons in mindfulness: Now time for healthy living.* Washington, DC: American Psychological Association.

Mindfulness practices help us to slow down and pay attention, without judgment, to our present-moment experience of ourselves, our relationships, and the world. When we learn to pay attention to what is happening in our present-moment experience, we can choose to respond with compassion rather than reacting automatically out of our fear, anger, or other negative emotions. Mindfulness practice has been shown to reduce stress, anxiety, and depression and improve the quality of our relationships and our lives.

Davis, M., Eshelman, E. R., & McKay, M. (2008). *The relaxation & stress reduction workbook* (6th ed.). Oakland, CA: New Harbinger.

This resource includes step-by-step instructions for learning and practicing positive coping skills, including assertive responding, meditation, dealing with negative emotions, and self-care (e.g., relaxation, nutrition, exercise).

Drinkwater, G., Lesser, J., & Shneer, D. (Eds.). (2012). *Torah Queeries: Weekly commentaries on the Hebrew Bible.* New York, NY: NYU Press.

"Brings together some of the world's leading rabbis, scholars, and writers to interpret the Torah through a 'bent lens.' This incredibly rich collection unites the voices of lesbian, gay, bisexual, transgender, and straight-allied writers, including some of the most central figures in contemporary American Judaism." (From the official book description.)

Riggle, E. D. B., & Rostosky, S. S. (2012). *A positive view of LGBTQ: Embracing identity and cultivating well-being.* Lanham, MD: Rowman & Littlefield.

This book illustrates the positive strengths and skills that help people who identify as lesbian, gay, bisexual, transgender, and/or queer (LGBTQ) to live rich and meaningful lives. Using these skills to foster a positive LGBTQ identity is important to effectively dealing with minority stress and creating narratives about LGBTQ issues.

Vines, M. (2014). *God and the gay Christian: The biblical case in support of same-sex relationships.* New York, NY: Convergent Books.

Highly readable and understandable, this book offers a positive model for reconciling conservative Christianity and LGBTQ identity using the heart and the head.

WEBSITES

- The American Civil Liberties Union (www.aclu.org/) provides up-to-date information about the rights of LGBT-identified individuals and same-sex couples. Their website includes information on parental rights, rights of children in schools, relationship recognition, discrimination, free speech, and the rights of transgender-identified persons and persons with HIV/AIDS.
- The American Psychological Association (APA; www.apa.org) works to end stigma and discrimination against LGBTQ

people and promote their well-being through solid science and scholarship, education, training, and advocacy. On this website, you can find links to many resources related to gender identity, sexual orientation, and sexuality. On the APA home page, you will find links to the LGBT Concerns Office, the Committee on LGBT Concerns, and several divisions that have LGBT interests, including School Psychology (Division 16), the Society of Counseling Psychology (Division 17), and the Society for the Psychological Study of LGBT Issues (Division 44). There are also important professional guidelines regarding psychological services for LGBTQ individuals. APA has been active in supporting equality for LGBTQ people around the world, including supporting policies for equal parenting and marriage rights. This website includes several links to bibliographies of the psychological literature on LGBTQ issues.

- The Association for Lesbian, Gay, Bisexual & Transgender Issues in Counseling (ALGBTIC; www.algbtic.org) is a division of the American Counseling Association. The website has many resources related to providing competent, affirming, and culturally sensitive counseling services. ALGBTIC also publishes a newsletter and an academic publication, *The Journal of LGBT Issues in Counseling*.

- Children of Lesbians and Gays Everywhere (COLAGE; www.colage.org) has the mission to "unite people with lesbian, gay, bisexual, transgender, and/or queer parents into a network of peers and support them as they nurture and empower each other to be skilled, self-confident, and just leaders in our collective communities." (From the website.) COLAGE sponsors online communities; community chapters; a family week in Provincetown, Massachusetts; and other programs. The website includes resources for LGBTQ parents and their children.

- The Family Equality Council (www.familyequality.org) provides a wealth of information and online community support for LGBTQ parents. There are many practical resources, including LGBTQ family-friendly book lists, guides for talking to your kids about your family, instructions for starting an LGBTQ parent support group, and tips for dealing with schools. On this website, you can also submit questions to experts on issues facing LGBTQ families.
- The Gay, Lesbian & Straight Education Network (GLSEN; www.glsen.org) states that its mission is safe schools for all students. Through research, training, and advocacy, GLSEN works to develop positive school climates and vibrant and diverse communities where all people are respected regardless of sexual orientation, gender identity, or gender expression. The GLSEN website has many resources for educators, students, and parents.
- The Gottman Institute (www.gottman.com) was founded by John and Julie Gottman. They and their team of collaborators are couple and family therapists and researchers who have designed and evaluated an approach to relationships that is based in relationship science and field tested in their clinical work. It is inclusive of same-sex couples and their families. Their website advertises resources including workshops for couples, DVDs, books, apps, and materials on parenting.
- The Human Rights Campaign website (www.hrc.org) has resources on religion and spirituality, parenting, marriage, gender identity, immigration, workplace, health and aging, and many other topics. Resources specifically focused on religion include coming out issues for Latino/Latina individuals and for African American individuals. Other topics address gender identity and faith communities. This website is also a good source for information about specific religions and

religious denominations and their position on same-sex relationships. Some information about affirmative groups within religious denominations is also provided.

- The National Black Justice Coalition (NBJC; www.nbjc.org) "is a civil rights organization dedicated to empowering Black lesbian, gay, bisexual, and transgender (LGBT) people. NBJC's mission is to eradicate racism and homophobia. As America's leading national Black LGBT civil rights organization focused on federal public policy, the National Black Justice Coalition has accepted the charge to lead Black families in strengthening the bonds and bridging the gaps between straight and LGBT people and communities." (From the website.) This website has some excellent publications on marriage equality, welcoming congregations, theology, and interviews with prominent and influential LGBT African Americans and allies.
- The National Center for Lesbian Rights (www.nclrights.org) has a useful collection of information relevant to same-sex couples and all LGBTQ-identified people. They provide information about current laws and policies, as well as easy-to-read interpretations of how these impact individuals and couples.
- The National Center for Transgender Equality (www. transequality.org) is "dedicated to the equality of transgender people through advocacy, collaboration and empowerment." (From the website.) The Resources page has information about transgender people, building community, federal issues, and how to become involved in the political process.
- The National Committee on Lesbian, Gay, Bisexual and Transgender Issues (www.naswdc.org/governance/cmtes/nclgbi.asp) was formed by the National Association of Social Workers to develop, review, and monitor programs of the Association that significantly affect individuals who identify as gay, lesbian, bisexual, or transgender. The Diversity & Equity link (www.

socialworkers.org/practice/equity/default.asp) has a number of position statements and citations for papers on LGBT issues.

- The National LGBTQ Task Force (www.thetaskforce.org) provides a state-by-state breakdown of laws and policies affecting same-sex couples and LGBTQ individuals. They conduct timely research and present findings on a number of issue areas, including aging, hate crimes, immigration, parenting, and racial and economic justice.
- NativeOUT (www.nativeout.com) is a "national nonprofit education and media organization, actively involved in the Two Spirit Movement. Our vision is to create social change in rural and urban communities that benefit Indigenous Lesbian, Gay, Bisexual, Transgender, Queer, and Two Spirit people" (From the website.) There are many interesting resources, including videos, available on this website.
- Out & Equal Workplace Advocates (www.outandequal.org) is a nonprofit organization dedicated to achieving workplaces whereas full equality extends to people of all sexual orientations and gender identities. On this website, you can find a career resource center, as well as information about diversity training and ally development in the workplace. Additional resources on this website include information on LGBT youth, marriage equality, and diverse cultural communities.
- The Queer Asian Spirit website (www.queerasianspirit.org) is "a welcoming forum to share queer wisdom, knowledges, experiences, communities, religiosities, theologies and spiritualities from men, women and transpeople of Asian and Pacific Islander descent of different faiths from around the globe! This website is a collection of resources for lesbian, gay, bisexual, transgender, intersex, pansexual, asexual, queer and questioning (LGBTIPAQ) people of Asian Pacific Islander (API) descent who are interested in spiritual and religious issues." (From the

website.) This website lists hundreds of resources from many faith traditions. There are also links to e-mail lists and faith communities around the world.

- Soulforce (www.soulforce.org) "is committed to freedom for lesbian, gay, bisexual, transgender, and queer people from religious and political oppression through relentless nonviolent resistance." (From the website.) The resource page has information on LGBTQ identity from the perspective of scientific research and theology. There are links to many other helpful organizations and resources for engaging in mutually respectful dialogues.
- The Williams Institute (williamsinstitute.law.ucla.edu/mission/) prepares research reports related to the impact of laws and policies on LGBT individuals and same-sex couples. These reports address many issues that affect people who identify as LGBT, such as safe schools, health, immigration, the workplace, violence and crime, and the military.

INDEX

ABOUT THE AUTHORS

Sharon S. Rostosky, PhD, completed her doctorate in counseling psychology at the University of Tennessee, Knoxville, in 1998. She is a licensed psychologist in the Commonwealth of Kentucky. She joined the counseling psychology program at the University of Kentucky in 1999, where she is currently a professor and director of training. Her research, published in more than 60 peer-reviewed journal articles and presented in numerous workshops for professional and general audiences, focuses on minority stress and well-being in individuals who identify as lesbian, gay, bisexual, transgender, and/or queer (LGBTQ) and in same-sex couples. She was honored in 2010 with the American Psychological Association (APA) Division 17 Social Justice Award.

Ellen D. B. Riggle, PhD, is a professor in the departments of Gender and Women's Studies and Political Science at the University of Kentucky. She is the coeditor of *Sexual Identity on the Job* and *Gays and Lesbians in the Democratic Process.* She has also published more than 60 articles in peer-reviewed journals and book chapters. Dr. Riggle has conducted research, lectured, and presented workshops on the impact of stigma on sexual minorities, legal status issues for same-sex couples, and the importance of positive well-being for LGBTQ individuals.

Dr. Riggle and Dr. Rostosky's 2012 book, *A Positive View of LGBTQ: Embracing Identity and Cultivating Well-Being*, was the winner of the APA Division 44 Distinguished Book Award. More information about the work of Dr. Riggle and Dr. Rostosky can be found on their website: www.prismresearch.org.

11/19/16